Black Neighbors

Black Neighbors

Race and the Limits

of Reform in the

American Settlement

House Movement,

1890–1945

Elisabeth Lasch-Quinn

The University of North Carolina Press

Chapel Hill and London

Library of Congress Cataloging-in-Publication Data
Lasch-Quinn, Elisabeth.
    Black neighbors : race and the limits of reform in the American
settlement house movement, 1890–1945 / by Elisabeth Lasch-Quinn.
        p.   cm.
    Revision of thesis (doctoral).
    Includes bibliographical references (p.   ) and index.
    ISBN 0–8078–2114–4 (cloth : alk. paper).—ISBN 0–8078–4423–3
(pbk. : alk. paper)
    1. Social settlements—United States—History. 2. Social work
with Afro-Americans—United States—History. 3. United
States—Race relations. I. Title.
HV4194.L37 1993
362.5'57'0973—dc20   93–18533
                                                                CIP

The paper in this book meets the guidelines for permanence and durability of
the Committee on Production Guidelines for Book Longevity of the Council
on Library Resources.

97 96 95 94 93   5 4 3 2 1

To Ray and my parents

"When [the soul] breathes
through his intellect, it is
genius; when it breathes
through his will, it is virtue;
when it flows through his
affection, it is love."
—Ralph Waldo Emerson,
"The Over-Soul"

Contents

2, 3, OR 4.

Illustrations

Acknowledgments

My gratitude goes to all those who inspired, encouraged, and assisted me in this endeavor. Bruce Laurie and Paula Baker did all this and more. Together with Jean Bethke Elshtain, Constance McGovern, and John Bracey, they provided helpful insights for revising the original manuscript of this book. I deeply appreciate the early and persistent interest of Lewis Bateman and the University of North Carolina Press as well as all the subsequent work involved in bringing the book to publication. Jacquelyn Dowd Hall and an anonymous reader for the University of North Carolina Press provided invaluable suggestions and encouragement. Ralph Luker, Judith Trolander, and Allen Davis gave heartening responses to parts of this work. In addition, I am deeply indebted to the interest and confidence of my colleagues and students at Syracuse University, with whom it has been my great pleasure to work. I am delighted to have found several true birds of a feather.

I am very thankful for the financial resources at my disposal. The University of Massachusetts and the department of history provided two University fellowships. The Henry J. Kaiser Research Travel Grant of the Archives of Labor and Urban Affairs of the Walter Reuther Library at Wayne State University and the Center for the Study of Philanthropy Research Grant helped defray the costs of research travel. Syracuse University provided funds for additional research through the Appleby-Mosher Fund and the Small Grants Program.

I have fond memories from the numerous trips to and long-distance communications with archives that this project entailed. The staffs at the Urban Archives Center at Temple University, Hampton University Archives, the Social Welfare History Archives at the University of Minnesota, the Sophia Smith Collection at Smith College, the Black Women Oral History Project at Radcliffe College, the University of Massachusetts Microfilm Room, the Civil Rights Documentation Project at Howard University, the Archives of Labor and Urban Affairs of the Walter Reuther Library at Wayne State University, Southern Oral History Collection, Archives of Industrial Society at the University of Pittsburgh, and others gave vital assistance. Fritz Malval of Hampton, David Klaassen of the Social Welfare History Archives, John Grabowski of Case Western Reserve Historical Society, and Michael Breedlove of the State of Alabama Department of Archives and History at Montgomery showed particular interest in the project.

Friends and relatives have made life during the production of this vast project worthwhile, pleasurable, and possible. Linda Pitelka, Lori Kran, my sister Kate Ramdin, and my grandfather, Henry Steele Commager, offered much early encouragement. And as always, I found I could rely on my brother, Chris Lasch, for help, interest, and friendship.

My parents, Nell and Christopher Lasch, deserve the highest praise and thanks for their unbounded love and support. This book owes its existence to theirs. My father's encouragement and example were, and always will be, wellsprings of inspiration.

Finally, I cannot imagine accomplishing this without the infinite, daily efforts of my husband, Raymond Lasch-Quinn. The vastness of his love and generosity defies words.

Black Neighbors

Introduction

In 1911, prominent Progressive Era reformer Jane Addams remarked that, everywhere in America, "a strong race antagonism is asserting itself."[1] Indeed, the migration of blacks from the rural South to the cities of the Northeast and Midwest that crested during and after World War I and again during World War II triggered racial tensions and cemented residential segregation. The early twentieth century witnessed what historian I. A. Newby called "the flowering of racist thought," a period of virulent racism throughout the nation. The enduring symbol of twentieth-century race relations is the black ghetto, which, soon after conception, deteriorated into an impoverished and permanent slum.[2] The settlement house movement grew out of an awareness of the severe conditions facing newcomers to the city. While it attempted to address the needs of white immigrants, it largely ignored the parallel situation of African Americans when they began to replace whites in settlement neighborhoods.

The first half of this study seeks to explain the tragic failure of the mainstream settlement house movement to redirect its energies toward its black neighbors. The second half aims to show how other institutions, which neither practitioners nor examiners of settlement work have traditionally considered part of the settlement movement, did conduct a version of settlement work in black communities. This history, however, articulates an expanded definition of settlement work that embraces those efforts among blacks incorporating the settlement movement's dual commitment to provide a vast array of social service, educational, and recreational programs, and to usher in sweeping social change. Expanding the regional scope beyond the northern and midwestern metropolis and the temporal reach beyond the Progressive Era predicates such an encompassing notion. Following the unfolding of the settlement movement in new eras and overlooked regions establishes important links among institutions formerly deemed inherently different. An expanded definition, geographical scope, and periodization of settlement work begins to shed light on the enigmatic role of race in American reform. This introduction will briefly present a review of the essence of the settlement house, a sketch of the main scholarly schools of thought on the settlement movement, an elaboration of the general thesis, structure, and purpose of the current work, and an outline of the specific aims of each chapter.

The settlement house, a community center staffed by volunteers, was a leading philanthropic institution in the United States, modeled after the example of Toynbee Hall in London. It sought to help the poor, usually European immigrants, adjust to the industrial city. Settlement workers actually resided in run-down areas of the city, encountering poverty firsthand and translating their experiences into concrete social reforms. Settlement work thus symbolized a unique marriage of direct delivery of social services and commitment to sweeping social change.

The settlement house also offered a remarkable range of activities that integrated social welfare services, vocational training, liberal education, cultural programs, recreation, and entertainment. The premises themselves served as everything from employment bureau to day-care center, public bath to night school, gymnasium to union hall, and soup kitchen to salon. Immigrants and migrant blacks who found the metropolis confusing and even dangerous often turned for assistance to their own kin networks, churches, families, and societies. While these groups fostered a sense of community, the settlement house attempted to offer the additional asset of bridging the gap between the "foreign colony" and the established institutions in the rest of the city. Settlement workers, mostly college-educated middle-class women, sought to make use of their privileged backgrounds to provide access to power and resources otherwise denied to workers or the poor. These early social workers managed to convey useful information and skills that could help their neighbors make their way in and eventually out of the city.[3]

Jane Addams, who founded the renowned Hull House in Chicago with Ellen Gates Starr in 1889, infused the movement with enlightened cultural pluralism. She viewed the settlement house as a catalyst for the eradication of prejudice. In *Twenty Years at Hull-House*, published in 1910, she gloried in the "indications of an internationalism, as sturdy and virile as it is unprecedented, which I have seen in our cosmopolitan neighborhood." She went on: "When a South Italian Catholic is forced by the very exigencies of the situation to make friends with an Austrian Jew representing another nationality and religion, both of which cut into all of his most cherished prejudices, he finds it harder to utilize them a second time and gradually loses them. He thus loses his provincialism." Addams firmly believed that the retention of cultural differences was compatible with social integration. Coexistence based on equality and mutual respect, she went so far to say, could lay in settlement neighborhoods the local foundation for world peace.[4]

The headworker of South End House in Boston, Robert Woods, wrote that "the typical settlement, under American conditions, is one which provides neutral territory traversing all the lines of racial and religious cleavage."[5] Still another leader of the movement, Graham Taylor of Chicago Commons, wrote that the essence of settlement work involved "the goodwill to understand one another, to interpret misunderstood attitudes and situations, to reconcile and be reconciled to differences of taste and temperament, race and religion, heritage and aspiration, and through service and sacrifice to promote the unity of spirit in the bond of peace."[6] Given this commitment to pluralism, peaceful coexistence, and social change, the settlement movement's failure to redirect its efforts from white immigrants to blacks requires careful analysis.

Most scholarly treatments of the settlement movement have taken it for granted that settlement workers directed their efforts toward the millions of immigrants whose advent daily caused a visible change in the urban environment. These studies usually concentrate on the years from 1890 to 1914, a period considered the apex of progressivism and of the settlement movement.[7] The sheer number of immigrants no doubt accounts for the early dedication of settlement activities to whites, and historians have tended to echo the emphasis of the settlement leaders themselves. However, extending this study of settlements beyond World War I necessitates an exploration of the domestic parallel to the "immigrant question"—the situation of black Americans.

A first glance at the record of the early settlement movement's response to blacks raises doubts about the sincerity of the goal of social integration. The majority of settlement houses either excluded blacks, conducted segregated activities, closed down completely, or followed their former white neighbors out of black neighborhoods. In addition, the National Federation of Settlements (NFS), a central organization founded in 1911, largely ignored efforts to conduct settlement work among blacks.[8]

Some historians have argued that most settlement workers merely shared the racism of their day. Thomas Philpott resolves the paradoxical formation of the black slum during the height of progressive reform by exposing the racism of most Chicago reformers. Others, like Howard Jacob Karger and Ruth Crocker, put in relief the impulse of early social workers toward "social control," suggesting that their treatment of blacks mirrored their treatment of immigrants. Settlement workers, in their view, sought to assimilate the poor and workers in order to ensure the perpetuation of their own middle-class values and security.[9]

The racism and social control arguments arose in response to the previous glorification of the liberal, progressive nature of settlement workers. Allen Davis and John Higham, for example, view settlement workers as exceptional and exemplary individuals who were genuine altruists in the heyday of the coercive professional, and enlightened pluralists in a time of racial and ethnic animosity. Without studying settlement work by and among blacks, these scholars assume that the pluralistic embrace of immigrants extended to blacks. Davis asserts that settlement workers must have been among the most racially liberal Americans of their time. Although he lists only a handful of settlements for blacks in contrast to hundreds for immigrants, Davis concludes that "the most important and most vocal settlement workers. . . opposed the dominant thought of their time and sought to aid the Negro by helping him achieve equality." [10]

Judith Trolander, who examines the settlement movement since the Progressive Era, calls for a revision of this portrait of settlement workers. She argues that the most vocal leaders like Addams and Lillian Wald of Henry Street Settlement in New York City best fit the description offered by Davis and Higham, while many lesser-known settlement workers were not as open-minded. She notes that "many reformers, including settlement house workers, were liberal on a variety of issues, but they had a blind spot on civil rights." Yet she does not make race a central theme of her analysis until she broaches the period after 1945. She concludes that the lack of an organized civil rights movement caused the "blind spot." [11]

While students of settlements have yet to embark on a concerted effort to analyze the complex role of race in the movement, several historians have recently uncovered fascinating evidence of less storied settlement work—that conducted among blacks. Historians of African American women, in particular, have produced both encyclopedic tomes and case studies that prove the widespread participation of women in supporting and providing for the black community.[12] Their work fleshes out the story—told by historians of the black church and voluntary associations—of the strong African American tradition of self-help and racial "uplift." Ralph Luker, historian of race and the social gospel, and Dorothy Salem, chronicler of black women's reform, for instance, acknowledge the existence of settlement houses in black communities as well as other community work encompassing both social service and reform.[13]

The current work seeks to allow settlement work to follow its natural contours. When permitted to do so, it embraces many other expressions of community work and reveals the more radical implications that some of that work had in its own time and context. By blurring the customary distinction between settlement and nonsettlement work, this book seeks to reinterpret community work in black neighborhoods as more than "uplift," but as an effort toward drastic social change that would have implications for all Americans. Proponents of these efforts shared the righteous and ambitious ideals of the mainstream movement, despite having to cope with the extra burdens of ostracism, inadequate funding, and demoralization. This work seeks to show how institutions that often worked precisely because of their conservative guise actually embodied a wide vision, one in which the development of African American communities and individuals was a metaphor for the ushering in of a better world for all.

The first half of the study addresses the reactions of the mainstream settlement movement to blacks. This part of the movement is easy to pinpoint, since it formed a national organization, the National Federation of Settlements, as well as local ones such as the United Neighborhood Houses of New York and the Chicago Federation of Settlements. In the 1930s, approximately 200 houses belonged to one of these three major groups.[14] Still others qualified as bona fide settlement houses. This aspect of the movement has received intense scholarly scrutiny, but, because it failed to develop potent leadership on the question of race, many expressions of settlement activity in black communities went unnoticed both by the movement and its chroniclers. Many white leaders drew distinctions between blacks and white immigrants. Although they were often among those Americans most aware of racism, most vocal about the need to address it, and most active in support of civil rights, their views had various flaws. Their particular view of African American culture and character allowed many listeners to persist in believing, along with most native-born and immigrant whites, that blacks could best progress on their own, through separate self-help or racially oriented organizations, but not through the settlement movement. The National Federation of Settlements unwittingly reinforced the idea that the issue of blacks was not of prime concern for the settlement movement when it made a rigid distinction between religious work and settlement work. The determination to rule out any work deemed religious translated into a failure to recognize many efforts among blacks as true settlement houses.

Beginning with Chapter 3, the second part of the book changes direction. Under the guise of the Young Women's Christian Association, the Women's Home Missionary Society of the Methodist Episcopal Church, South, the black women's club and community movement, the National Urban League, and southern industrial schools, a vast number of community centers formed in the first half of the twentieth century. While the first half of the book does suggest some of the types of work undertaken, the second analyzes several key examples in greater depth. Because of the distinctions settlement workers made between their work and that of other organizations, scholars have tended to repeat this bifurcation of settlement work and other community work. Yet an examination of several key examples of institutions and individuals requires a more flexible and inclusive definition of settlement work. From the YWCA black branch or hostess house to the Bethlehem House or the southern school-settlement, these efforts sought to integrate a variety of social services with a dedication to social change. The inability of the mainstream movement to broaden its definition to include all similar efforts severely limited its potential as a mass movement. Since scholars have accepted uncritically the self-image developed by the settlement movement, they have not linked similar movements. An expanded definition brings into focus an entirely new settlement movement. While scholars have studied these other institutions, they have not interpreted them as expressions of the settlement philosophy. Analyzing them as part of that movement reveals aspects of these movements that have remained obscured. The expansion of the definition of settlement work not only points to numerous examples of settlement or settlement-type work, including that conducted among African Americans, but calls for and results from a lengthier periodization and broadened regional scope. Former settlement studies end with World War I and concentrate on major metropolises. Extending the time frame and regional base yields a variety of settlement houses established after or continuing well beyond the so-called waning of the movement; it also reveals a number of unexpected forms of settlement work, including examples from the rural South and small cities throughout the country as well as the usual major urban areas. It is necessary to look beyond the Progressive Era, beyond the cities of the Northeast and Midwest, and beyond the restricting definition of settlement work to uncover evidence of another settlement movement, to grasp its essence, and to examine critically the mainstream settlement movement.

More specifically, to carry out these themes, the first half of the book begins by focusing primarily on the responses of the mainstream settlement movement to African Americans. Chapter 1 delineates the views of blacks held by mainstream settlement leaders. It argues that settlement leaders, hardly ignorant of the problems facing black Americans, made significant distinctions between immigrants and blacks. Many held a view of African American culture as severely deficient. Because of the brutality of the system of slavery, blacks had lost the very rudiments of culture, the argument went; thus they lacked social organization, family ties, and the basic foundation of inner moral restraint. Most settlement workers sought to interpret the needs of their neighbors for the purpose of changing an inhumane social order. They disagreed with nineteenth-century charity workers who blamed the poor for their supposedly inherited moral frailty and instead faulted the environment. Blacks, however, did not benefit from this reorientation. Since they had allegedly lost all culture during slavery, they needed to educate themselves in the basics of "civilization." This attitude contributed to the settlement movement's failure to take a concerted stand on race and redirect its efforts toward blacks. Instead, most settlement workers encouraged either organizations uniquely devoted to civil rights, or blacks' own efforts at self-help. Besides a few exceptional individuals, whose fascinating stories require future scholarly attention, they lent their names to separate organizations devoted to improving particular aspects of the black experience. Their inability to grasp the significance of race to their movement is an agonizing shortcoming of the movement as a whole. Yet some settlement workers did aim their efforts at blacks. Chapter 1 presents an overview of these efforts, with key examples of the various approaches and choices, along with an analysis of their limitations.

Chapter 2 pursues the failure of the National Federation of Settlements to enact a consistent policy regarding race relations. Considering their claims of liberalism, cosmopolitanism, and pluralism, the sources of this weakness are complex. In the early twentieth century one of the ideas most emphasized by settlement workers was the differentiation of their work from that of religious missionaries. The distinction between settlement and mission constituted an essential aspect of the movement's very identity and self-definition. This chapter argues that the settlement movement's attempt at cosmopolitanism suffered from a secular, urban, and northern bias that systematically excluded blacks from the movement. Still based largely in the rural South, most African Americans shared a culture in which religion played a central role. Therefore, those whites and blacks who wished to conduct settlement work among blacks, especially in the South, often did so through missions, institutional churches, or other organizations with a strong religious component. Several examples illustrate the diversity and number of such efforts.

The second half of the study moves away from the mainstream settlement movement and concentrates on a few telling examples of little-known forms of settlement work conducted among blacks. Chapter 3 examines the workings of the Hampton- and Tuskegee-inspired rural southern school-settlement. Usually lacking contact with the National Federation of Settlements, these settlements nevertheless tried to combine social services, educational and recreational facilities, and community revitalization and self-sufficiency. The Calhoun Colored School and Social Settlement in Lowndes County, Alabama, the Penn School on St. Helena Island, South Carolina, and the People's Village School in Mt. Meigs, Alabama, relied for funding on supporters of industrial education for blacks. Yet in their rural settings, the black and white women who headed the schools sought to expand their purpose. Their schools served as community centers and represented efforts to instill local pride and to bring about land ownership and other significant reforms. These schools earned recognition as models for New Deal programs of community regeneration.

Chapter 4 delves deeply into three main expressions of settlement activity, which tellingly coalesced in the women's interracial movement of the early twentieth century. Lugenia Burns Hope's Neighborhood Union in Atlanta, the Bethlehem Houses of the women's home missions movement in the Methodist Episcopal Church, South, and the local black branches and hostess houses of the YWCA all functioned as settlements. These examples show the remarkable accomplishments of black and white women who combined delivery of sorely needed services with agitation for social reform. An ideology of moralist womanhood helped them transpose modest local attempts to improve conditions for their own children and those of their neighbors into a greater movement for social justice through interracial cooperation. Their efforts not only helped sustain their families and communities but also brought about a new era of cooperation between black and white women. In the course of their community activism, their ideology of activist, moralist motherhood transformed into a credo of Christian, humanitarian citizenship.

The conclusion summarizes the role of race in the decline of the settlement movement. It briefly reviews the trajectory of the settlement movement from the Progressive Era to the 1940s, with a brief foreshadowing of developments occurring in the 1960s. Not only did the settlements' failure to welcome black neighbors universally into their programs contribute to their long-term decline, but their restrictionism left the great promise of the movement unfulfilled. When racial tension erupted in the 1940s, settlements finally recognized that their future relied on their successful grappling with the issue of race. The National Federation of Settlements enacted a policy of integration, but local situations did not lend themselves to a smooth transition. In addition, the ensuing new style of community activism that took root from the fruition of the civil rights movement in the 1960s made the settlement seem outmoded. The Great Society's emphasis on indigenous leadership and staffs combined with black militancy to oust whites from the movement along with the goals of integration and cooperation. A new separatism replaced the old, neither of them assisting blacks in their quest for access to power, resources, and full participation "as co-worker[s] in the kingdom of culture."[15]

This small contribution to the understanding of the relationship between race and reform raises a variety of unanswered questions. Future studies might take advantage of the plethora of sources on black settlement activity hitherto generally sidestepped by scholarly analysis. Local archival materials on black branches of the YWCA, school-settlements, Urban League affiliates, institutional churches, religious settlements, missions, and community centers should provide access to more detailed information on the attitudes and behavior of the neighbors of settlement houses. While their role in the transformation of the settlement movement is implicit in the current study, more explicit illustrations would surely enrich and perhaps alter current interpretations. Further transcending of the usual temporal, regional, ethnic, and geographical bounds will yield fresh insights, as will comparative approaches. This study only begins to reevaluate American reform in light of the African American presence and to hint at the omnipresence of race as a crucial factor in all attempts by Americans to change themselves.

One

The Mainstream Settlement Movement and Blacks

A 1943 report on the William Byrd Community House, a social settlement in Richmond, Virginia, noted that the white "neighbors" were moving out as blacks moved into the section of the city served by the center. Whites did not want to walk through neighborhoods inhabited by blacks, so they attended settlement house functions in diminishing numbers, many of them convening instead in private houses. Meanwhile, having no recreational facilities at all, the new black residents eyed the center's activities with envy. The report recommended establishing a new settlement house for the white neighbors and relinquishing the William Byrd House to blacks. The author justified turning over the old house to blacks by stressing their deserving behavior: "We have been fortunate enough to have a high type Negro moving in." [1]

Surprisingly, this was a typical response of settlement workers to racial tension in settlement neighborhoods in the first half of the twentieth century. Given the settlement movement's ostensible commitment to pluralism and integration, the conditions at the William Byrd Community House are disconcerting. Did the vision of a new cosmopolitan culture based on the coexistence of diverse groups include everyone but blacks? Did settlement workers follow the lead of many white Americans who rated ethnic and national cultures on a scale of advancement and desirability as citizens, placing American blacks at the very bottom of the scale? Or were they ignorant of the dire living conditions faced by blacks in the early twentieth century?

This chapter seeks to begin to unravel the views that many settlement workers had of blacks as well as to delineate some of the ways workers actually responded to their black neighbors. While there was undoubtedly a great range in both views and policies, key examples serve to document a movement that was thrust into great confusion over the issue of race, an issue that contributed to its decline. First, a discussion of the views put forth by four authors, with whose ideas settlement workers would have been familiar, sketches some of the confines of their thinking about African Americans. Then, the elaboration of the ways in which settlement houses themselves responded to blacks completes the portrait of a movement in crisis. Even some of the settlement houses established primarily for blacks require critical attention. But in light of the failure of the rest of the movement to address the needs of blacks, these efforts stand clearly apart from the fray.

Several individuals connected to the settlement movement broached the subject of race head-on. Jane Addams, Louise de Koven Bowen, Frances Kellor, and John Daniels stand out as fascinating examples of a small group of individuals whose sensitive interest led them to dedicate much thought to the peculiar problems facing African Americans. While they differ from many of their white colleagues in this regard, their writings are both intriguing and frustrating. This small sample hardly illustrates how all settlement workers thought about blacks; no four individuals can speak for such a multifarious group. Nevertheless, their views are highly significant; they symbolize the inability of the larger settlement movement's vision to provide guidance on the issue of race. Greater familiarity with the situation of black Americans, working experience among them, or more encompassing intellectual frameworks might have helped prevent their misunderstandings, and, in turn, prohibited self-defeating and discriminatory policies.

These four writers did not share similar backgrounds or ideologies, the same relationship to the settlement movement, or even the same views of blacks. Yet their sociological analyses, no matter how piercing, help piece together an explanation for the limited response of the settlement movement to African Americans. This contention does not aim to question these reformers' accomplishments and pioneering efforts on behalf of a more humane society. A study of their limitations merely underscores the incredible sway held by the period's conception of black history and personality; their narrowness derives not from outright racism but from a certain generalized view of blacks that developed out of the particular conditions in the United States.

These thinkers, to varying degrees, all described the character of blacks as somehow maladjusted and their culture as lacking. The harsh system of slavery, they believed, had obliterated morality, family integrity, social organization, and even culture and civilization itself. While settlement workers distinguished themselves from nineteenth-century charity workers by emphasizing the environment and not hereditary moral weakness as the root of poverty, they did not use this reorientation to the benefit of blacks.

The debilitating depiction of the black individual as lacking the most basic capacity for self-control buttressed the settlement movement's failure to redirect its efforts from white immigrants to black migrants. Rather than responding to black migration by welcoming the newcomers, settlements largely ignored blacks. Instead, their leaders tended to advocate black self-improvement organizations, which they thought would begin the slow "civilizing" process. Like most white Americans, including even those who donated money and served as board members, these settlement workers accepted unquestioningly the innocuous demeanor of such institutions. Some supported the Urban League, which publicly emphasized that it delivered services and helped individuals assimilate to society rather than altering social structures. Others supported institutions such as the black industrial schools in the South, which professed primarily to teach "manual training," the basics of running a household, manners, and moral "decency." A few settlement workers lent their support to the National Association for the Advancement of Colored People, an organization dedicated to equal rights for blacks. The support of these institutions did show concern, and for a few exemplary individuals it represented true compassion, understanding, and experienced judgment. But for most, the support of these institutions came at the expense of a commitment to reorient their own movement toward their black neighbors. They generally promoted reforms that lacked the settlement movement's purpose of community revitalization through change in the local political economy and provision of social services. Ironically, many of these same institutions, beneath their veneer of conservatism, ran programs that mirrored those of the settlement houses. Nonetheless, the views of settlement spokespersons often helped perpetuate a faulty interpretation of black culture that underpinned the movement's failure, as a movement, to address the problems of blacks. This failure represents the tragedy of the movement.

Settlement Leaders' Views of Blacks

Early in the twentieth century, settlement workers did actually recognize race relations as an important social issue, and their very distinctions between blacks and immigrants determined the different approaches taken by their reform efforts. The philosophy of settlement workers, the policy of the National Federation of Settlements, and the reaction of individual settlement houses to the influx of blacks into immigrant enclaves showed a hypersensitivity to race relations as a crucial issue. Their Achilles' heel was not their lack of information or awareness of the situation of blacks but their perception of the nature of African American individuals and culture.

Well before the "great migrations" of blacks from the rural South to the cities of the North and Midwest during World War I, the 1920s, and World

War II, early social workers showed their awareness of the difficulties facing black Americans. In 1905, *Charities* (later *The Survey*), a leading journal of philanthropy, devoted an entire issue to the emerging black ghetto or "the negro city," with articles on the significance of black migration, the meager industrial opportunities for minorities, and the dearth of social services for blacks. In the manner of early social work and sociology, many observers went about collecting detailed information on nascent trends that helped determine the experience of blacks throughout the entire twentieth century.

The articles in *Charities* followed the approach of progressive social reform, intending to expose shocking conditions in order to effect social change. New York Charity Organization Society worker Lilian Brandt observed the large number of black migrants leaving the rural South for industrial cities. University of Pennsylvania professor Carl Kelsey rooted out causes for migration, citing especially "economic discontent" and perceived urban opportunity. Frances Kellor, founder of the National League for the Protection of Colored Women, warned of the dangers awaiting black women who were recruited for jobs as domestic servants but were often forced into prostitution instead. Boston settlement worker John Daniels presented research on the lack of opportunities for blacks in the industrial city where job discrimination caused black men to become "industrial scavengers" or "men-of-any-work." Some researchers stressed the need among black families for earnings from both spouses for mere survival. Other articles displayed the role of blacks as strikebreakers, the disproportionate number of black criminals, and the minimal social services available to blacks. An article by Booker T. Washington entitled "Why Should Negro Business Men Go South" completed the issue, urging blacks to stay in the South because "we should see to it that we do not lose in the South that which we possess. We should not grasp at a shadow and lose the substance."[2]

This issue of *Charities* reflected an early concern of some progressives for the specific plight of blacks as well as a general knowledge of social problems, which historians of black migration, the black ghetto, black workers, and black women have since corroborated.[3] During this period, a number of reformers researched and wrote on the subject, acknowledging that the trends of migration, urbanization, immigration, and industrialization called for a reevaluation of the American race problem. Studies revealed how difficult it was for blacks to overcome poverty because of the discrimination in housing and employment, inadequate education and diet, and disproportionate rates of delinquency, crime, death, and infant mortality they faced. Usually focusing on a particular city or region, writers showed the omnipresence of black poverty and white racism. These pioneering works in the social history of African Americans included W. E. B. Du Bois's *Philadelphia Negro* (1899), Mary White Ovington's *Half a Man: The*

Status of the Negro in New York (1911), Louise de Koven Bowen's *Colored People of Chicago* (1913), and John Daniels's *In Freedom's Birthplace: A History of the Boston Negro* (1914). Besides these and other books, numerous articles on specific topics relating to blacks appeared in journals of social work, philanthropy, sociology, and religion. Many of these authors either engaged in settlement work or were associated with the settlement community. Settlement workers, in addition, contributed significantly to the founding during this period of the National Association for the Advancement of Colored People and the National League on Urban Conditions among Negroes. In addition, settlement workers like Jane Addams contributed articles to the journals of these organizations, *The Crisis* and *Opportunity*, and other organs of the black press.[4]

While they attempted to employ "scientific" methods of observation, settlement workers did not stand united on the ideas and policies that resulted from their thinking about blacks. In fact, even issues concerning immigrants divided them. Some espoused assimilation and Americanization programs, often serving as the social arm of industrialists' scheme of corporate welfarism.[5] Others celebrated the diverse cultures of immigrant groups as "gifts" that enriched American culture; these settlement workers sought to preserve old world traditions in activities such as art exhibits, classes in living crafts, and the celebration of holidays. On the far right of the spectrum, some settlement workers joined the ethnocentric trend of the 1910s and 1920s and fought for immigration restriction.[6] Such a range of opinion on the nature of immigrants' role in the future of the United States inevitably appeared in discussions of blacks.

A vast historiography has focused on the dichotomy between Booker T. Washington and W. E. B. Du Bois, gradualism and immediatism, and industrial training and higher education.[7] While this division undoubtedly dominated public discourse, it tends to obscure subtleties of opinion, ideas, and action. Categorizing settlement workers, for instance, obscures important nuances and contradictions within even a single individual's thinking on race. The theories of leading settlement workers and associates of the movement—Jane Addams, Louise de Koven Bowen, Frances Kellor, and John Daniels—exhibit the great range of ideas of those rare mainstream settlement workers who did address the situation of black Americans. Their ideas help piece together an interpretation of the African American past that puts them in neither the Washington nor the Du Bois camps, but on shaky ground in between. They blamed the perpetuation of poor economic and social conditions among blacks partly on society but primarily on what they considered the weakness of the black family, the degradation of the black individual's psyche, and the annihilation of culture all resulting from the system of slavery. These ideas dominated the thinking of many reformers in the Progressive Era, and others since.[8]

While these reformers sought to overthrow what they considered the racist biological view of racial differences, their focus on environmental causes still led many of them to accept a portrait of blacks as inferior or maladjusted. Although some saw blacks as only temporarily backward, they settled for a stereotyped polarization of all African Americans into good and bad categories that could actually help legitimize opposition to social intermixture. This was an ambiguous term that could mean anything from miscegenation to integration of neighborhoods, and its use by those who celebrated the melting pot for immigrants established a clear boundary beyond which blacks were not to cross. Their reasoning articulates a certain way of thinking about race that emerged in the particular historical convergence of massive European immigration and the birth of social work and persisted throughout the first half of the twentieth century.

Jane Addams, ardent proponent of the doctrine of "immigrant gifts," and thus most likely to espouse an enlightened view of blacks, made a crucial distinction between blacks and white immigrants. In a 1911 article entitled "Social Control," she warned that, everywhere in America, "a strong race antagonism is asserting itself." In the North, racism took the concrete form of residential segregation. Seclusion denied blacks access to what she called "inherited resources" among which numbered psychological and familial resources that established the basis for "social restraint." As a result, she went on, "in every large city we have a colony of colored people who have not been brought under social control." To Addams, "social control" did not mean the imposition of the values or power of one individual or group on another. Instead, it meant the ability of the family to re-create the inner moral structure composed of elements such as family bonds, parental discipline, and generational continuity that instilled respect and led to socially desirable behavior. Unlike the strong families of Italians, for example, black families' "lack of restraint" caused black girls to yield to the city's "temptation" since their lives lacked the family customs necessary for assimilation into civilization. In Addams's view, residential segregation in the city exacerbated an already volatile situation. Since blacks had to rent near the vice districts, she concluded, "the family in the community least equipped with social tradition is forced to expose its daughters to the most flagrantly immoral conditions the community permits."[9]

Addams assessed the problems facing blacks as resting both on unfair social arrangements and on what she saw as the resulting weaknesses of the black family. Addams supported W. E. B. Du Bois and served on the NAACP board as a founding member. In her *Second Twenty Years at Hull-House*, Addams called the plight of blacks "the gravest situation in our American life," especially "because we are no longer stirred as the Abolitionists were, to remove fetters, to prevent cruelty, to lead the humblest to the banquet of civilization." The primary emphasis of her social work, however, remained immigrants. Another reformer and Hull House associate, Louise de Koven Bowen, criticized Hull House for not taking a leading role in bridging racial divisions. She noted that few blacks lived near Hull House, but the few who occasionally attended a club meeting or a class "were not always welcomed warmly." Some Hull House residents helped start Wendell Phillips, a settlement in a black district on the west side of Chicago; Jane Addams helped raise money for Frederick Douglass Center, a settlement for both blacks and whites on the fringe of the south-side black ghetto, founded by Unitarian minister Celia Parker Woolley. Louise de Koven Bowen questioned this approach, however: "The settlement seemed unwilling to come to grips with the 'Negro problem' in its own environs, yet Hull-House was willing to be concerned with the same 'problem' elsewhere in the city." [10]

Bowen, who later served as president of Hull House from 1935 to 1944, studied the living conditions for blacks in Chicago and analyzed her results in 1907 in *The Colored People of Chicago*, published by the Juvenile Protection Agency, of which she was founding president. She differentiated between the opportunities for blacks and immigrants:

> The enterprising young people in immigrant families who have passed through the public schools and are earning good wages continually succeed in moving their entire households into prosperous neighborhoods where they gradually lose all trace of their earlier tenement house experiences. On the contrary, the colored young people, however ambitious, find it extremely difficult to move their families or even themselves into desirable parts of the city and to make friends in these surroundings.

Bowen noted that most blacks had concrete reasons for lacking motivation since little opportunity awaited them upon adulthood. The crowding of blacks in the lowest paying, least desirable jobs and the need for earnings from both spouses were facts of black family life. Bowen's pamphlet expressed outrage at the disproportionate number of blacks in jail, the practice of bringing black women to the North as maids that often ended in prostitution, and the entrenched "black belt" that had the highest rents and the worst living conditions in the city. Her observations called for social change: "the life of the colored boy and girl is so circumscribed on every hand by race limitations that they can be helped only as the entire colored population in Chicago is understood and fairly treated." [11]

Historian Thomas Philpott shows that no white Chicagoans were "more conscious of Negro conditions than" settlement workers like Addams and Bowen. But despite their exposés of poor living conditions for blacks, they stopped at a certain line that few whites would cross. Philpott writes that Bowen "asked

Louise de Koven Bowen. (Jane Addams Memorial Collection, Special Collections, University Library, University of Illinois at Chicago)

her city to grant its citizens everything but equality . . . equal treatment before the law, access to employment and admission to public institutions and accommodations." [12] Bowen concluded that the black man "does not resent social ostracism." [13]

Jane Addams's focus on the lack of "moral restraint" in the black family and Louise de Koven Bowen's belief that blacks required equality but not integration were among the attitudes that dominated twentieth-century thinking on race relations across the political spectrum. These two themes predominated even among those reformers most committed to improving the conditions for blacks. Frances Kellor, an early proponent of the environmental school of criminology, began her career with a study of southern blacks and crime and later established the National League for the Protection of Colored Women (one of three reform agencies consolidating into the National League on Urban Conditions among Negroes). Kellor's participation in the League and her study of crime reflected her belief that blacks needed outside help from their moral superiors. The emphasis on environmental factors such as poverty and discrimination represented a view that appears open-minded when compared to racial determinism, but the preoccupation with the supposed disintegration of moral tradition rendered blacks hapless victims in the eyes of reformers. This portrayal of blacks paved the way for a paternalistic, moralistic style of reform. Rather than establish integrated settlement houses, most settlement workers turned to different types of reforms when their efforts targeted blacks.[14]

Frances Kellor's study of the "criminal negro" orchestrated a particular, revealing variation on the idea of environmental causes for criminality. Her theory provided the basis for a replacement of inherited racial factors with historical, environmental ones. Both concepts, however, sought to explain basically the same character traits. Kellor asserted that determining the relative influence of environmental and hereditary factors in crime had ramifications for policy: "Habitual-criminal acts recognize the physical basis of the crime; parole laws recognize the influence of environment." She contrasted the "more humane system" of the North, which entailed "more moral and mental instruction" with the South's system of "revenge and punishment" which was "neither systematic nor scientific." The reason cited for this difference was that the South's "criminal class is largely Negro."[15]

Kellor saw the disproportionate number of blacks in the penal system as inevitable given the "agencies that produce crimes." Rather than faulting discriminatory law enforcement or poverty itself, Kellor interpreted "environmental factors" quite literally. Conditions conducive to crime include the southern climate, she asserted, which encourages "crimes of passion and licentiousness" and predisposes one to "idleness" rather than "frugality and forethought." Southern soil requires a smaller "expenditure of energy" than soil in the North, so a black person "rarely labors a full week, even if he knows the necessity exists; for he feels assured of a livelihood." She went on: "Every race for whom Nature provides lavishly, and in whom there have not been developed desires aside from those incident to self-preservation, will not exert itself. The necessity does not exist. It is the obstacles that have assisted the Anglo-Saxon race in its upward course." Unwittingly contradicting her own attempt to root out the causes of the high rate of black criminality, Kellor stated that southern whites shared the indolence of blacks, whom she believed "were lavishly provided for under slavery." White men lost their lethargy when they entered the industrial city, yet this new competitive environment also fostered crime. Southern women had a low crime rate because they "are not subjected to the temptations offered by industrial and professional life." In this analysis, Kellor decided on a some-what anachronistic course of action. A black man, she concluded, "needs that training which will take him out of the class of unskilled labor and put him in a position to attain the interests of a small farmer in the North." [16]

The most important factor predisposing blacks to crime and the most prom-ising area for crime prevention, Kellor thought, was "the domestic life and the training surrounding the child." She declared that "there is no race outside of barbarism where there is so low a grade of domestic life, and where the child receives so little training, as among the negroes." The explanation for this back-wardness was that "in slavery, the negro knew no domestic life." In the forty years since emancipation, Kellor said, the educational system that should aim "to create and establish all the sound principles and practices of domestic life" had failed "to enlighten or reform the negro." "Instruction in reading and writ-ing, history, arithmetic, theology" has little value without teaching "the need of morality, sobriety and fidelity." The latter, in addition, had to begin with the most rudimentary aspects of life itself. Kellor lamented that "in matters of cleanliness, sanitation, prevention of disease, etc., he [the African American] has been left to look out for himself." [17]

Kellor thought blacks lacked inner moral strength and thus had "loose domes-tic relations." While white slaveholders bore the brunt of these reformers' anger, Kellor also blamed black women for yielding "to white men as readily as in slavery" and for not being "virtuous when they enter matrimony." She criticized marriage among blacks as "more of a religious ceremony . . . [that] does not give them the consciousness of new legal and social obligations." Care of chil-dren declined since slavery, she asserted, when "whites were interested in the life of the negro child" for its "cash value." The "relatively crude and simple" social life of blacks likewise worsened since the abolition of slavery severed their contact with whites. Social life among blacks, Kellor scolded, centered not on organizations and clubs, but on the church, which "is lacking in the fundamental principles that should make it a governing agency." The church organizes "most of the excursions, picnics, parties, entertainments, cake-walks and festivals." Its provision for the leisure of blacks "permits of much social intercourse" but only "leads to an expenditure of money for finery and unnecessaries that keeps the race impoverished," she judged. [18]

Kellor's view had contradictory implications. On the one hand, she tried to show the role of the antebellum, Reconstruction, and post-Reconstruction

South in the devastation of the personality, morality, and social organization of blacks. On the other, she helped further racist assumptions about the inferiority of blacks by blaming them for their situation. Black politicians had bungled Reconstruction, she thought, and while disfranchisement of all blacks was unethical, most blacks (and many whites) should be barred from voting on the grounds of illiteracy. Kellor concluded that "the Negro at present has neither the perceptions nor the solidity of character that would enable him to lead his race" since he has "not yet attained the position where he is regarded as a man rather than a Negro." As for the future, she proposed the cooperation of whites in advancing "such economic, financial, cultural and educational conditions as will enable him to maintain similar grades in his own race and to have literature and recreations of equal standards." She made it clear that the theory of racial progress did not favor "mingling at the white's social functions, or invading his home," for "the free intermingling of the two races is impossible, at least for many generations." Like Louise Bowen, she acknowledged a boundary to reform and advancement, reassuring whites that "the Negro will not demand . . . social equality with the whites. He will find within his own race what he needs and desires."[19]

The Progressive Era witnessed what scholar I. A. Newby called a "flowering of racist thought." Even those believing themselves interested in the welfare of blacks debated "whether or not the black man's presumed biological differences from whites made him less capable of civilization." While reformers like Addams, Bowen, and Kellor rejected a biological explanation for the subordination of a black individual, they failed to answer the "unresolved question of his capacity to function in civilized society." Their focus on environmental origins of varying capacities failed to contradict the portrayal of blacks as inferior. This stress on cultural deficiency created, in the minds of many whites, a new rationale for discrimination.[20]

This limiting schema did not sufficiently challenge the theoretical underpinnings of outright segregation. Thomas Philpott cites Henry Bruère, a Boston settlement worker and director of New York City's Bureau of Municipal Research, who took these ideas to the extreme when he applied immigrant restrictionist views to blacks. In a 1904 article, he advocated industrial training rather than higher education because he thought it would keep blacks in the South. While possessing very different intentions from Frances Kellor, he nevertheless shared her view that, after "long years of comfortable slavery," blacks sought to keep from working. Blacks needed to develop their very selves, and to aim ultimately at self-improvement, not assimilation. Bruère explained that, unlike immigrants, blacks "cannot be raised by a process of assimilation" as their race is "so foreign."[21]

In a time when racist tracts and the eugenics movement spread the specter of race suicide, and professors Edward A. Ross and John R. Commons and others spouted quasi-scientific methods of ranking racial and ethnic groups, the settlement workers no doubt put forth some of the most enlightened white views of blacks.[22] Jane Addams strongly supported the antilynching campaign of Ida B. Wells.[23] Bowen and Kellor worked to prevent the victimization and forced prostitution of black migrant women in northern cities. Others participated in the social survey movement, studying "the negro problem" and publishing books and articles on the subject. Applying the same techniques to the study of blacks and summoning up as much reformist fervor, some even drew the analogy between blacks and immigrants.

In 1914, South End House resident John Daniels wrote *In Freedom's Birthplace*, a lengthy study of blacks in Boston from the time of early colonial settlement to the First World War. His study did make an important statement about the contributions of notable African Americans to American history. Though escaping the usual ignorance of the efforts of blacks, he interpreted their achievements as exceptions. In addition, his proposed reforms stumbled on several obstacles. He rejected "social intermixture" of the races and furthered a stereotypical portrait of African Americans. Camouflaged in the writings of prominent progressives, and presented as the analytical summary of social scientific research, these ideas were all the more insidious.[24]

John Daniels's mentor, Robert Woods, head of South End House, wrote an introduction to Daniels's study. Woods noted that the book represented the culmination of a project undertaken in 1904 that led to the establishment of a black auxiliary to South End, the Robert Gould Shaw House. Woods encouraged philanthropists who donated funds to industrial schools in the South to become aware of a new northern issue involving not only racial "equality" but also "contact." Since white racism erupted as black migrants arrived in increasing numbers, the fate of the city and the fate of blacks could not be separated from the fate of the entire nation. The particular historical moment, Woods thought, provided an unequalled opportunity to alter all three. Comparing blacks to immigrants, he stated that the situation of blacks could be approached from a "normal and ultimately manageable angle" if only "the Negroes can be considered as an unassimilated social factor analogous to the different immigrant nationalities." Woods went on, however, to undermine his own argument. The European immigrant and the African American were not similar in every respect, he said, for "it is true that the analogy is incomplete:—at the point of racial intermixture it ceases."[25]

Woods elaborated the ways he thought black migrants should take advantage of the opportunity offered by the city for permanent change in their position. Following in the footsteps of immigrants who also had to overcome bitter prejudice, blacks should establish political, economic, and religious allegiance within their own group. The "secret" to success, he said, was "the power of association based on racial loyalty." He admitted that his theory implied that "a certain sort of segregation" was "provisionally a blessing." Blacks' inability to marshal respect from whites resulted from their "incapacity for loyal, continuous, result-getting team work among themselves" and not from white racism. Blacks needed self-imposed, "constructive discipline," Woods contended.[26]

However enlightened this approach initially appeared, its unfavorable view of blacks rejected the very analogy between blacks and immigrants.[27] While urging blacks to follow the example of immigrants toward assimilation and self-help, Woods placed road blocks on both paths, first by invoking the taboo of racial intermixture and then by tracing African Americans' defeats to stunted self-improvement. While he ostensibly faulted white prejudice, he ended up blaming the moral failings of blacks even more: "It is not fundamentally in the outward hindrance to vocational success or cultural recognition, but in the confusion and ineptness with which color prejudice affects the productive moral faculty of a whole racial group."[28]

In the text of *In Freedom's Birthplace*, Daniels meticulously depicted the social and economic odds against blacks. After reviewing the record of black history, which included valiant black participants in the Revolutionary and Civil Wars, and renowned blacks from poet Phillis Wheatley to "the greatest Negro intellectual," W. E. B. Du Bois, Daniels concluded that slavery determined the experience of most blacks in this nation; blacks were brought "from their native African jungle, where from time immemorial their ancestors had lived in a state of primitive savagery." Slaves "were savages themselves, utterly ignorant of civilization, having no religion above a fear-born superstition, and lacking all conception of reasoned morality," Daniels went on. Slavery itself worsened the state of blacks in the South, "where for two centuries and a half their race was held in subjection even more degraded than the savage state of their ancestors, so far as concerned its prohibition of all independence and independent progress, and its disregard of any germs of personal chastity and marital loyalty." Because social conditions had hardly been more than "slavish" since emancipation, Daniels concluded that black migrants from the South remained virtually unchanged from his unflattering portrait of black slaves. Even in the North where blacks were free since the Revolutionary period, and in possession of "political and civil rights equal to those of white citizens," Daniels claimed, they "remained the most backward group in the community." The obstacles to their advancement to higher positions in industry resulted from "obvious shortcomings in the basic qualities of trustworthiness, responsibility, accuracy and thoroughness." Daniels went on: "Their social order and organization are still the most rudimentary. Their churches are the weakest. Their part in political affairs is the least." The typical black person worked in "menial or common labor" and except for a few exceptions, in all respects failed to "measure up to the average white man." [29]

The crux of Daniels's portrait of blacks alarmingly resembled that of the more charitable Jane Addams, and those of Frances Kellor and Louise de Koven Bowen. Blacks, he maintained, were the "farthest in the rear" of any race, in "the inculcation among its members of any positive code of morality and any general ethical standards." He saw this lack of morality as reflected in a "lesser reproductive power" and a "lesser resistance, not only to disease, but to the general wear and tear of present-day urban conditions." Rather than the result of those very conditions, this weakness derived from a lack of "stability," an "incapacity for cooperation" and independence, a reluctance to "take fuller advantage" of voting strength, and undeveloped religious activity. What religious activity blacks did engage in included tolerance, which Daniels interpreted as a sign of "a serious defectiveness of moral vision." Their "excess of religious emotionalism" indicated "a shortage in the power of restraint and self-control." [30]

Daniels interpreted the dire straits of the African American individual as signifying "an intrinsic weakness or flabbiness at the very root and core of his make-up," a lack of "fundamental moral stamina." He thought that racial animosity in the North existing since the earliest Colonial settlements abated during the Abolitionist and Reconstruction phases when blacks were "indulged" and failed the test. Racism reached new heights after 1895, springing from "legitimate" acknowledgment of the "inferiority" or lesser "actual racial worth" of blacks, Daniels believed. Antipathy resulted from the breaking away of whites from the "abolitionist propaganda of unrestricted inter-association between the two races, and [turning] in the direction of the Negro's segregation." [31]

In spite of his damning view of blacks, Daniels went on to call for the "advancement" of the race. An already apparent sign of progress was the growing equality before the law of a black individual, so recently a nonentity. In addition, his turning to "self-endeavor" and focus on "earning his daily bread" and then on education, and on "gradually bettering his conditions of life" in the manner recommended by Booker T. Washington, symbolized fine "intuition." Evidence of "the evolution of a general social order," based on "independent progress," began to lay "a foundation upon which to build his future." Daniels defined the "fundamental moral stamina" required for equality as that "stern and exacting discipline of centuries of civilization slowly acquired." Daniels deemed a comparison of blacks and immigrants "neither fair nor intelligent," for "both justice and accuracy demand that the situation of the Negro to-day be compared, not with that of the white man to-day, but with his own condition in the past." Ironically, Daniels ended his study by claiming that prejudice would dissipate as blacks made progress. He believed that prejudice was much greater in the South, but because blacks were a more "distinct and self-reliant group" there, they would probably develop faster. It is up to blacks alone to "attain the position" of "self-respect and worthy recognition," he declared.[32]

Daniels and other leading settlement workers clearly differed on their ideas about blacks. But several recurring themes emerged, none more prominent than African Americans' cultural deprivation, their lack of "moral" or "social restraint," their weak families, and the natural social distance between blacks and whites. While reformers stressed environmental, not biological causes, they failed to challenge the portrayal of blacks as inferior. This focus, though not shared by all, had critical implications for the way settlement workers would translate philosophy into policy. In assessing the overall response of the settlement movement to blacks, it is important to note that the influx of black migrants to the city slums was apparent to those with heightened social concern as early as the turn of the century, but became obvious to all during World War I and afterward. While most scholars have treated the issue of race as tangential to the study of the settlement movement, any study transgressing the usual boundary of 1914 must consider the black neighbors as perhaps the major influence on the subsequent history of the movement.

Settlement Houses' Responses to Blacks

In 1936, Sidney Lindenberg and Ruth Zittel, of Neighborhood Centre in Philadelphia, observed that increased black migration during and after the war decreased immigration, and the subsequent alteration in the composition of many settlement neighborhoods changed the very nature of the "settlement scene." They thought the future of the settlement movement depended on its ability to adapt to the changing needs of its new neighbors. They reiterated the observations of the Progressive Era reformers that blacks, more than any group, faced the greatest challenge of warding off poverty in the twentieth-century city: "Because of an inferior economic position and pressure from a white group, which through control of recreation, housing and education restricts his freedom of movement, the Negro is forced into the most densely crowded, unsanitary areas . . . those areas which have already degenerated through years of 'population packing.'" The overpopulated black ghetto suffered from an exceptionally "high rate of delinquency, a high morbidity and mortality rate and a low standard of living." These conditions caused the authors to ask, "What is the Settlement, the sponsor of the underprivileged and the champion of the immigrant, doing for the Negro who has settled on its doorstep?" Lindenberg and Zittel answered their own question with the comment that "we can say upon observation that comparatively few of the settlements have even scratched the surface of this problem." "Let's face the issue!" they urged.[33]

Not until the early 1940s did the settlement movement as a whole make a concerted effort to address the situation of blacks, when the National Federation of Settlements engaged in a long-overdue analysis of its interracial policies. Throughout the first half of the twentieth century, a settlement confronted by the appearance of blacks in its environs responded either by closing down, by following its white immigrant neighbors and moving out of the neighborhood, by excluding blacks, by conducting segregated activities, by establishing or urging the establishment of a separate branch for blacks, or by attempting integration. In addition, some black and white workers erected independent settlements for blacks or for a mixed clientele.[34] This list of choices reflects the wide range of responses within the settlement movement. Yet in both closed- and open-minded reactions, similar themes echoed the views of the movement's leaders and etched in the boundaries of reform.

Those scholars interested in the settlement houses' responses to blacks have conducted case studies of individual houses, cities, or periods. Some of their findings, when accompanied by new examples, yield instructive patterns. A few illustrations serve to suggest the various choices made by reformers and the translation of their theories into practice.

Judith Trolander describes Hull House's response to blacks, for instance, as inaction. Although the second largest black neighborhood in Chicago enveloped the settlement, "blacks were hardly represented in the Hull-House program." Jane Addams began a black mothers' club in 1927, a picture of which appeared in the institution's yearbook with the assertion that "Negroes were taking part in the program." Yet these mothers were not invited to any community activities or put on the mailing lists. Thomas Philpott notes that the Hull House summer camp and its boarding house for working girls—the cooperative Jane Club—were both open only to whites in the first four decades of the century, and other activities kept black participation to a minimum by imposing a "quota" that did not reflect the true racial composition of the surrounding streets. Not until 1938 did headworker Charlotte Carr and Works Progress Administration race relations advisor Dewey Jones, the only black staff member of Hull House to date, make an effort to enlist the participation of blacks. While some black boys began to use the game room, blacks did not join most of the activities. When Jones died in 1939, efforts at integration faltered. Although unintentional, Trolander concludes, "the feeling developed that Hull-House was for whites only."[35]

Many other settlements allowing black participation organized separate activities along the lines of the Hull House black mothers' club. In his study of settlement work in Columbus, Ohio, Jon A. Peterson elaborates the functions of the Godman Guild House, established in 1898 in Flytown, a factory slum district in the northwestern section of Columbus inhabited originally by Irish Americans and German and Welsh immigrants. Godman Guild workers helped establish the city's first neighborhood library, the first free public bath, the first public gym, and one of its first kindergartens. Inspired by the example of Hull House, it founded playgrounds, a summer vacation school, a pool room, clubs for boys, an employment bureau, an infant welfare clinic, dental and prenatal clinics, a public park, and a family summer camp qua health resort.[36]

In the 1910s, blacks from the rural South arrived in Flytown. Some whites and even the few blacks who had lived in the neighborhood moved out, and in 1919 and 1920, reports of racial conflict elsewhere caused Godman Guild Headworker James Wheeler to put into effect a policy of strict segregation of facilities. Blacks and whites could use the house on alternate days for classes, clubs, and teams, while Sundays were open to adults of both races. The summer resort, "The Reservation," did not admit blacks at all; a separate one got off the ground in 1926. Wheeler explained that "it would be fatal to the success of the Reservation as a place of resort for the white race, if colored people were admitted there." He offered a dubious rationale: "*This is a condition and not a theory.* The whites would simply withdraw and fail to come if the Camp were opened to colored, and the camps will be either white or colored as the case may be, but not both. . . . Therefore segregation, which is bitterly opposed by advanced colored people and colored agitators, is really necessary to *any* progress at all." Only the clinics, the employment bureau, and other general services were officially unrestricted. This policy continued until 1956, when criticism initiated in 1952 by the NAACP and the National Federation of Settlements finally brought about the integration of activities, ironically at the same time that Godman Guild and other settlements lost their central importance in the city.[37]

Other houses refused to follow even this biracial policy and either closed down or voted to move out of the neighborhood, following their departing white neighbors. These decisions did not transpire easily, as they often meant reevaluating the original settlement leaders' intentions. Given the pioneer generation of settlement workers' murkiness about African Americans, later settlement workers often stewed over the choices and the future of their houses. They struggled over whether settlements had primary allegiance to the geographical neighborhood or to the actual neighbors. While this could be a real dilemma, it also provided a loophole that allowed settlements to neglect some of their neediest neighbors.

Abraham Lincoln Centre, founded in 1905 in Chicago, was one of the exceptional attempts to direct local efforts to improve race relations. Judith Trolander writes that, in the 1930s, the Centre was one of only two settlement houses (the other was the Ada McKinley Center) to have a sizable group of black participants. With a white director, Curtis Reese, and an integrated staff, the house stood between black and white communities and fostered equal and integrated participation in all of the Centre's activities, including social events.[38] According to Thomas Philpott, the Centre tried harder than any other Chicago settlement to cross the color line. It began as a program of the Unitarian All Souls Church, intended by one of its founders as "a factory where men were made." Above its door read the church's motto: "Here let no man be stranger." Yet the tenement district inhabited by Germans, Irish, and Jews began to empty as the Black Belt expanded eastward, eventually enveloping the house. The settlement tried to keep its programs integrated, but had increasing difficulties attracting whites, and thus found its plan of improved race and ethnic relations stymied by neighbors' attitudes. Whites refused to use the facilities when blacks attended and when the settlement sheltered blacks during the fierce race riots of 1919, it "stood accused of forcing 'social equality' on the community."[39]

In the wake of the riots, Abraham Lincoln Centre retained its ideal of "interracial brotherhood" while confronting the problem of recruiting and maintaining white membership. The house allowed groups to be self-selective, unwittingly causing segregated activities. During the 1920s, whites used the settlement less in spite of the proximity of a large white neighborhood. The All Souls Church meanwhile abandoned the neighborhood for an all white section of Chicago. In 1929, Philpott notes, Curtis Reese reaffirmed the staff's commitment to integration and many more whites withdrew. In the 1930s, the settlement tried to keep whites through "controlled registration" in which only one black person could be admitted for every nine whites. The price of an interracial policy seemed to be de facto discrimination.[40]

Another alternative available to those interested in conducting settlement work among blacks was the independent house established primarily for blacks. These houses were not exempt from controversy and tension. On the one hand, a segregated facility raised questions about the viability of the house's proclaimed goal of enhanced race relations. On the other, assumptions about the nature of the neighbors influenced the specific types of reforms undertaken, or the very definition of racial advancement itself.

While those rare settlements dedicating themselves to blacks provided valuable resources and a source of civic pride, they sometimes reflected, though in a milder form, a stereotyped view of blacks as falling into categories of either "good or bad," or likely versus unlikely to succeed. To different ends and varying degrees, settlements with integrated or all-black staffs, which worked predominantly or completely with black neighbors, often expressed this polarization. A *Southern Workman* article published in 1906 described Eighth Ward House in Philadelphia, "a Northern settlement for Negroes . . . a settlement that bends its efforts to the helping of a degraded Negro community." The author wrote that "it is only the weaker element in the Negro race that comes drifting into the Northern cities." The view that migrant blacks lacked the most basic social restraints or civilized traditions often led to an emphasis on hygiene: "And how has the settlement attacked its problem? First of all it took the neighborhood as a mother takes a naughty, dirty child, and washed its face." Unlike the efforts of a Hull House or a Henry Street Settlement, this clean-up activity was not the beginning of a process, but an end in itself. A worker described the goal of Eighth Ward House: "At the present stage of the neighborhood development, the settlement stands, perhaps more than anything else, as a disinfecting agency to the community—a sort of moral Platt's Chlorides—striving by the radiation of such spiritual power as lies within its command to make a purer, sweeter atmosphere for the more normal growth of all who respond to its influence."[41]

Similarly striking language characterized the 1908 report of a Clifton, Massachusetts, Conference of black leaders, philanthropists, and educators, which read that "legislation can never shape this granite of African origin for its appropriate place in the temple of civilization." The conference report went on in a self-laudatory manner about "our endeavor to help the members of the 'child race' in their efforts to rise."[42] It is tempting to dismiss this denigration of black character and culture as the product of the paternalism of white philanthropists. However, even middle-class black settlement worker Janie Porter Barrett, later founder of the Virginia Industrial School for "wayward" black girls, began Locust Street Settlement in Hampton, Virginia, by sorting her "neighbors"; some "were ruled out if they weren't clean, or if they used bad words." Barrett, too, inordinately stressed appearance and hygiene. She sacrificed a bathroom for her own house to use the money to build a clubhouse. "You see," she reported, "we needed this more and it helped the people to whom I preached cleanliness, cleanliness, cleanliness all day and every day to know that I had exactly the same inconveniences that they did." Many of the activities of Locust Street Settlement constituted an attempt to make members project an appearance that would counteract negative stereotypes of blacks as uncivilized and unclean. Its Homemakers Club, for example, aimed "to make the home more attractive" and "to keep boys and girls off the street." Its "'flower lovers' department distributes plants, seeds and cuttings to beautify the yards of the community and preaches the gospel of clean back yards."[43]

It is important to note that these were the views of those whites then considered the most liberal on the issue of race and even of many black reformers.

Janie Porter Barrett in photo entitled "Mr. Harris Barrett's Home," by Frances Benjamin Johnston. (Courtesy of Hampton University Archives)

This ideology combined good intentions with a view of blacks as victimized by their heritage in slavery to buttress gradualism and to emphasize individual shortcomings as the source of low social and economic status. Placing the blame primarily on slavery took the attention away from more immediate conditions caused by ongoing exploitation and prejudice. This view in turn inspired reform measures appropriate for this so-called primitive stage of development of African American culture and personality. In a time when settlement workers and others stressed that the environment, not individual weakness, caused poverty and the suffering of groups, blacks did not benefit from this reorientation. Instead, a historical environmentalism kept alive the stress on individual moral and personal deficiency. The Eighth Ward Settlement, for instance, received letters continually asking whether it trained servants. Rather than the outrage one might expect from an institution dedicated to social work among blacks, the workers responded, "No, we do not train servants. The very best we can hope to do is to prepare the material out of which servants or any other workman helpful to humanity can be trained."[44]

The terms with which these reformers articulated their views of blacks, their very language, had implications for the types of reform undertaken. When Albert Kennedy noted that slaveowners "debauched Negro morale," he no doubt had good intentions. In his attempt to lay the blame where it did indeed need to rest, he expressed an ideology that in turn helped perpetuate a new set of unequal social relations. Slavery, he thought, had created "a white-negro work relationship that encouraged laziness, thievery, lying and rebellion."[45] These traits, usually voiced as a lack of innate moral restraint imbued by a vacant cultural tradition, went on to reinforce in the minds of many Americans that the identity of the black personality itself was inferior and deviant.

The theory that black migrants and white immigrants differed fundamentally underpinned many settlements' policy of establishing a separate branch for blacks. In practice, these houses at times managed to conduct integrated activities. Lincoln House in Manhattan, initially called Stillman House, a branch of Henry Street Settlement, was founded by Lillian Wald. She took pride in the integrated classes, though the house also conducted activities composed entirely of blacks or of Jews, according to the wishes of the neighbors themselves. Because of the extensive research on living conditions among blacks conducted by Lincoln House, Wald earned a reputation as an advocate for blacks and for interracial advancement.[46]

The Robert Gould Shaw House also formed as a branch of another settlement, the South End House in Boston. The Shaw House offered all of the usual settlement activities such as choral groups, a Mothers' Club, a Fathers' Club, athletic teams, after-school functions, and a variety of classes. Although located in a predominantly black neighborhood, it too welcomed others. Melnea A. Cass, who was active in Shaw House in the 1920s, recalled that the white and black people "mingled in together very nicely." The story of her experiences at Shaw reveals that a separate black branch could become a thriving community center and source of community pride, as well as a springboard for further involvement on behalf of blacks. Cass described the House's "Friendship Club," which began as a meeting of mothers of kindergartners and went on to build a nursery school, raise funds for the settlement house and a children's camp, and conduct other social service activities. In 1949, Cass helped found Freedom House, another community center dedicated to improving social conditions for blacks, and served as president of the Boston NAACP in the 1960s.[47]

Several independent settlement houses successfully challenged the precepts both of the need for a "civilizing" regime and of separate organization as the only strategy. One remarkable example was Karamu House, a settlement house established in 1915 to provide cultural opportunities and interracial contacts to its Cleveland neighbors. Working for decades against overwhelming odds, marked by white hostility and poor funding, Karamu managed to become a thriving center for the arts, a bridge between races, and a source of pride for the community and eventually the city. Many actors, dancers, musicians, and other artists got their start at Karamu, and the Karamu Theatre earned world renown for its encouragement and training of African American dramatists.[48]

Russell and Rowena Jelliffe, founders of Karamu, were called by one con-

Karamu House rehearsal. Action from Eugene O'Neill's The Long Voyage Home, *Arena Theatre, Karamu House, Cleveland, Ohio. (Western Reserve Historical Society, Cleveland, Ohio)*

temporary journal "Banner Bearers in the field of Negro-White relations in the American Settlement House Movement." While Karamu emphasized the importance of educating whites and blacks together, the Jelliffes differentiated between white immigrants and blacks. They stressed that the disadvantaged background of blacks necessitated "social engineering" to help them achieve equality. "European immigrants had the good fortune to bring with them a nucleus of professionals, men and women, and well established cultural patterns," while blacks' main heritage was an absence of these patterns.

The most disadvantaged ethnic group in the U.S. today are Negroes though they have been here nearly as long as any other segment of population. Ravaged by their ethnic birthright, they have not been permitted to be themselves. The subculture which they have erected [of] Anglo-Protestantism, music and political life is yet profoundly affected by their native endowment in the way of rhythm and tonal sensitivity, strong group sympathies and the traumatic experience of slavery. Unlike all other immigrants, Negroes have had to build a group life without benefit of professional men of their own group to advise and assist, and to challenge the knowledge and morality, as well as the physical and legal power of their exploiters.[49]

While the Jelliffes attempted more than most of their white contemporaries to understand and address the abhorrent situation faced by blacks, their view had limitations. While promoting blacks, it devalued their traditions and institutions. While favoring a challenge to the knowledge, morality, and power of the exploiters of blacks, the exclusively urban vision undervalued rural culture in general. A 1942 article on Karamu read:

> In most homogenous Negro areas the institutions through which the populations express themselves are small and highly stereotyped. They reflect what might be called a "hamlet," "neighborhood" or "village" rather than an urban level of culture. The human potential of aggregation of from 15 to 50,000 households can in no sense find expression, be focused on group interests and be integrated into the poly-cultural life of the metropolitan city with such meager and inadequate structures. The local institutional apparatus, far from freeing, smothers the vitality of the populace.

This view presents an alteration of the settlement philosophy to apply to blacks. Rather than striving for social integration of the neighborhood as a microcosm of the city and nation, settlement leaders often turned to a different style of reform when blacks were involved. Albert Kennedy wrote that "the unit structure to perform this functional task must be at the city level, since Negro ethnic life is so poorly and thinly structured in neighborhoods."[50] The 1942 article called Karamu "America's foremost Negro art center" as well as a bridge between the isolated, rural southern life and the new national culture. "Karamu is the story of how the Negro stepped at last out of the dead-end streets onto the main highway."[51]

In translation from ideal to practice, this thrust could create the active and thriving cultural center that Karamu became. However, the emphasis on progress as artistic achievement and metropolitan culture could lead to the neglect of those blacks who remained on the "dead-end street," as well as the abandonment of many functions of a settlement house. In 1946, a Karamu House report explained that the house would be moved out of the slums to find better neighbors. In the new neighborhood, which had a higher degree of home ownership, "live those earlier and former clients of Karamu who have 'come up a notch in the world.'"[52] Other changes occurred simultaneously. Those activities that could "earn community acceptance" like art and music enjoyed

Karamu House actors behind the scenes. Preparations for The Taming of the Shrew. *(Western Reserve Historical Society, Cleveland, Ohio)*

emphasis because they "became a bridge across a great and hurtful separation." In a 1946 field report, the NFS recommended that these cultural activities replace "emergency programs" such as canteens and daycare. Instead, the report recommended the use of psychiatric social workers in place of those trained in group work or progressive education.[53] At the same time, the report noted that the house had changed from a mixed to an all-black clientele. Becoming tied to a citywide or national culture could mean sacrificing attention to the least advantaged group of blacks, social work aimed at the neighborhood instead of the individual, and the conducting of welfare and other community services in addition to cultural and recreational work.

This is, perhaps, a subtle distinction to make about a period so torn by blatant racism as the early twentieth century. Some of those who characterized blacks as lacking "self-control" or accepting "social ostracism" were among that small group paying special attention to the horrendous situation facing black Americans. These individuals risked ostracism themselves, just by expressing their views publicly. And those institutions seeking to ameliorate some of the worst conditions in black communities did add an invaluable presence. The failures of those settlements that conducted biracial activities or separate facilities for blacks are easily overshadowed by those whose doors simply closed in the faces of their black neighbors. Criticism about ideology, attitudes, and policies does not slight the real dedication and sacrifices of those few outstanding settlement workers. And no matter how flawed their programs, some aspects of their efforts proved crucial enough in their neighborhoods to sustain and even expand their offerings. Their policies, in addition, did not always reflect their deepest beliefs. Clearly, many who believed in integration had to face a white clientele that did not. Settlement workers considered responsiveness to community needs and desires a cardinal principle of their work. Unfortunately, that often meant bowing to the demand for segregation, curtailing the settlement house's commitment to activism as well as service, or limiting its integrated activities to those blacks considered desirable neighbors.

There were exceptional settlement workers who did not share the view that slavery had deprived blacks of fundamental social and cultural attributes, and instead called attention to the forces still at work to deprive and debilitate African Americans. In addition, several independent settlement houses devoted themselves entirely to blacks, such as Flanner House in Indianapolis, Phyllis Wheatley House in Minneapolis, Plymouth Settlement House in Louisville, and Neighborhood Union in Atlanta. The Wharton Centre illustrates some of the strengths of these houses, as well as some of their limitations.

Susan Parrish Wharton, a Quaker and a graduate of Vassar College, founded a settlement house called the Starr Centre with the intention of addressing the needs of blacks in Philadelphia. When the Centre began devoting itself primarily to Italian immigrants, she set up a separate center, which was incorporated as Whittier Centre in 1916. Its activities fell into three categories: thrift, health, and housing. In 1916, the settlement also incorporated its housing activities; the Whittier Centre Housing Company bought and improved low cost housing and rented it to blacks, even lending money at low interest rates to tenants who agreed to fix up the residences.[54]

The Whittier Centre conducted surveys of over a thousand households to determine housing and health conditions. It sent a medical social worker to visit families and its Committee on Health and Sanitation held meetings on health issues such as tuberculosis prevention. Settlement workers also conducted preventive health programs, visiting families with infants and giving instructions about "feeding, cleanliness, bathing, ventilation," and other contributors to good health. The Centre's efforts led to clinics for infants, a prenatal clinic, and provision of black nurses and physicians for the community.[55]

In 1930, the Welfare Federation of Philadelphia conducted a study of blacks that showed significant migration into Philadelphia, especially into north-central neighborhoods. The survey also revealed a severe shortage of affordable

Wharton Centre, main entrance, 1708 North 22d Street, Philadelphia. (Urban Archives, Temple University, Philadelphia, Pennsylvania)

housing, a lack of recreational facilities, and a high delinquency rate. It cited only a few local efforts to address these problems, calling the North Philadelphia League a "quasi-political organization . . . for recreational activities and other welfare work," with no paid worker, little money—"bare, dingy, pathetic." The YMCA had shut down, and the Whittier Centre faltered. The study concluded that this section of the city sorely needed a settlement house.[56]

The Whittier Centre regrouped, moved into more adequate buildings, and opened as the Susan Parrish Wharton Settlement of the Whittier Centre, known locally as—and eventually changing its name to—"The Wharton Centre." The first week at the new Centre brought 1,500 blacks; this high attendance was a harbinger of the Centre's enduring popularity. The new facilities included a main building at its current site, 1708 North 22nd Street, that housed class-rooms and meeting places, and an annex in the rear, that provided a gymnasium (formerly a movie theater) and an assembly hall. All staff members were black.[57]

Headed by Claudia Grant and John Caswell Smith, Jr., the settlement sought to attack the problem of delinquency with a recreational program that included athletics, crafts, hobbies, and other activities that would "divert much anti-social energy into more useful channels." A Doll Club formed when Centre workers found that many young girls attending the settlement had never owned a doll. The number of children desiring these toys so far exceeded the number of donations that a Circulating Doll Library was instituted. A total of 935 ex-changes took place in the first five months alone. Older girls formed the Home Makers' Club, the Cooking Club, Girl Reserve, and Girl Scouts.[58]

An examination of the activities of Wharton shows that, in its first decades, it managed to undertake the complete settlement program of combining social services and reform. The clubs and classes addressed the immediate social and recreational needs of the neighborhood, providing a place to play after school for "latch-key" children of working parents, an athletic outlet for the excess energy of teenagers, a relief from isolation for the elderly, instruction in crafts for all ages, and classes in practical skills such as running a household economically.[59] The provision of meeting space, facilities, supplies, instruction, organized ac-tivities, and a warm welcome undoubtedly made the Centre an oasis in the overcrowded, impoverished neighborhood.

Letters from former participants in house activities indicate the importance of the Centre in their lives. In 1952, John N. Doggett, Jr., pastor of the Scott Meth-odist Church in Pasadena, California, wrote: "Although twenty years, more or less, have passed since the days of my frequenting the Centre, participating in Cooking, Craft, Model Airplanes, and Basketball Clubs, the memory is still very vivid. Even as I write, I can visualize the settlement and recall the names of those who had a part in making this useful experience thrilling." Doggett went on to say that he had first met his wife, Frances Brown, through the settlement's ac-tivities, and that he was currently "trying to do for the youth what you have done for me and hundreds of others" at the Centre—developing "those elements of character that are so necessary for potential adults who must make their way in life." Though years had passed, he still cherished the "self-confidence gained through my role in the Dramatic Club."[60]

Wharton Centre boys, off to clean lot. Wharton Centre, Philadelphia. (Urban Archives, Temple University, Philadelphia, Pennsylvania)

Indeed, the actual workings of the clubs belied their somewhat innocuous titles. What began as sewing or craft clubs often embraced a gamut of other activities. In time, members gained a sense of self-worth from participating fully in small group activities. In addition, the gatherings, which initially centered on a particular craft or skill, often led to weighty discussions. One Mothers' Club, for example, began in 1931 for the purpose of sewing children's clothing as well as sharing conversation and comradery. In 1936, now called the Mothers' Sewing Club, a group of about forty women over the age of twenty-five, sought "to teach cooperation, economy, ethics, [and] household and community appreciation." The Mothers' Knitting Club, a slightly smaller group, had as its goal "to learn how to knit; [and to discuss] civics and current events." The requirements for this group's leader were "to teach knitting; [and to] interpret housing, labor, social problems, and current events."[61]

Meticulous records kept by the clubs' leader, Bessie George, illustrated that conversation and instruction in the Mothers' Clubs covered a vast range of topics. The groups discussed personal hygiene, planned rummage sales to raise money for bread and milk for needy families, performed musical programs, and hosted a demonstration by a floral arranger as well as "a talk to domestic workers" about "fight[ing] poor wages." The combination of practical house-

Wharton Centre ladies' sewing group. Wharton Centre, Philadelphia. (Urban Archives, Temple University, Philadelphia, Pennsylvania)

hold skills and civic consciousness shone through the club records. An observation for February 10, 1937, found one group of women crocheting tablecloths and signing a petition generated by one member "against moving Central High to Germantown." Other meetings featured a heated debate over education, the singing of the "Negro National Anthem," a discussion of current events in Germany, and practical nursing lessons. At one meeting, women considered a protest to be held at a local school. At another, they discussed teenagers and birth control; in a discussion of children's problems, the women wondered what to say to a "child who asks, what can one do to keep from having a baby?" The year 1942 found the mothers enrolling in First Aid and Red Cross classes and discussing the domestic ramifications of World War II. They had moved "from a personal interest in handicraft . . . to a broad interest in all things that affect not only us as individuals, but affect our country." [62]

The Wharton Centre aimed at "strengthening the moral and social fiber of the individuals in the community," but it did not appear to take a paternalistic stance. Its staff considered the work in small groups as "an organized way of working with individuals in a group to help develop their abilities to participate more fully with others." Club records indicated a willingness on the part of group leaders to give club members the freedom to direct activities and raise concerns. The leader played a minimal, mostly passive role, merely ensuring that all participated openly and equally, prohibiting the dominance of "cliques," and providing some direction.[63]

By the 1950s, the Centre had established a day-care center, a summer camp, and a notable program called "Operation Streetcorner." According to the guidelines of this program, a settlement worker would target a popular local hangout and spend some time with young gang members, neither condemning nor praising their activities and ideas, until they considered him one of them. Eventually, the worker would try to redirect the abundant energy of the youths into constructive projects. The provision of meeting grounds and recreational facilities at the house fulfilled a major need. The settlement would not try to abolish the gangs, but boisterously recognized "the wonderful quality of togetherness which gangs afford" along with a much-needed sense of self-esteem. Instead, "Operation Streetcorner" sought to redirect this collective power toward positive ends. In one case, a gang called the "Saints" decided to clean up an abandoned lot near the Wharton Centre and transform it into a playground for youngsters. Others cleaned neighbors' basements and sold the junk; the proceeds went to the purchase of softball uniforms. As a result of this project, eleven gangs met in the neighborhood and became involved in settlement activities. A dramatic piece written in honor of the Centre's twenty-fifth anniversary proclaimed "Operation Streetcorner" one of the Centre's main successes: "What's the program? They visit places like the United Nations. They hold forums, work camps. They have singing sessions, hikes, dances, dramatic presentations. They get scholarships for college studies. They get jobs. . . . They, then, are tomorrow's citizens . . . good ones, mind you . . . men of whom all can be proud."[64]

While this program achieved much success and recognition, the Wharton Centre also faced many problems. The most glaring was underfunding; the perpetual difficulty of providing adequate staff and facilities for the number of neighbors who wanted to participate in the Centre's program was exacerbated by the Great Depression, and persisted afterward.[65] The Whittier Centre Housing Company eventually folded because of lack of funds.[66] Related to the financial stress were the social conditions against which Wharton struggled. While programs addressing particular individuals were invaluable, personal problems were interwoven with those of society itself. The activities conducted by Wharton, however crucial, increasingly focused on the individual at the expense of social change. Headworker Claudia Grant expressed frustration with the situation when she called on Wharton to look beyond providing a mere recreational outlet and to take a broader approach to reform:

> Recreation is very important in the lives of both adults and children. There are many other factors, however, that must go into decent living, without

which recreation loses much of its value. Employment in peace times as well as war, adequate housing facilities, education geared to the individual needs of people, an effective church, good wholesome neighborhoods in which people can take pride, and above all, parents with a personal sense of responsibility towards their homes and their children, are the ingredients that give a secure basis for good citizenship. Recreation centers have a contribution to make, but, before they can be used effectively, basic and minimum needs of people must be met. Our first job is with the parents and children who seek our services. The second and equally important one is that of participating in all community planning and activities having a bearing on the welfare of these parents and children.[67]

In spite of the few black settlements in its membership, the erection of black branches by some of the most nationally renowned settlements, occasional committees on race relations, and several truly well-meaning settlement workers, the National Federation of Settlements failed to develop a strong policy to deal with the influx of black neighbors into settlement environs during and after World War I. Even the establishment of black settlements, like the Phyllis Wheatley House in Minneapolis, founded in 1924, often merely furthered racial segregation. Providing a separate facility for blacks legitimized their exclusion from the rest of the city's settlements. While large cities often had several settlements for white immigrants, one was usually the limit for blacks. As Howard Jacob Karger writes, "the creation of [the Phyllis] Wheatley [House] provided a convenient excuse for the white settlement houses of the 1920s and 1930s to relinquish their responsibility to serve the black community."[68]

The hostile racial climate of the early twentieth century contributed to the shortcomings of the settlement movement by driving many of those sincerely interested in the plight of blacks to support other types of organizations, such as the NAACP or the National League on Urban Conditions Among Negroes (the Urban League). The Urban League was formed in 1911 by the combination of the National League for the Protection of Colored Women, the Committee for Improving the Industrial Conditions of Negroes in New York, and the Committee on Urban Conditions. Supported and staffed by a coalition of upper- and middle-class whites and blacks, many tending toward conservative politics, the Urban League tried to project a nonthreatening public persona. Yet its local affiliates conducted activities throughout the country along the lines of settlement work.[69]

Generally, historians' tendency to focus on the League's accommodationist image has overshadowed this settlement activity. Historian Nancy Weiss describes the program of the League as one dedicated to fostering "manners and morals," motivated partly by an altruistic desire to help black newcomers adjust to the industrial city, but also by a self-interested, middle-class desire to crush stereotypes of blacks that intensified discrimination and segregation. Instructors taught the rudiments of housekeeping, diet, health, and especially hygiene—all essential aspects of the League's "civilizing" regime. Weiss concludes that, compared to the NAACP and the settlement movement, the League's program and ideology were basically accommodationist and thus offered "useful services, but unspectacular results." While the League helped people get jobs, she writes, it generally accepted that attainable jobs would be domestic, or unskilled, and often undesirable and insecure, and advised black people accordingly. Weiss asserts that most League members differed ideologically from other progressives, focusing on changing the "private practices" of blacks instead of laws or public opinion. Settlements, for instance, sought to change both the behavior of their working-class neighbors and the discriminatory practices affecting their lives.[70] Because white reformers largely failed to integrate their programs, organizations like the Urban League had to take over functions falling outside their original purview. Weiss concludes that "because settlements and charitable agencies . . . rarely dealt with blacks, it fell to the Urban League to adapt their programs and methods and create new ones to fill the void."[71]

There is no doubt that the League sought a nonconfrontational posture, and that it willingly accepted the contributions and efforts of whites. It also often emphasized the goal of assimilating blacks to their new neighborhoods and not vice versa. Beneath the surface, however, many of the Urban League's local affiliates established community centers that were the equivalent of settlement houses. While not usually formally tied to the National Federation of Settlements, the extensive settlement work conducted by the Urban League comprises a significant aspect of the movement. Urban League settlement houses included Douglas Community Center in Springfield, Illinois; Armstrong Association in Philadelphia; Tampa Urban League Social Center; Frederick Douglas Community Association in Toledo, Ohio; Hallie Q. Brown Community House in St. Paul, Minnesota; Pearl Street Community Center in Waterbury, Connecticut; Warren Urban League Community Center in Warren, Ohio; Lincoln Urban League Community Center in Lincoln, Nebraska; Wheatley Social Center in Fort Wayne, Indiana; the Detroit Urban League Community Center; and many others.[72]

League-affiliated branches differed dramatically from one another. Some merely ran offices and acted primarily as job and social service referral agencies. Others, however, conducted full programs that included active employment bureaus, day-care centers, social work, social research, housing placement, recreation, legal council, clubs, and classes. The Frederick Douglass Community Association of Toledo, Ohio, epitomizes these active branches. It offered numerous classes and activities in the categories of music, drama, recreation, welfare and relief, athletics, and education. Welfare and relief work included "1. House Visitation, 2. Distribution of Coal, 3. Neighborhood Clubs, 4. Christmas Basket Distribution, 5. Quarters for Social Service, 6. Cooperation with Welfare Agencies, 7. Free Employment Service, 8. Summer Camps."[73]

Another settlement, the Douglas Community Center in Springfield, Illinois, and many others like it, attempted not only to help individuals adjust to difficult living situations, but to use the settlement activities as a springboard for wider change. One report noted that, at the Center, "the most beneficial result" of the clubs and classes was "*group unity*, *loyalty*, and *cooperation*." It went on: "Many examples are to be found of people who previously were isolated and who had no contact or mutual interests in their neighborhood but now have become *enthusiastic and interested supporters of civic and domestic improvements*." The Douglas Center made it clear that its community service activities were dedicated to broader social change. In one report, it noted that, in three and a half years, some 1,062 individuals had registered for work through its employment bureau. While the placement average was 75 percent, the Center was dissatisfied; the jobs obtained were nearly always "odd jobs" for men and domestic service jobs for women. As a result, the Center's workers attempted to pressure local businessmen and manufacturers to give consideration to black applicants. The Center also initiated a Vocational Opportunity Campaign, the purpose of which was to raise public awareness about the restricted employment opportunities available to blacks. The topic was broached in a variety of forums, including women's clubs, manufacturers' associations, and a public interracial meeting.[74]

Other centers protested and sought to change the conditions they observed by discontinuing their placement of women in domestic service jobs, and meeting with local officials to discuss police brutality against blacks, the lack of affordable housing, and the need for an expansion of employment opportunities. Local League affiliates pursued improvements in employment, health, housing, recreation, and social service, albeit through cooperation and not confrontation. They cast black advancement as primarily a social concern, and not a political one. Yet their vision rested on a staunch belief in racial equality, mutuality, and integration. In a time of virulent discrimination in housing and employment, this stand was both bold and reformist by implication. League settlements acted much as other settlement houses did, by conducting a thorough investigation of the community and then, armed with accurate information, agitating for concrete changes. Leagues fought for black membership in unions, established libraries offering works by black as well as white authors, and promoted African American culture in other ways. The affiliates also engaged in a variety of activities aimed at interracial understanding that represented direct rejections of segregation. They conducted integrated summer camps and other recreational activities, conveyed interested white college students and others on "Goodwill Tours" through black neighborhoods, and arranged interracial mass meetings and dinners. Many of these Urban League settlement houses successfully conducted activities that were not only racially integrated, but culturally mixed as well.[75]

A final example illuminates both the possibilities represented by, and the difficulties encountered by, those who wanted to transpose the settlement project to African American communities. Mary White Ovington's attempt to establish a settlement house for blacks in New York City illustrates the kinds of limitations even these individuals encountered; Ovington had a much fuller appreciation of the achievements and institutions of blacks, yet a restricting set of social precepts inhibited the implementation of her plans.

Settlement workers who had a commitment to blacks turned to the Urban League or the NAACP, though often they merely contributed their names in support. Mary White Ovington, however, provides an example of a reformer genuinely interested in improving the living conditions for and treatment of blacks. Frustrated by unsuccessful attempts to establish an integrated settlement designed primarily for blacks, she concluded that American reformers needed to battle racism on the national front. She thought that the dire conditions faced by each African American resulted from his treatment as "half a man," and not from lack of culture or civilization. In 1909, partly in response to the race riot the year before in Springfield, Illinois, Ovington met with William English Walling and Henry Moskowitz to call for a "Conference on the Status of the Negro in the United States." The 1909 conference adopted a platform of fundamental rights for blacks—the abolition of all forced segregation, equal educational advantages, enfranchisement, enforcement of the fourteenth and fifteenth amendments, and the establishment of a permanent committee "to organize a complete plan of defense for the legitimate rights of the Negro race in this country" that became the NAACP. Over half of those on executive committees had done settlement work. According to Allen Davis, "it has been noted that the three who organized the NAACP were a southerner, the daughter of an abolitionist and a Jew; it seems even more significant that all three were settlement workers." [76]

Ovington represents those settlement workers who became aware of the need for a national organization for black civil rights during their experiences in community work. Before espousing this type of reform, Ovington was headworker at Greenpoint Settlement in New York City from 1895 to 1903 in a model tenement she helped establish. Her abolitionist family had endowed her with sensitivity to the issue of race, but it had also taught her that Reconstruction

Mary White Ovington. (Archives of Labor and Urban Affairs, Wayne State University, Detroit, Michigan)

had ended the "Negro problem." In 1903, at the age of thirty-eight, Ovington heard a lecture by Booker T. Washington at the Social Reform Club in New York City that alerted her to the extreme prejudice facing black Americans. As a fellow of Greenwich House, headed by Mary Simkhovitch, she began a study of black Manhattan published in 1911 as *Half a Man: The Status of the Negro in New York.*[77]

In 1904, Ovington wrote to W. E. B. Du Bois expressing her newfound interest, beginning a correspondence and friendship that lasted over thirty years. True to the calling of the settlement worker, Ovington insisted that she would investigate the economic and social conditions in black communities with the goal of "helping to start social work among them." She hoped to model her work on Du Bois's *Philadelphia Negro*. His research, inspired in turn by a settlement worker in Philadelphia, took the form of a mammoth volume on all aspects of life in the city, including employment, the family, and crime.[78]

Meanwhile, Ovington told Du Bois that she had spoken to several people about the idea of starting a settlement for blacks. Although they had given their approval, she added, "I know that I shall want to recommend the two races working together in a settlement and that I shall seem very radical." She went on to say, "You speak of the need, if I am to undertake this work, of my meeting with Negroes and not shrinking from them. Indeed, I think it is you who must shrink from me. When I read the nauseating magazine and newspaper writing on the race question I feel ashamed and abashed. This is not a time for an Anglo-Saxon to rejoice in his race's generosity or greatness of spirit."[79] Ovington resolved "that I must do some work among the Negroes, that I couldn't go on any longer at settlement work, because I wanted to do work among that race and no other." She embarked on a rigorous schedule of inspecting tenement houses and working with boys' and girls' clubs. After four months of inspections, she explained to Du Bois that although blacks suffered from segregation, they impressed her with their self-sufficiency, their low crime rate, their household skills, and their strong religious values.[80]

House-to-house inspection clarified Ovington's goal of building a model tenement "in one of the crowded Negro quarters" from which to conduct settlement work. "Where I feel very strongly and where I may slip up," she confided in Du Bois, "is that I want the work carried on by colored and white." She thought whites could assist blacks, not as superiors who would "civilize" them, but as members of a privileged race and class who could help them gain access to the city's resources. "Every month I feel that the two races must work together in any philanthropic work in the city," she commented, reasoning that "it must be isolation that creates much of the difficulty in the South, and why should we try to produce unnecessary difficulties for ourselves in the North?" In understatement, she added, "Of course, you know there is a school that will oppose any bringing of the races together."[81]

To "ease the tension," Ovington first proposed the construction of a model tenement with two black and two white settlement workers living in apartments in the building. Lillian Wald described this arrangement in *The House on Henry Street* as helpful for dissolving both the reformers' and the neighbors' intimidation. Rather than integrate the entire tenement, Ovington suggested that only

Mary White Ovington (middle) and W. E. B. Du Bois (left). (Archives of Labor and Urban Affairs, Wayne State University, Detroit, Michigan)

black neighbors reside there so that the public would not have to face total inter-mixture. "Wouldn't this suit those who think themselves fastidious?" Ovington asked Du Bois, adding, "but who really are vulgar at heart?" She feared that an integrated staff might take deserved recognition away from blacks. "But grant-ing that a worthy point of view," she concluded, "there will be more glory if the Negro here in New York has the white man to push him forward than if he tries to get an audience alone."[82]

Du Bois responded that Ovington's idea of white and black management was "the only sensible way." Within the next month, she wrote that she had received money for the model tenement and shortly thereafter she lived among blacks, continuing her "social study." Du Bois replied that he was happy both for her sake and for the sake of blacks. In spite of her success, however, she was the only white who consented to live in the black tenement and she did not achieve her goal of a settlement for blacks with an integrated staff.[83]

Ovington's correspondence with Du Bois made it clear that social conven-tion severely curtailed her plans. She faced an issue that limited her freedom to act—her sex. She wrote of meeting a Columbia professor who "patted me on the back—I think literally not figuratively—and made me feel that I was a good, but over-enthusiastic little girl." A few months later, at a Settlement Associa-tion dinner, the guest of honor, a German professor, spoke to her. Although she could not understand most of what he said, she easily deciphered one of his comments: "Sociology, ah, what is that? Sociology is political economy for women!" In another instance, Du Bois asked Ovington to attend a meeting of the Niagara Movement of which Ovington was one of the select few white associate members. She replied, "Will any women be present?" Yet another time reformers had planned a march to protest the showing of "The Birth of a Nation." Ovington and others had intended to participate until they received many letters stating that the spectacle of white women and black men walking together would destroy the cause. Ovington wrote that people advised her "that it would be a great mistake for white women and colored men to walk in the parade," as the papers would simply capitalize on the idea and read, "White Women . . . Niggers . . . The Birth of a Nation!" She ultimately accepted the idea that the parade had to be "all men or all colored people."[84]

The climate of public opinion about relations between whites and blacks undoubtedly limited the extent to which white women could actively engage in reforms among blacks, at least on the level of the local community. In 1910, Ovington sat beside a black man at a public dinner. The next day, one newspaper's account of the dinner at the New York City Cosmopolitan Club called her a "high priestess" who "affiliates five days every week with Negro men and dines with them at her home in Brooklyn, Sundays"; it called the dinner a "Bacchanal feast." Ovington wrote of the newspaper account that "those who wrote it up did not comment on the white man who sat next to the negro woman, but they poured spleen on the white woman who sat next to a colored man. We were described as drinking and making love."[85]

Ovington and others genuinely interested in the welfare of black Americans thus understood from experience the tremendous obstacles of racism and segregation. They devoted their efforts either to agitation for basic political rights and legal justice or to delivery of vital social services. The settlement house, a unique combination of those different functions, tragically failed to transcend the greater inability of mainstream American culture to allow blacks or whites to cross the color line. The NAACP differed greatly from the settlement movement. Similar in its spirit of reform, the NAACP was not designed to offer services aimed at improving the economic situation of blacks or at revitalizing neighborhoods. A movement dedicated to full citizenship, it played an essential role in American life. But as W. E. B. Du Bois realized in the 1930s, the NAACP represented a style of reform that moved away from an emphasis on the local political economy.[86] The settlement movement's failure to adapt its plans for drastic community change to blacks hastened the fragmentation of social service and civil rights activities into other organizations dedicated only to aspects of the integrated, ambitious goals of settlement work.

Two

"A Social Church" but Not a Mission

At the turn of the twentieth century, renowned black sociologist W. E. B. Du Bois noted that "the social life of the Negro centres in his church—baptism, wedding and burial, gossip and courtship, friendship and intrigue—all lie in these walls."[1] Sixty years later, E. Franklin Frazier illustrated that African American churches traditionally served as much more than promoters of doctrine, but as mutual aid societies and fraternal organizations that laid the foundations for institutions ranging from insurance companies to black colleges.[2] Historian C. Eric Lincoln wrote that the black church served as everything from community forum to lyceum.[3] In fact, the black church has historically combined functions as diverse as daycare, welfare, employment counseling, education, entertainment, and social activism.

Ironically, such integration of community services and reform resembles the ideal settlement house. In light of this similarity, comments by many settlement workers about the weakness of African American culture, morality, social organization, and religion, seem inexplicable. While evocation of universal racism would handily resolve this paradox, the blindness of settlement workers requires further examination. Their inability to unite their own efforts with those of religious activists, both black and white, partially explains their failure to adapt their program to the black migrants who replaced their immigrant neighbors during and after World War I. Reflecting a tendency of settlement workers to see their reforms as directly opposed to the efforts of church missions, the National Federation of Settlements (NFS) followed a policy of excluding from membership most religious settlements. This exclusionary policy contributed to the organization's elitism and eventual decline. The exclusion of religious workers also symbolized the narrowness of the "liberalizing creed" preached by settlement workers. This creed aimed to integrate racial groups, cultures, and social classes, through urban, secular, "progressive" institutions. This ideal appears inclusive, but lost its potential in translation into an exclusive policy.

The first section of this chapter will explore the ideas of early settlement leaders who clearly differentiated between settlement houses and missions even while receiving sustenance from the Social Gospel movement. It will then trace the codification of these ideas in the antidenominational policy of the National Federation of Settlements from its formation in 1911 through the 1940s. The second section will illustrate the great extent of settlement work conducted among blacks under the auspices of both black and white churches. The NFS was ignorant of the extent of settlement work among blacks for the precise reason that it insisted on excluding what it considered missions, even when they fulfilled all of the functions of settlement houses.

Religion and the Settlement's Struggle for Self-Definition

In 1945, Albert Kennedy, settlement worker and former NFS Secretary, justified confining his discussion of "Settlement Contributions to the Understanding and Improvement of Negro-White Relations" to northern cities by blaming universal southern racism. "There were few settlements in the South and with the best will in the world, southern head workers could not singlehandedly defy the public opinion on which their work for whites was based," he wrote. This view reflected the belief among many northern liberals that the South was a bastion of racism and provincialism, and caused Kennedy to ignore evidence produced by his own survey of southern settlement work conducted among blacks. Historians have since reinforced this assumption that southern settlement work did not exist by focusing primarily on reforms undertaken in Boston, Chicago, and New York, with only an occasional foray into cities like Minneapolis or Indianapolis. Allen Davis writes that the South's few settlements, except for a few exemplary houses such as Eleanor McMain's Kingsley House in New Orleans and Francis Ingram's Neighborhood House in Louisville, "were of very little importance." "Most of them were modified missions," he adds, unintentionally reflecting the hitherto unexamined bias of settlement workers themselves. The portrait of the mission as the antithesis of progressive reform, a contrast delineated by settlement house reformers from the 1890s to the 1950s, guaranteed the continued silence in the historical record of religious workers, a group often deeply involved in efforts to improve race relations.[4]

While settlement workers and their central organization, the National Federation of Settlements, acknowledged the religious influences on the early settlement movement, they insisted upon differentiating between their work and work conducted under religious auspices. While trying to carve out an inclusive ideology, the regionalism, urbanism, and secularism of their movement actually

Albert J. Kennedy. (Social Welfare History Archives, University of Minnesota Libraries)

limited their vision. Students of the settlement movement have largely failed to transcend these biases, and thus have left uncovered the southern and religious dimensions of the settlement movement. Those dimensions offer clues for understanding efforts to transpose "the settlement idea" from immigrant to black neighborhoods.

Albert Kennedy's ignorance of the extensive settlement work conducted among blacks is best understood not as malicious racism but as part of a limited cultural vision through which his understanding of blacks was filtered. He and other progressives sought to apply a scientific approach to the study of society that they believed would lead to specific reforms for the betterment of society. Kennedy wrote that the purpose of settlements was, first, "to subject the contemporary social order to continuous critical review for the purpose of discovering ways and means of bringing about a more equitable and more harmonious local and national life and secondly, the use of a particular method." [5] This "particular method" entailed a type of social work that settlement workers thought unique. They spent a great deal of time elaborating "the settlement idea."

American settlement workers cited the distinction between settlements and missions continually in the first five decades of the movement, insisting that the paramount feature of "the settlement idea" was the very absence of an idea. Kennedy wrote: "By the uninformed, the two may be, and often are, taken to be identical, or there is, perhaps a vague idea that a mission is conducted on lines rather more religious or 'churchy' than those of a settlement. The two are in fact distinct efforts: differing in conception, in constitution, and in methods, and agreeing only in their object which is for the good of mankind." The crux of the distinction rested on the difference between what Kennedy called "open" and "closed intellectual systems." The religious houses, by definition, worked within a closed system since they tried to purvey dogma, and "any belief or activity which does not fit within the dogma can hardly qualify as 'the higher life.'" This view reflected the struggles of urban settlements to realize "the opportunities of life in America" by "crossing stereotyped loyalties of race, religion and culture" and by shedding religion as "a divisive force." [6] Ironically, this very attempt at freedom from doctrine created a new creed that annulled the greatest opportunity facing the second generation of settlement workers.

At the turn of the century, much of settlement workers' identity rested on their view that their work differed from religious work. They sought to separate themselves from earlier forms of social work as epitomized in the Charity Organization Society that focused on the needy individual rather than trying to alter social conditions.[7] Canon Samuel A. Barnett, considered the mentor of the British settlement movement after inspiring a group of students who founded Toynbee Hall in London, wrote a classic and often-cited essay published in the late 1890s and reprinted in 1909 by Canon and Mrs. S. A. Barnett. The essay, "'Settlements' or 'Missions,'" noted that most people "regard the Settlement as a sort of Mission—another form of the proselytizing spirit." The authors set out to dispel the confusion. In the great project of the day, answering the "social question" by "promoting good fellowship between man and man" meant for the educated a choice between two ways—"the way of Missions and the way of Settlements." [8]

The Barnetts summed up the difference between the settlement and the mission: "A Mission has for its object conversion. A Settlement has for its object mutual knowledge." A mission served best in "agitated times," a settlement in "quiet times" when it "feels its strength to be in the gradual infusion of higher thought, the slow gaining of confidence and of mutual respect between rich and poor who have learnt to be friends." The way to bridge the gap between "Capital" and "Labor," in the Barnetts' view, was through the dissemination of culture. "The State and voluntary bodies" could not achieve this goal, because "culture comes by contact and true learning by example." [9]

The Barnetts criticized missionaries for failing to provide an example of high culture, for they often stooped to the level of the people they intended to uplift: "They have become untidy, less regardful of dress by which to signify their respect of others and of themselves, less scrupulous as to the cleanliness which is recognized as the best safeguard of health, less careful of courtesy which is necessary to equal intercourse." At the same time, "a missionary, be it even a clergyman, in a poor neighborhood, is liable to become conscious of superiority," whereas in a settlement's "community of equals . . . every form of conceit is checked by constant contact with people of varying points of view." [10]

Accepting diverse opinions, rejecting narrow goals, and residing in poor neighborhoods all aimed at the ideal of making "brotherhood a practical reality and not a dreamer's theory." While deploring the "conceit" of religious missionaries, however, the Barnetts outlined a type of cultural missionary work based on the assumption that culture itself appertained to "Capital" and needed to be taught to "Labor" by the go-between, "University men and women," all for the purpose of social unity. While disclaiming any dislike of missions and insisting on their importance, the Barnetts gave the impression that missions were out of touch with the scientific or "reasoning spirit of the age," suffered from the weight of their own "machinery," and focused too narrowly on the limited end of conversion. "A Mission exists to proselytize," they concluded, while "a Settlement's distinguishing feature is the absence of programme." [11]

In 1911 Gaylord White, worker at New York's Union Settlement, professor of Applied Christianity, and director of Student Christian Work at Union Seminary, expressed surprise at the continued "confusion of mind regarding the method and the aim of the social settlement." Some still confused it with " 'mission work,' as if it were some new form of religious propagandism; others with charity or education." In his article, "The Social Settlement after Twenty-Five Years," White deemed it necessary to repeat the distinction, insisting that "there is perhaps no more serious blunder concerning the social settlement than that which confounds it with the mission." Unlike the mission, the settlement professes "no definite propaganda, no clear-cut social theory to apply." Nevertheless, he outlined the goal of organizing "all the local forces for good, in some co-operative programme for the common welfare." Rather than enjoining the cooperation of church workers in the effort, he considered any linkage in the public mind with specific ecclesiastical organizations detrimental to community solidarity. The settlement ought to establish neighborly relations "with every element of the surrounding life." Yet its theorists seemed to contradict this purpose by excluding the impoverished when they insisted that the settlement, unlike the mission, "is not dealing primarily or as an essential part of its work with the dependent class. It is simply a neighbor among neighbors." [12]

Also in 1911, the year of the founding of the National Federation of Settlements, Robert Woods and Albert Kennedy, both settlement workers at South End House in Boston, coauthored a *Handbook of Settlements* that engraved the distinction between religious and settlement work on the formal policy of the NFS. They wrote that the settlement house that "provides neutral ground" and "is wholly unsectarian not only from the point of view of its staff, but as judged by the various elements in its neighborhood," exemplifies "the kind of social enterprise here set forth." Woods and Kennedy listed religious settlements separately, for although some had "a high degree of settlement spirit," they included churchly functions and thus did not qualify as settlement houses. However, "where such specific religious effort is conducted without willing or conscious invasion of other religious loyalties, it has not been construed as carrying the house in question beyond the distinctive limits of the settlement field." [13] This vague exception later created difficulties for translation of philosophy to policy since it put the burden of definition on the leaders of the NFS.

A partial explanation for the desire to distance the settlement house from the church is the perception of the increasing secularization of American life.[14] In 1898, Robert Woods wrote about the grave situation of the churches that failed to reach "the majority of their natural constituency." The Protestant churches, he thought, needed increased efficiency and enhanced proselytizing among other groups, and a unified movement to recapture the interest of "the working people" who "regard the churches with more or less indifference, if not with actual hatred." Woods blamed the "dogmatic creeds" for the constantly increasing "estrangement between the working classes . . . and the churches." He warned Protestant churches that the Catholic church had a stronger sense of devotion and better captured the popular imagination because it created a compelling vision of "the nearness of God" and evoked "essential religious feeling" rather than dwelling on sectarian dogma. Social betterment, in Woods's view, required a much broader application of religiosity and moral fervor.[15] It is interesting to see that thirteen years later, Woods and Kennedy defined a settlement in such a way that an estimated 2,500 Catholic settlements did not fit the definition of a bona fide settlement house. At that time, roughly 400 settlements met the criteria for inclusion in the formal movement.[16]

*Founders of the National Federation of Settlements. From left to right: front row—
Graham Taylor, Mary McDowell (seated), Robert A. Woods; second row—Cornelia
Bradford, Jane Addams (in striped blouse), Lillian Wald (seated), Elizabeth Wil-
liams, Dr. James Hamilton; back row—Helen Greene, Helena Dudley, John Elliott,
Meyer Bloomfield, Mary K. Simkhovitch, Ellen W. Coolidge. (Social Welfare History
Archives, University of Minnesota Libraries)*

Viewing the "settlement idea" from the vantage point of religious activists
shows not only that this concept was itself contested terrain, but also that the
absence of dogma translated—at least to some listeners—into precisely its
opposite. As early as 1903, another definition of the settlement house's function surfaced in an article in the *Nashville Christian Advocate*, the organ of the
Methodist Episcopal Church, South. Unlike northern settlement workers who
emphasized the need to distinguish between religious activity and social work,
these southern workers thought that "social settlement work does not usually
give promise of usefulness or permanence unless it has behind it the backing
and the faith of the Christian Church." The article portrayed northern settlement workers, usually university students, as possessing "a certain immaturity
of judgment and a certain inexperience of complicated problems." These students, only temporarily interested in reform, thought that "organizations for
social betterment, for the care of the outcasts and the better distribution of labor
among those who wish to work, will do more for the world than the church."

These "men . . . have not very modestly insisted that independent organizations for these purposes are more desirable, and even more useful, than is the church," the article continued. The point was not to malign settlement houses, but to argue that institutions founded to improve "moral and material conditions" should address the salvation of the individual as the means of perfecting society.

> It is an excellent thing to have free baths and reading rooms and gymnasiums. Agencies for the placing of the unemployed often serve a most useful purpose. But it is a truth which this generation is coming to see more clearly every day, that the only way to save a man's body is to save his soul. Let us, therefore, openly accept also the corollary that the best way to save his soul is by the time-honored and spirit-honored agency of the Church of God.[17]

This opposing view only helped support settlement leaders' view of religious work as dogmatic. In 1912, however, Graham Taylor of Chicago Commons observed that the white women of the Methodist Episcopal Church, South, had established many social settlements that represented the most advanced church effort toward social progress. Significantly, he wrote that they attested to "the awakening of southern people to their social obligations and opportunities," an awakening symbolized by the Southern Sociological Congress, which met in 1912 to dedicate the South's resources to modernization. These women pledged their lives to "Negro education, community and social agencies," Taylor noted, with great praise for these southern efforts.[18] During this same period, however, the formation of the National Federation of Settlements led to a codification of the settlement philosophy that neglected most similar efforts.

Ironically, settlement workers and their chroniclers usually paid homage to the Social Gospel as a primary motivation for their movement.[19] Many first-generation settlement workers actually had formal religious training. Union Settlement worker Gaylord White, a theological seminary graduate, underlined the religious impulse in 1911 when he reflected on the early years of the settlement movement: "We may safely conclude that the settlement has a contribution of peculiar value to make to the work of setting up that new order of society which those who follow the lead of the Christ believe shall be eventually realized in the Kingdom of God."[20] During a symposium on the settlement movement fifteen years later, William McLennan, resident of Welcome Hall in Buffalo, said that "the settlement cannot survive where its friends have lost the vision of a New Jerusalem coming down out of heaven from God." Another worker urged greater attention to the spiritual needs of the neighbors: "I believe that one of the greatest needs in many of our neighborhoods is a strengthening of essential religious faith in the minds and hearts of thousands of people." "I feel that the settlement has an opportunity to meet which it cannot entirely throw upon the churches," the speaker continued.[21] While these comments reflect the religious motives of these speakers, many settlement workers saw a much more vague connection between the church and social work. While they too sought a more perfect society, the attainment of a "Kingdom of God" on earth was only a figurative rendition of a more ideal participatory democracy. Most settlement workers aimed at a more secular version of the Social Gospel than did the churches.

As standard histories of the Social Gospel in the Progressive Era have failed to note, the movement swept the South as well as the North.[22] The pivotal role of the church in southern life insured that a strong element of religiosity would dominate the movement, which in the North tended toward more secular interpretations.[23] Regional differences in culture created divergent reform movements. Even within the southern Social Gospel movement, tensions arose that paralleled the conflicts between North and South, and between secular and religious activity. The effort to make their work interracial, for instance, frustrated many reformers. Attempting to form organizations that expressed their essential credo of interdenominationalism, which they considered the most progressive characteristic of the Social Gospel, these reformers encountered a major obstacle—the people whose lives they sought to reform.

In the proceedings of a 1907 conference at Greensboro, North Carolina, of the International Sunday School Association, field superintendents and state secretaries wrote, "we soon discovered by further personal investigation that Negroes are intense denominationalists." They found that blacks felt tremendous loyalty to their own denominations, and had "little time or money left for interdenominational organization." The nature of the living and working conditions for blacks in the South partially explained their reluctance to participate in the movements associated with the Social Gospel. Meager incomes often prevented blacks from giving money to causes outside their denomination. In addition, the cost of conventions prohibited participation by blacks and their inability to control their own time "presented a serious obstacle to our work," the report continued. Its disappointed conclusion was that "the Negroes were not ready to reap the advantages of interdenominational work."[24]

Other evidence reveals similar tensions between reformers' ideas and the ideas and behavior of those blacks whose well-being they sought to ensure. A conference of philanthropists, business people, religious activists, and black leaders met in 1908 in Clifton, Massachusetts, and published a book based on their meeting entitled *An Era of Progress and Promise: The Religious, Moral and Educational Development of the American Negro since His Emancipation*. The report emphasized that political change would not remedy the dire conditions for blacks and "industrial training and the acquisition of property must be underwritten by morality and religion." The authors praised the effects that religion had wrought in transforming blacks from "savages" to "Christians" but lamented that, because "no other organization is so encouraged by the white Neighbors of the Negroes," it has forced blacks to be "shut up to the church" and caused educated black men to be "shut up to the service of the church." [25]

These reformers also complained about the intense denominationalism of African Americans, which they interpreted as a "stage in the development of Negro churches":

> The point has not been reached, however, in the progress of these denominations, when cooperative relations in carrying forward special phases of religious activity, now so generally recognized as common to all evangelical churches, may be entered into and maintained. Denominationalism makes demands up to the limit of the ability of the average church member to answer. It follows from this that in whatever way help is extended to the Negro churches in advancing any of their departments of work, full recognition must be given to their denominational predilections. [26]

Albeit tinged by a sense of the superiority of nondenominational thinking, these comments did represent a realization that conditions in the black community itself would frustrate the best-laid plans of extending the cross-denominational Protestant crusade to blacks and would influence the nature of reform work among them.

No less authorities than W. E. B. Du Bois and E. Franklin Frazier noted the same tendencies among African Americans toward strong denominationalism. Du Bois went further to say that social life was centered on the congregation. In 1903, his Atlanta University study on religion among blacks stated that "today the Negro population of the U.S. is virtually divided into church congregations which are the real units of race" experience. He attributed this localism to the African American past. White domination during slavery caused the church to be "the first distinctively Negro American social institution" because religion was "the sole surviving social institution of the African fatherland." The suppression of other organizations caused the church "to become the center of amusements, of what little spontaneous economic activity remained, of education, and of all social intercourse." As a result of the centrality of the local church, strong loyalties to particular denominations persisted. [27]

E. Franklin Frazier interpreted denominationalism as resulting from the backwardness of black religion. "A social atmosphere of repression" prevented the "self-realization" of African American individuals, creating a "psychology of the sick" including a deviant personality, culture, and even physique. "The religion of the Negro," he wrote, "has been characterized as the religion of death. It is for 'dying souls.'" While critical of the black church, however, he blamed the harsh social environment for what he called the "malady" of blacks and their institutions. Equating that environment with white oppression, his interpretation thus implied a need for social change.[28]

Some settlement workers, however, cited what they considered the primitive stage of development of the black church as a reason not to engage in the reform of race relations. Charles Cooper of the Kingsley Association in Pittsburgh showed intolerance of African American traditions when he stated that "I am personally certain that the best colored leadership is not sufficient for the best [settlement] work today." He wrote that blacks "themselves are behind" and black leaders "immediately thrown out of gear" when the issue of race came up in conversation. Particularly, Cooper faulted their denominationalism:

Denominational lines in the colored churches are what they used to be in the white churches forty years ago. They are so jealous of one another and have not reached the spirit of cooperation and tolerance that white Protestants have; and in the second place they are jealous of the settlement especially if any of its activities fall on hours in which the neighborhood churches have their meetings and services. In a colored neighborhood where there are several colored churches it is almost impossible to find hours in which some church may not have some activity.[29]

The denominationalism among African Americans seemed to some white settlement workers sufficiently frustrating to suspend "the spirit of cooperation and tolerance" altogether.

Many of the most successful institutions conducting activities with African Americans managed to work through denominational churches or, at the very least, to keep a main focus on religion itself. In 1930, the Federal Council of Churches of Christ in America published a handbook entitled *The Social Work of the Churches* that revealed a remarkable number of efforts during the previous decades for improving interracial relations and living conditions for blacks. The handbook's editor, F. Ernest Johnson, included religious organizations as diverse as the various Protestant denominations, the Society of Friends, the Unitarians, the Catholic church, and the Jewish communions. The book summarized specific techniques and theories of social service, and included social pronouncements of the various churches on issues ranging from minimum wage and maximum hours legislation, regulation of labor for women and children, unemployment insurance, legalization of unions, collective bargaining, housing improvement, and health measures.[30]

A significant concern of the churches was interracial cooperation. Social pronouncements from the Unitarian, Congregational, and Catholic churches, the Federal Council of Churches, and the Methodist Episcopal Church, South, favored equal rights for blacks. In addition, the Baptist, Episcopal, and Jewish organizations all condemned mob violence and advocated antilynching legislation. The Federal Council of Churches stated that

> Negroes should be fully recognized as Americans and fellow citizens, given equal economic and professional opportunities, increasing participation in all community affairs; a spirit of friendship and cooperation should obtain between the white and the colored people, North and South. They should have parks, playgrounds, equal wages for equal work, adequate schools, equal facilities and courtesy when traveling, adequate housing, lighting and sanitation, police protection and equality before the law. Especially should the barbarism of lynching be condemned by public opinion and abolished by vigorous measures and penalties.[31]

These pronouncements represented concerns that led to concrete actions on the part of some churches. As subsequent examples will illustrate, their work often included all the functions of a settlement house, and sometimes more.

On the other hand, the National Federation of Settlements remained committed to avoiding what it deemed unenlightened denominational community work. Coupled with a northern, urban bias, this view translated into policies that unintentionally, but systematically, excluded many southern settlement houses from their organization, and especially most of those conducting reform work among blacks. The NFS believed that denominationalism or extreme religiosity would enhance racial and ethnic hostilities, and so contradicted the very purpose of settlement work.

In fact, in order to articulate their ideal, settlement workers often felt the need to define their work in opposition to church missions. In the formative years of the national organization, settlement workers thought they needed to carve out a more defined self-image. Refusing to follow the dictates of a religious creed fit the progressive trend of secularism as well as the modernist movements of scientism, cosmopolitanism, and experimental social education. The Ethical Culture Society, with which the settlement movement exchanged participants and ideas, was the guiding spirit of many northern and midwestern urban settlement workers.

John Lovejoy Elliott, one of the mentors of the Ethical Culture school, wrote that "ethical religion" stressed social morality, whereas churches and schools merely addressed individual morality. In 1915, he defined Ethical Culture as a new religion based on cooperation and mutual respect—the inspiration for a "new social work." Rather than charity, he thought, settlement workers helped instill self-respect, which was necessary for social regeneration. This view held that conversion entailed more than the personal experience of the divine, but also an awakening of social conscience. The convert grasped the divinity of daily human life; like the breath of God, the inspiration for becoming a good citizen infused the individual. "We are learning to say Man, Humanity, with a significance not less sacred than that which men formerly meant when they said God," Elliott wrote.[32]

Unlike the church, which did not tend to awaken social conscience, he thought, the group work conducted by settlements encouraged cooperation, fraternity, and awareness: "The settlement should become in the long run a kind of social church, engaged in developing the cooperative life of the neighborhood, developing social vision." Settlement work should aim at drawing out the "creative social powers" of all people, a task Elliott likened, in an interesting simile, to that of a "religious mission."[33]

A later article in *The Standard*, the organ of the Ethical Culture school, contrasted, as its title indicated, "The Community Church and the Ethical Movement." It portrayed the settlement and the Ethical movements as far superior to the community church. While the church might try successfully to create an ecumenical "civic family," it could never wholly escape "the preposterous sin of sectarianism." While a church might embrace "Hindus, Bahaists, Christians, Jews, Mohammedans, Theists, Atheists, Liberals, Orthodox," it has the impossible task of finding a method of worship that suits all alike. Ethical religion more closely approaches the ideal of a "people's university," complete with spiritual and moral functions, by abandoning the element of worship.[34]

This theoretical universalism did not translate well into practice, however, at least in the case of the St. Louis Ethical Culture Society. Reflecting on the World War I and postwar era, both blacks and whites surveyed suggested that the Ethical Culture Society and its settlement house did nothing memorable for race relations. In fact, the Society failed to take a strong position on the race question and one person revealed its policy of segregation in a simple statement: "I wish they would admit Negroes to Membership in the Ethical Society."[35]

After the war, the settlement movement underwent a period of self-criticism and revision of goals. The failure of the ethical vision in the First World War, the debate over immigration restriction and its outcome in the National Origins Act of 1924, the hegemony of capital over labor, the development of corporate welfarism, the advent of Community Chest funding, and the introduction of psychiatric social work were some factors that caused this self-examination.[36] Regardless of the influx of blacks into urban areas during and after the war, settlement workers still appeared to believe that their primary clientele was the immigrant population. Although leaders of the NFS maintained an eerie silence on the issue of blacks, the raising of questions about the purpose of the movement significantly coincided with the great migration of blacks into the immediate neighborhoods of settlement houses.

Settlement workers' concern with reevaluating their work also arose in response to outside attacks. *The Century Magazine,* for example, ran an article that questioned the very purpose of settlements. It especially faulted the movement for trying to conduct courses of liberal education among working people who would rather have evenings free for recreation. Rather than taxing "tired bodies and tired minds" with "history or geography or mathematics or language," "settlements should find a type of educational work more directly related to a student's social and economic advancement; that is, focus on the problems of the job rather than depending upon the mere itch for culture." The article proposed that settlement workers, disguised as floor managers, "but who would be in reality teachers," should observe workers on the job, using "the mistakes and the problems that arise hourly as cues for direct instruction in the finer and more effective carrying out of the employees' duties."[37] This plan plainly portrayed settlements as nothing more than an arm of capital, an image that would be anathema to any settlement worker.

Other criticisms took more subtle forms. Published in 1922, Sinclair Lewis's popular novel *Babbitt* depicted Babbitt's daughter, Verona, as an aimless young woman with a vague desire to do social work, but more for the image she had in mind than genuine concern: "I want to contribute—I wish I were working in a settlement-house. I wonder if I could get one of the department-stores to let me put in a welfare-department with a nice rest-room and chintzes and wicker chairs." Babbitt sputtered furiously in response about how "all this uplift and flipflop and settlement-work and recreation is nothing in God's world but the entering wedge for socialism."[38] While Lewis invited the reader to laugh at Babbitt's attitude, the lame portrait of the settlement house nevertheless makes a strong impression.

In their meetings throughout the 1920s, settlement workers themselves experienced doubts about the success and direction of their work. Many workers thought the movement had become too staid because of the growth of bureaucracy, the passing of the pioneer phase, and the obsession with efficiency and method. One settlement leader concerned with the drift away from activism, Paul Kellogg, editor of the leading social work journal, *The Survey,* urged reformers to carry on the tradition of "turning the results of their swift experimental studies into action." He went on: "We have a tremendous vacuum in American life today; there is a stronger tendency toward research and specialization than toward common action." Eva Whiting White of Elizabeth Peabody

House in Boston thought that the 1920s had brought a period of reaction and with it a "fad" in social work to use "a kind of mechanical technique, or the ABC steps of procedure." [39]

Many blamed the shift from private donors to the Community Chest, a centrally administered citywide fund donated by businesses for a variety of philanthropic efforts, for a trend among settlements toward political conservatism. Kellogg asserted that "the Community Chests are rather nervous when any organization takes up a thing with teeth in it." [40] Jane Addams's stress on the settlement as an experimental institution, forever responding to the needs of a particular neighborhood, seemed threatened by the dispersal of many settlement functions into other specialized agencies. In a society of increasingly institutionalized services, the settlement had to reconsider its role. A reevaluation of the difference between church and settlement work, still a primary concern, inevitably ensued. A concerted effort to unite with the church in improving conditions for black Americans might have answered the settlement workers' questions about the future of their work, but instead their struggles with the issue of religion helped rule out this possibility.

The Topics for Discussion of the Executive Committee of the NFS for a 1923 meeting included "discussion of questions raised by the growth of settlements organized under denominational auspices and carried on by leaders supplied through missionary training schools." "What shall be the policy of the National Federation toward the admission of such houses?" it asked.[41] Following the theoretical guidelines of the mentors of the movement, the Executive Committee decided in 1924 "that care be exercised that no organization or settlement formed for propaganda of religion or other dogma be included in membership." [42] Ironically, around the same time, a discussion of interracial work took place. Mary Simkhovitch pointed out that it is easy for settlements to limit their work and influence to one or two dominant races in the neighborhood. "Spot maps" that charted the ethnic composition of settlement neighborhoods showed "queer holes" and "these sometimes mean local colonies of foreign groups not reached by the settlements," she said. Hindsight suggests that these "queer holes" were often inhabited by recent black migrants. The only concrete action proposed for working with blacks, however, was inviting "an outstanding Negro" to address the next NFS Conference on Interracial Cooperation.[43]

Tortured discussions of the settlement's changing role and position in the community continued to revolve around the issue of religion. In 1928, the question of admitting religious houses into the National Federation arose during a discussion about whether to admit a particular house. Graham Taylor of Chicago Commons thought the question involved much more than the policies of one house. "What is [a] religious institution? What is [a] mission? What is [a] settlement house?" the minutes of an Executive Committee meeting read. Another worker thought that a religious house that served a partisan neighborhood was acceptable, although "personally [I] think religious propeg[ation] a great mistake." He wondered what would happen if the composition of the neighborhood changed, an increasingly pressing matter as blacks moved into immigrant neighborhoods. Albert Kennedy questioned whether churches should be able to use settlement houses, and Charles Cooper chimed in, "[the] swim[ming] pool [could be] used for baptisms!" Mary Simkhovitch advocated admitting religious houses as long as they did not use propaganda, but Graham Taylor judged it too "hard to determine propaganda." They eventually agreed that "it always got back to what is a Sett[lement]. No one knows. That's the trouble."[44]

In 1928, the Executive Committee of the NFS again addressed the issue of religion, revealing the reasons for their great concern. Graham Taylor feared public misunderstanding of the settlement house, saying that he was "afraid of propaganda and religious agencies since [the] public regards all on [an] equal status." About the committee's policy on church settlements, Taylor thought it would be better to exclude those religious agencies that were "the real thing" than to include those that did not conduct true settlement work, "and so guard our fundamental power." Revealing that this power was already somewhat threatened, Taylor insisted that the NFS needed a "group standard" to avoid being "prey to points of view of [the] stray inquirer." His words took on an even more embattled tone when he said, "if we don't hang together, we will all hang separately."[45]

Other members of the Executive Committee shared this defensiveness, expressing a need to distinguish between the settlement house and other organizations they saw encroaching on their territory. Lillian Wald, New York's Henry Street Settlement founder and pioneer in settlement work, announced that "the time has come again to have a definition [of a settlement house]!" Albert Kennedy obliged her by citing four types of agencies calling themselves settlements, along with their raison d'être: "1. Missions, to change opinion, 2. Jewish, Protestant, Catholic, to reinforce faith and mode [of] life, 3. Clubs and organizations like Y[MCA and YWCA]'s, and 4. Settlements which are strictly local and belonging to one definite district."[46]

In response to a statement about the great number of agencies that sought membership in the NFS, Kennedy alluded to the possible threat to the funding of other houses by the Community Chests: "[I] think Settlements would be hurt by [the] inclusion of Missions . . . [It would] debase currency as it were . . . [It would] appear representative to the public. They do stereotyped work rather than [a] pioneering and experimental type of work. [The Community] Chests might take [the] average as representative of [the] whole!" The issue of the need to please the Community Chests arose in the same meeting as the issues of labor and interracial relations. Citing the example of businessmen's withdrawal of support from Jane Addams because of her pacifism during World War I, Graham Taylor wondered whether houses could take stands on controversial questions. If settlement workers expressed their views, "how long would we remain in [the] chest?" Helen Hall added that "controversial questions [were] taboo" and Frances Ingram cited a case where "a child labor group was asked to cease propaganda until after [a] campaign." Other members cited criticism from schools of social work and comments by academics to "keep the whole sociological movement in [the] realm of the transcendental—the safest place of all!" George Bellamy, of Hiram House in Cleveland, thought the Chest system led to a "lot of other agencies getting disciplined as well," adding, "we're not the only ones sweating under this situation." He suggested that outside endowments would make settlements independent again, though they could still rely on Chests for support for the "accepted type of activities." Other committee members disliked the restraining presence of the Chest, but thought Bellamy's proposal would never meet Chest approval.[47]

Kennedy proposed detaching the settlement "altogether from philanthropic work" and becoming devoted entirely to education by having all houses associate with a university. John L. Elliott exclaimed that this would constitute "education at [a] low level!" Others pointed out that settlements had many other functions that they would not want to sacrifice. Elliott admitted that other institutions could conceivably conduct some programs such as those in the "arts, music and health," but that the settlement used these uniquely in "the interests of a higher life." The daily concerns of practical programs put the burden of keeping up a broader vision upon the national organization, and, "this vision has failed us," Elliott believed. He expressed the general sentiment of the committee: "We need a new emphasis."[48]

In the 1920s, this "new emphasis" was clearly a bone of contention. Some settlement workers did propose cooperating with other national groups working on similar issues such as "emigration." Mary Simkhovitch also thought that "more hospitality" and not more exclusiveness would make the settlement's future more promising. Cooper acknowledged that "religion does motivate [the] life of many of our people. [The] Settlement has [the] function of getting religious groups to appreciate and understand each other." He continued: "[There] must be some other way than aloofness. [We] should unite all other groups."[49] While these sentiments hinted at a tantalizing possibility for united reform, the fear of propaganda dominated, as did the need to establish the settlement as different from all other institutions. In the same year, plans to set up an interracial conference ironically revolved around united "social and religious organizations," the two types of organizations admittedly most interested in improved race relations. The failure of settlement workers to grasp the impact of their exclusive policy toward religious work reinforces Elliott's idea that their original vision had somehow failed them. At the moment of redefinition of the movement, narrow vision, paranoia resulting from the fear of budget cuts, and concern with institutional uniqueness and image, along with fears of losing power, all limited the possibilities latent in the settlement movement's second generation.

The question of admitting religious houses to the NFS arose perennially, allowing for continual possibilities for a reversal of this stance. The NFS's intense commitment to discouraging denominational work, coupled with a northern, urban bias, translated into concrete action that systematically excluded reformers from other regions, and those most likely to conduct work among blacks. The view that denominationalism would enhance racial and ethnic hostilities and contradicted the very purpose of settlement work led to a policy that inadvertently furthered social disunity. As an indication of the severe implications of this policy for houses in the South, the example of Kingsley House run by Frances Ingram, known fondly as "the Jane Addams of the South," stands out. It had a policy of working out race divisions, reasoning that "all helpful experiments will have a national and even an international meaning." Following the NFS's ideal, which was forged in a northern, urban context, meant sacrificing power in the South. Kingsley House had a great difficulty affecting policy, for the very reason that it was the only nonsectarian house in New Orleans.[50]

Regardless of the cultural differences between the northern and southern context for settlements, reservations about admitting church-related houses continued to preoccupy the NFS. White women of the Methodist Episcopal Church, South, ran a number of settlements for both whites and blacks. This activity took root in the 1880s with the establishment of the Women's Home Mission Society, which arose partly out of the urge to provide assistance to the freedmen and women. By the 1930s, integrated staffs operated settlements throughout the South, although the clientele remained segregated into Bethlehem Houses for blacks and Wesley Houses for whites.[51]

In 1935, the Bethlehem Center in Nashville applied for NFS membership. In response to this particular request for admission, the NFS warned that admission might "make a precedent in regard to certain houses having church connections." A subsequent visit revealed that the house in question was an exemplary settlement house in a black neighborhood with an interracial staff dedicated to improved race relations. The house conducted religious work, but "not of any denominational character" in spite of its backing by the Methodist Episcopal Church. The house won a favorable recommendation and the NFS circumvented the religious question by making clear the exceptional quality of the particular house: "As to the question of precedent for other houses under the direction of the Methodist Episcopal Church, South, it is of considerable higher standard than their other centers. . . . These would not be considered eligible, either in standard of work or in attitude on the religious question."[52] The admission of Bethlehem House was accompanied by the assurance that "there is some religious work, . . . but this is a Protestant inter-denominational school in a totally Protestant community"; therefore, it was acceptable.[53]

The belief that those settlements that included a significant element of religion in their programs were doctrinaire made the NFS continually stress the distinction between what they continued to call "missions" and settlements. The Membership and Standards Committee developed a list of criteria for admission, trying to articulate the nuances that made a religious settlement unacceptable. A shift began to occur in the late 1930s, however, as settlement workers underwent yet another period of self-examination. This time, causes for alarm included the New Deal's assumption of many roles traditionally played by local agencies, as well as the departure of workers from the Works Progress Administration who had greatly assisted settlements during the early and mid-1930s.[54]

Increasingly, the NFS became engulfed in a growing awareness that the Hull House model no longer applied, and thus the new guidelines for admission into the national organization required updating. In 1937, the original requirement spelled out in 1911 by Albert Kennedy, that a settlement operate within an "open intellectual system," underwent review. The Board of Directors realized that actually "we did take a stand within a closed intellectual system which had as its basis democratic ideals," although "we are open minded in our approach in that it coincides with demands of democratic procedure." That procedure only came into play after exclusion of those settlements not considered qualified, as they admitted: "Sometimes we act in a dictatorial way in the interests of what we think is right."[55]

At the same time, a slight softening of the rigid stance on religion took place: "Some felt that the religious needs of the neighborhood are just as important as others, but if the settlement is working in a given district and the examination of the needs of the neighborhood showed that religious needs were not being met, it would be the function of the settlement to develop that aspect of its need." The address of religious "needs" reflected a new approach toward settlement work that was increasingly reactive, professional, and systematized. Criteria for admission of new houses no longer stressed open-mindedness, but efficiency, stability, and adequate facilities. This change paved the way for the long overdue recognition and admission of religiously affiliated houses. Yet this occurred well after the pioneering years of both these church missions and the settlements, when both sought to effect lasting social change as well as to help individuals. Settlement workers acknowledged that they had a new focus, emphasizing the "adjustment of the particular individual" as much as the alteration of the basic structures of local and national life. In fact, in a list of the purposes of settlement work, community work was only one item along with work with individuals and groups and the delivery of services. The fundamental definition of settlement—residence in a poor neighborhood—also diminished in importance at this time.[56]

These trends helped change the NFS's view toward religious work. No longer seen as competitors, missions and religious settlements seemed bona fide if they offered the types of services offered by settlement houses. When Albert Kennedy conducted his national questionnaire concerning interracial work in settlements, he was bombarded with information about the religious work that had been conducted for decades. In the 1940s and 1950s, the NFS thus suddenly "discovered" religious work and interracial work simultaneously. The heightened awareness of racism brought on by the experience of black soldiers in World War II, the nascent civil rights movement, Nazism, and postwar racial conflict startled the NFS into the sudden realization that improved race relations should be their primary concern.

The 1950s finally revealed the problems of a policy of exclusion of most church-related work. Religious work, involving both blacks and whites, had attempted to confront race problems for decades, problems that the NFS only belatedly acknowledged as critical. Evidence that the religion barrier needed to be broken much earlier surfaced in a statement of the Women's Division of the Board of Missions in May, 1952. These women hinted at the existence of conflicting views within the ranks of religious workers themselves when they stated that clergymen had often objected to their work precisely for the reason that it was not missionary in type.[57]

Religious Settlement Work among Blacks

In the 1940s, the survey conducted by Albert Kennedy provided a plethora of information on religious settlement work that concerned race relations, tragically filling in a picture retrospectively of an opportunity missed by the settlement movement. The blindness of many leaders of the mainstream movement, which resulted from regionalism, urbanism, and nondenominational progressivism, fortunately need not be repeated by students of the movement. Ironically, it was the very religious emphasis that led to a true cosmopolitanism and paved the way for an emphasis on social justice.

A review of the many attempts by organizations with religious affiliations to address issues concerning race reveal the limits of the settlement "method," which actually worked against its own stated goals when it came to blacks. The desire to be scientific, secular in a style they thought democratic, cosmopolitan, and progressive kept settlement workers from approaching their ideal of responsiveness to the nascent social problems of their neighborhoods, cities, and nation. Their ideals thwarted a potentially powerful union with those groups interested in improving race relations and foiled the possibility of infusing these movements—admittedly often provincial and limited by their own goals—with the broader vision of social ethics.

In 1937, Frances Ingram of Neighborhood House in Louisville published an article entitled "The Settlement Movement in the South," in which she described an extensive number of houses in that region. She noted that at the turn of the century, "the settlement movement gained impetus in the South": "Churches, missionary societies, federations of Women's Clubs, kindergarten associations, the Council of Jewish Women, nurses, sororities, and individuals, were all fired by its idealism." She described settlements piloted by industrial schools, the Woman's Christian Temperance Union, colleges, and church organizations, in communities from Washington, D.C., and Baltimore to the mountains of Harlan County, Kentucky. Citing the economic structure as the primary problem of the South, she noted that the system of tenant farming was considered the "curse of the South." The sharecroppers, "a dissatisfied group," migrated from "farm to farm and from state to state" and eventually into the city. "Unadapted to the city conditions, he [the migrant worker] is unequipped educationally and industrially to compete with the city man. He is most likely to travel into the poorer sections and become discouraged by a lack of opportunity, whereupon he returns to the country; soon dissatisfied, however, he returns to the city." [58] Ingram's observation echoed that of settlement workers who aimed their work at white immigrants.

Aware of these conditions, certain churches and associations, by establishing settlements and centers, tried to help migrants adapt to new communities since the turn of the century. Ingram cited the Women's Missionary Society of the Methodist Episcopal Church, South, which established its first settlement in 1901 and later built many others "in cotton mill districts, in foreign-speaking sections, in mining centers, near fish canneries, among Mexicans, Cubans, French Arcadians, and Negroes, also in rural districts." Others conducting work included Presbyterians and the Women's Missionary Union, an auxiliary of the Southern Baptist Convention.[59] These southern efforts were mirrored by various organizations in other regions. Religious associations particularly interested in improving race relations included the YWCAs, other white Protestant denominations, and the black churches, especially the African Methodist

Episcopal Church. Several examples will illustrate the scope of social reforms conducted under religious auspices well before the onset of an organized civil rights movement, and also well before the NFS's recognition of the primacy of the situation of blacks in America in the goal of social harmony and national self-improvement.

Black churches themselves often conducted settlement work along with their worship services, to the best of their abilities considering their often tight or nonexistent budgets. In particular, the AME institutional churches often combined welfare, employment, education, insurance, savings and loan, and many other functions. The AME Institutional Church on South Dearborn in Chicago, established by Reverend Reverdy C. Ransom, was built in 1900. Founded to administer social work among what was then the largest black community in the city, the settlement included a building with a 1,400-seat auditorium, a Sunday School, a church, a kindergarten, a day nursery, music classes, a reading room, a library, a voice-training department, and an employment bureau. It conducted clubs, classes, lectures, and night classes in stenography and typing. This ambitious work was, however, curtailed because of lack of funds, and Ransom left within a few years.[60]

Another effort in Chicago, the Olivet Baptist Church, had a huge membership of 9,069 in 1919. The center maintained an employment department, a rooming directory, a kindergarten, and a day nursery. Its organization included forty-two auxiliaries and sixteen employees. The Riot Commission Report published after the Chicago riot of 1919 found that the church was one of the strongest institutions among blacks, as it was often the only "social institution with an unhampered opportunity for development." The Commission observed a multitude of churches conducting employment bureaus, lectures, community programs, parties, meetings, recreation and amusements, social service departments, basketball teams, and literary societies. One such center, the People's Church and Metropolitan Community Center, organized by a group that withdrew from the Bethel AME church in 1920, raised $22,000 from its members in five months in order to establish a community center for several thousand blacks in Chicago. An explosion of churches with extensive, integrated programs akin to those of settlement houses accompanied the migration of blacks during and after World War I.[61]

Other institutional churches included the Trinity Mission established a few years later by Bishop R. R. Wright, Jr., who after World War I became president of Philadelphia's Colored Protective Association, an association dedicated to defending blacks against racial persecution. The Association and the AME church established the Richard Allen House for black migrants to "come and get free lodging, meals, and service until they could locate a permanent place," but it only operated during the years of peak migration during and after the war. Later Wright founded the Goodwill Service Center, an AME community organization in Memphis, Tennessee.[62]

Another example reveals a concrete reason why efforts among blacks sometimes might not have appeared to equal the renowned northern settlements— lack of wealthy donors. The Congregational Church established the Barnwell Community Center in Beaumont, Texas, named after a superintendent of black Congregational churches, H. S. Barnwell. The center aimed at promoting "community solidarity, happiness, health, good citizenship and highest Christian ideals" among the black neighbors it served, through the departments of "Religious, Moral and Health Education." It provided a meeting place for the Boy Scouts, the community Recreation Council, the Goodwill Council, and other civic organizations, and organized the local YMCA until it became a branch of the white YMCA funded by the Community Chest. Paralleling the settlement's goals and "having no interest in creeds, it seeks to lift to higher levels the lives of those who come within her sphere of influence."[63]

In the 1920s, the church bought property for an adjoining playground, and established a social service department during the 1930s. The department investigated 700 cases of blacks in need, distributed 700 cords of wood and 3,000 garments. Responding to the severe crisis of the depression, Barnwell also established eight "community unemployment gardens and wood yards" as well as a clinic for those who could not afford medical care. Called the Community Health Home, the clinic served as the only hospital providing competent care to blacks and allowing black nurses and doctors to practice. In 1939, the center was self-sufficient and able to separate from the Congregational church, but continued to be supported primarily through donations and denominational contributions from throughout the country. In 1940, Barnwell initiated an insurance program, the Barnwell Sympathetic Benevolent Association, which resembled the mutual aid societies prevalent in black communities since the eighteenth century. Members paid one dollar per month in return for free clinical care, twenty-five days of free hospitalization per year, and "a respectable burial at death." The elderly for whom obtaining old-age insurance was difficult or impossible "found it a balm." In 1942, a Home for Negro Youths opened its doors to assist juvenile delinquents and a yearly Community Christmas Tree was set up to help the poor. In addition, the center housed a branch of the public library. In 1946, the General Director of the house wrote, "The center has made itself felt in many ways; reclaiming the lives of those it has worked with physically, socially, morally and spiritually."[64]

In Philadelphia, Benezet House attempted to work among both blacks and whites to improve race relations as well as living conditions for blacks. Under the auspices of the Society of Friends, the house formed in 1920 as a combination of Locust Street Mission Association, the Western District Colored School, and the Joseph Sturge Colored Mission Sunday School. The City Welfare Federation helped support the settlement until 1935, when dwindling funds from the Quakers caused the house to disband. Under the Crime Prevention Association, a boys club of 2,000 members continued, as did an Adult Bible Class of 80 members, which had existed since 1910. In spite of its religious orientation, Benezet directed settlement work through its day nursery, kindergarten, school classes, boys and girls clubs, and family visiting. The house sought to conduct interracial work with the unique combination of offering "first, the type of social work which is needed by thousands of Negroes in a big city in common with many other groups—and second, cooperation and fellowship without fear or favor between members of the two races."[65]

With classes in "hygiene and habits," as well as sewing and cooking classes for women and day-care programs for children, the house aimed to address the needs of the entire family "from toddling beginners with pigtails erect to grey-haired old ladies and their toothless husbands." It provided babysitting, classes in carpentry, basketball tournaments, and other athletic opportunities, and claimed to direct "youthful energies into more wholesome channels than the nearby poolrooms and dance halls." While this definition of "wholesome" is subjective and has paternalistic overtones, the provision of daycare and classes in trades alone were welcomed warmly by the working-class blacks reached by the house, judging by its membership. The house offered daycare to twenty to thirty children, including bathing and food. In regular activities, the average attendance was 150, ranging in age from six months to ninety-eight years old. In the 1920s, the house's concern with race relations far surpassed the norm for most whites and from the vantage point of Benezet House, the Friends had an optimistic outlook: "As we try to help, in our various capacities as workers, visitors, Sunday school teachers, and board members, we find that 'color lines' are quietly disappearing of our common concern."[66]

This kind of interracial work, a rare effort in settlement work, encountered great obstacles. Many religious organizations pressed on anyway. The Rankin Christian Center, for instance, developed as a project of the National Home Mission Societies of the Northern Baptist Convention, in cooperation with the Pittsburgh Baptist Association following a survey of the Inter-Church World Movement. In 1920, the survey found that ten percent of the Rankin, Pennsylvania, population were blacks, about sixty percent recent immigrants, and the rest native-born whites. Settlement work began primarily for immigrants, but in 1924, blacks applied to use the facilities. Like some settlements, the house initiated a biracial policy, allowing blacks to occupy the building for one day a week, under the supervision of their own leaders, while the regular staff took a day off. By 1930, the black population had doubled and a second day was added, along with a separate club room. Gradually, a policy of scheduling blacks and whites on all days in the same building got under way. If they could afford it, native and immigrant whites deserted the neighborhood.[67]

By 1940, blacks constituted nearly 30 percent of the community, but made up a much higher concentration of the immediate environs of Rankin house. In the 1940s, the city opened a Housing Project at the urging of the center. Racial tensions flared and kept the project segregated, eventually prohibiting cooperation between the community center and the housing project. Whites resented the presence of any blacks, especially since the black population was growing. Blacks who had inhabited the neighborhood for years resented the influx of southern blacks as well as the new segregationist tendency of whites. Whites refused to associate with blacks at tenant councils and recreational activities. From 1930 to 1945, the center operated as a settlement house with denominational backing, and not as a missionary group. Racial tension flared in certain activities and receded in others, such as educational classes, leaders' institutes, the track team, and the well baby clinic. Mass activities like the library, gameroom, and playground, were integrated but usually dominated by blacks because "1. Other facilities for Negro youth are almost non-existent in this area, 2. White young people have more places to go, and 3. Parental approval of interracial policy by Negro parents versus disapproval by white parents." The integrated staff persisted in running most activities, presenting their plans as a "de facto development" to the Board of Directors, which did not approve of "programs and policies designed to promote inter-racial participation."[68]

Other interracial experiments conducted under religious auspices included the efforts of the YWCA, which as early as 1915 organized a conference to explore work among black girls in the South and within decades had established some of the earliest integrated social institutions.[69] The Board of Home Missions of the Congregational Christian Churches, through the American Missionary Association, also attempted to better conditions for blacks by establishing rural life schools, which aimed "to bring whole groups of farmers out of the Sharecropper or Tenant class into the class of landowners and home owners." The schools helped train black ministers, offered classes in cooperative canning, cooking, and homemaking, and provided important information on farming and crop rotation. Schools helped in cooperative communities such as Dorchester, Georgia, with programs such as the Friendly Service Department, which reconditioned and sold clothing at low cost.[70]

Other similar efforts included centers such as the ecumenical Church of All Nations and Neighborhood House in New York City, which sought to "demonstrate that people of various races, nationalities and religions can live and work together." An integrated staff of African Americans, Asians, and Caucasians, with religious leanings from Greek Orthodox to Jewish, set an example for the membership whose composition reflected the house leaders' diversity.[71] While this type of effort was unusual, denominational work often aimed at a similar acceptance of diversity, as did settlements conducted under the auspices of the Lutheran and the Presbyterian ministries. In 1945, Albert Kennedy also mentioned the Bronx House and Council House in New York City as settlements that conducted work with blacks under Jewish auspices.[72]

Albert Kennedy acknowledged that Presbyterian community centers in Louisville had long been on the forefront of combatting white racism while offering needed services to blacks. These included the Hope Community Center and the Grace Community Center, both operated by the Presbyterian Colored Missions.[73] The Board of National Missions also established a Presbyterian church and "Christian Service Center" in the heart of the "inter-racial" area of West Oakland, California, sending a black pastor, Reverend John Dillingham, to develop a social center. With degrees from Shaw University, Crozer Theological Seminary, and Yale University, Dillingham had a great range of experience, from teaching in a southern college to pastoring churches and attending international conferences. The petition for the organization had signatures and support from Texas, Arkansas, Louisiana, and Oklahoma, as well as California. In addition to the church auditorium, the center enjoyed the use of additional rooms, adjacent playgrounds, and athletic fields. With a much broader goal than merely offering a place of worship, the settlement housed a health clinic, a counseling center, boys and girls clubs, and other activities composing an integrated program of "worship, education, and fellowship" seven days a week, not just on Sundays.[74] The center aimed at improving the quality of life in the community.

Some of the most striking examples of attempts to conduct work among blacks were those of the Women's Home Mission Society of the Methodist Episcopal Church, South. From the time of its founding in the 1880s, the Society endeavored to address the problems of the "Freedwomen of the South."[75] The organization formed in Cincinnati in 1880 and as early as 1897, president Belle Bennett asserted that the society had "done nothing for the Negroes." She declared that "the path of duty is plain before us. . . . We must enterprise some special work for this great race of people."[76] In spite of resistance from the male leaders of the church and from local whites, the Society increasingly focused on the plight of blacks. It aspired not to evangelize, but to improve living conditions with the cooperation of the black community by establishing settlement houses. The church women set up Bethlehem Houses or Centers in black neighborhoods throughout the South, braving the hostile forces of racism and poverty. As detailed in Chapter 4, these houses were usually separate from those for whites, the Wesley Houses. Yet they did provide much-needed services and activities and, when successful, fostered community pride and cohesiveness.

While this work no doubt had its paternalistic element, these examples represent a drastic contradiction to the image proffered by the northern settlement workers who stressed the provincial, dogmatic, sectarian nature of religious "propaganda." The women of the Methodist Episcopal Church, South, had genuine motives, as evidenced by the great amount of time and energy poured into celebrating the achievements and potential of African Americans.[77] To a limited degree, this type of organization improved community life, if only by offering facilities hitherto unattainable to impoverished neighbors. Merely establishing a gymnasium for blacks in a slum district in the context of the early twentieth century was a reform. Providing for the most basic needs of working-class life, through day-care centers, kindergartens, night schools, and grounds for recreation and religious worship, represented an authentic attempt to infuse the Social Gospel into the less glamorous, more neglected neighborhoods than the sites of Hull House or Henry Street.[78] While these religious organizations differed in some ways from their more cosmopolitan sisters, the northern and midwestern settlement houses, they came a step closer to addressing the perennial and still unsolved domestic parallel to the immigrant question—the situation of black Americans.

In the 1950s, the National Federation of Settlements and Neighborhood Centers, as the NFS was then renamed, reported on a conference designed to develop an awareness of work that resembled settlement work but operated under religious auspices. It noted the formation of the National Council of the Churches of Christ out of twenty-nine denominations interested in social betterment. The Women's Division of the Methodist Church, the report went on, operated sixteen Bethlehem Houses with integrated staffs in largely black neighborhoods. These women thought that their work should not be missionary and thus had "come into conflict with the local clergymen who questioned why the women should be putting in time and money for neighborhood work which was not missionary or evangelistic in nature." The NFSNC had the belated opportunity to glean from the information it now had that work under denominational auspices often constituted the best way to gain financial support, buildings, community acceptance, volunteers, and membership. It also had another chance to unite with religious activists interested in lasting reform. Instead, the national organization evoked its time-honored but misguided rule: "Since settlements are meant to provide a common ground where peoples of all sorts can meet together, certain formal religious practices are excluded and Houses which evangelize cannot become members of the NFSNC."[79]

At about the same time, the Ethical Culture Society's journal, *The Standard*, reprinted articles written thirty years earlier that established the strict distinction between the "dogmatic creeds" and ethical religion. One article stated: "The Society has never attempted to substitute a moral creed for the dogmatic or doctrinal creeds which it repudiated at the outset. . . . If an Ethical Society were to lay down a moral creed then it would automatically exclude not only all those persons who in theory dissent, but all those who in theory assent." [80] By struggling so valiantly against dogma, the leaders of the settlement movement created a new dogma, a new criterion for exclusiveness, a "closed intellectual system." In spite of the ideals of objectivity, progressivism, and cosmopolitanism, the movement carved out its own provincial sphere in the midst of the burgeoning industrial city. Theorists of settlement work erected an edifice of discourse; they thought that this blocked the path of their own vows to respond immediately to the most pressing social problems of their day and to extend what they saw as the blessings of American citizenship to the neediest. Settlement leaders tragically failed to grasp the truth of their own words, that "morality is a matter of practice." [81] They broke the promise of their own ideals.

Three

Southern School-Settlements for "Total Education"

In 1912, Mary White Ovington, settlement worker and cofounder of the National Association for the Advancement of Colored People (NAACP), described a dichotomy in early twentieth-century thinking about African Americans. One school of thought stressed education and supported industrial training in the South. Adherents thought that the only solution to the problems of blacks was "the slow education of all of the people," and therefore refused to dwell upon "injuries and persecutions." The second school, she explained, asserted that "the policy of 'time and patience' is outworn." Violence against blacks, discriminatory treatment by the courts, disfranchisement, and unequal distribution of school funds all mandated what this school's advocates considered more direct action, such as the activities of the NAACP.[1] Paradoxically, it was the former school, represented by the Hampton-Tuskegee tradition, that gave birth to a significant form of social settlement work—the southern school-settlement.

These two opposing views were embodied, in the eyes of many contemporaries and scholars since, in the persons of two of the greatest black leaders, Tuskegee Institute founder Booker T. Washington and sociologist W. E. B. Du Bois. The differences between these two thinkers have often been simplified as a debate over industrial education versus liberal education, and accommodation versus agitation. The rhetoric and ideology of these two leaders undoubtedly clashed. Yet the abstract polarization of all efforts for social betterment into Washingtonian and Du Boisian camps has obscured the day-to-day functions of many social reform organizations, especially those in the rural South. While the Washington–Du Bois split prevailed in public discourse, their approaches mingled in an entirely new and complex recipe when put into practice.

Positioning the spotlight on this great debate between two renowned figures has also eclipsed the efforts of lesser known individuals, such as a cadre of women, both black and white, who undertook reform work in the South. This chapter will focus on three of these women and their efforts to conduct a form of settlement work in the rural South. These and other women engaged in similar efforts have not ordinarily appeared in accounts of reforms characteristic of the Progressive Era because of the usual bias toward urban and northern reformers. Under the guise of industrial training, however, women dedicated to improving race relations conducted ambitious work among blacks living in some of the most impoverished regions of the Deep South. They founded elementary and secondary industrial schools that served as nothing less than community centers integrating a variety of social service organizations, local improvement programs, and educational services. Although white racism and economic exploitation severely handicapped their efforts, these school-settlements aimed at a radical reconstruction of indigent and demoralized communities.

Booker T. Washington modeled Tuskegee on his alma mater, Hampton Normal and Agricultural Institute in Hampton, Virginia. Under the leadership and ideological inspiration of founder Samuel Chapman Armstrong, Hampton self-consciously styled itself as different from the usual college or university. It sought to combine higher education and technical training, "the training of the hand and eye, as well as of the mind." Armstrong's nineteenth-century missionary upbringing was reflected in his belief that effective education built moral character and that the education of blacks would lead to their social uplift.[2] While criticized by those who thought him paternalistic or patronizing toward blacks, and too accommodating toward racist whites, Armstrong undeniably inspired many blacks and whites to dedicate their lives to working for the betterment of social conditions among blacks and for improved race relations. Booker T. Washington, his best known protégé, drew inspiration from Armstrong and established a Hampton outgrowth in the Alabama countryside. Tuskegee wielded enormous influence on all aspects of race relations in this country, including the views of whites toward blacks and the approach of black activists, to say nothing of the broader spheres of education, politics, and American culture. Like many Hampton graduates, Washington nurtured a lifelong commitment to Armstrong's ideas, which he immortalized in a memorial service address after Armstrong's death in 1893. Washington went so far as to say that Armstrong was much more than a teacher "to hundreds of us who knew no man that we could call father."[3]

When Washington wanted to convey the "Hampton idea," he often related a vignette about "a young girl educated at Tuskegee" who foraged into "a dense, ignorant mass of 30,000" where she encountered "the slavery of the mortgage system like a cancer eating up soul and body, leaving the Negro in debt, landless, homeless and too often with empty stomach and clotheless body." The school term lasted less than three months and the people lived in one-room cabins, "groaning under a load of debt, with worn and haggard countenances, without hope for themselves or their children." This young graduate immediately went to work using the Hampton approach she had learned at Tuskegee.

> She went among the parents, gave instruction in housekeeping, organized a sewing class, advised here and reprimanded there. Soon she organized the older people into a club that met every week. In these meetings she would tell them in a plain, simple, common sense manner how to save, what to buy and what not to buy, how to sacrifice, how to live on bread and water, if need be till they could get out of debt and stop mortgaging. Thus by showing them how to use the results of their labor, how to turn their earnings in the direction of their mental, industrial and moral uplifting, the first year she caused many to stop mortgaging and make contracts for the buying of homes. In addition she showed them how by their own efforts to build and supply with proper apparatus a neat, comfortable schoolhouse to replace the wreck of a log cabin. . . . Now my friends, I wish you could have the privilege that I have had of going into that community and seeing the complete revolution, yes regeneration, that has been wrought in the mental, industrial and religious life of this community by the efforts of this one girl.[4]

Washington used this story to describe the methods of Hampton and Tuskegee, stressing that the money for community regeneration originated from the inhabitants and that the effort represented a revival of "that sense of self-dependence, habit of economy and executive power" discouraged during the 250 years of African American bondage.[5] The agent of this "complete revolution" of community life was an education that aimed beyond the teaching of academic subjects to the inculcation of high standards of conduct and achievement. Washington thought other whole communities, and blacks as a group, could undergo a similar awakening simply by witnessing what he called "object lessons." Rather than employing traditional pedagogy, handing out charity, or preaching hope for the future, the graduates of Tuskegee, Hampton, Fisk, Talladega, Tougaloo, and other schools would send out "a class of leaders" to guide the people, he said.[6] Teaching by "object lesson," Washington believed, constituted the best approach toward whites as well. Rather than reciting the wrongs inflicted on blacks, he promoted the following plan:

> Let a graduate go out from this or some other school, settle near them, live a good life, keep a clean house, with a yard full of flowers, raise forty bushels of corn instead of twenty to an acre; and by and by the white neighbor is going to notice it, and stop by the gate to look at the flowers and talk about the crop; and gradually he will conclude there are exceptions, and

after a while find other exceptions, and find common ground of interest, and in this way our problem will gradually work itself out. We have been depending too much on the power of the mouth instead of object lessons.[7]

While the catalogues of Tuskegee and Hampton listed courses in manual trades and other aspects of industrial training, one of the most important points of Washington's interpretation of the Hampton imperative—community development—has often remained veiled under the stigma of industrial training itself.[8]

James Anderson, among many other scholars, as well as Hampton's contemporary critics, has portrayed the Hampton model as possessing the mission of training "a cadre of conservative black teachers who were expected to help adjust the Afro-American minority to a subordinate social role in the Southern political economy."[9] Washington's rhetoric was certainly milder than the language used by Du Bois and the Niagara Movement. As symbolized by his Atlanta Exposition Address, Washington urged peace between the races and counseled blacks to have patience. On the so-called slow road to equality, however, the Hampton-Tuskegee model encouraged efforts that sometimes were far from conservative. Anderson and others have left no doubt about the racist motivations of those northern white philanthropists and white Southerners who supported industrial training for blacks to the exclusion of any type of liberal education. Yet the records of certain school-settlements suggest that, despite the racism and paternalism of their donors, actual efforts on the community level ranged beyond their ostensible accommodationism. Anderson implicitly questions the stereotype of the industrial school itself by showing that the emphasis on Hampton's industrial program obscured its primary mission—to train black teachers for the South. This goal, articulated by both blacks and whites in a time when southern blacks daily encountered the realities of a violent, openly racist culture characterized by lynching, disfranchisement, Jim Crow, and dire poverty, hardly aimed to support the status quo.

The late nineteenth and early twentieth centuries witnessed sweeping educational transformations that bore such innovations as the industrial education movement, expanded public school systems, the rise of black colleges, progressive education, the adult education movement, agricultural extension work, and the expansion of higher educational opportunities for women. The Hampton idea flourished within the broader movement of industrial education, which had a variety of meanings. It could connote applied science and technology programs that trained professionals, trade schools that prepared workers for certain occupations in industry, or manual instruction. Common schools often adopted the latter to supplement the academic curriculum "in order to promote habits of industry, thrift, and morality."[10]

Hampton Institute promoted manual training along with its academic program for the declared purpose of "moral uplift." Another essential motive for including this type of education involved the need to procure much-needed funds for what amounted to a type of upper level secondary and higher education for blacks at a time when other opportunities were scarce. The late nineteenth and early twentieth centuries brought about a tidal wave of reform dedicated to improving the quality of modern life, but at the same time they witnessed one of the most severe racial backlashes in U.S. history. Scholars have amply illustrated that the North and South were both characterized by brutality against blacks, social ostracism, residential segregation, and other horrors that made simple existence an anguished struggle. Racism was not confined to one hostile group but included many prominent politicians, intellectuals, and other leaders, as well as unfriendly white neighbors. The economic realities of entrenched black poverty in the northern and midwestern slums and the permanent indebtedness of black workers under the southern crop-lien system combined with custom to buttress a racial caste organization.[11]

Within this context, reformers interested in altering the plight of blacks did indeed see an emphasis on education as a way to appease and appeal to those in control of scarce financial resources, namely northern white philanthropists with cash and southern businessmen with land. Hampton reformers valued manual training, as they expressed in their resounding praise of its benefits. It also undoubtedly lent a legitimacy and persuasiveness to their fund-raising efforts. Hampton and Tuskegee ostensibly supported industrial education as the long-term solution to the social inequality facing blacks, and this appealed to potential donors both for its harmless demeanor and its tangential benefit of keeping blacks in the South. Within the context of race relations in the 1890s, Washington thought it best to underemphasize what he saw as Tuskegee's mission of providing an "education for life" with its full connotations of teaching teachers as community activists to revivify impoverished rural regions and teach self-sufficiency. While photographs of Tuskegee portrayed students dressed in their Sunday best to feed chickens or hoe a garden, the vague epithet "industrial training" covered a much broader expanse of educational experience.[12]

Historian Elizabeth Jacoway points out that the word "industrial" had different implications in the early twentieth century from its current meaning. Many scholars who criticize the industrial education movement as a southern attempt to control and exploit blacks economically and socially provide as evidence the failure of industrial education to prepare workers for modern industry. Some suggest, Jacoway writes, that Southerners implemented an obsolete educational program to keep blacks in a subordinate position. Jacoway argues against this interpretation, however, by showing that Northerners and not Southerners controlled industrial schools and also that "industrial" training never aimed to equip blacks for new jobs in industry. Instead, she writes, "industrial education was a moral program designed to inculcate the primary virtue of *industry*." It neither sought to instill readiness for life in the industrial city nor to deliver vocational instruction, but to provide an "education for life." This education included practical skills but revolved around building character, or "the development of manhood and womanhood," in the words of contemporary education reformer and sociologist Thomas Jesse Jones.[13]

Jacoway's interpretation of the industrial schools provides a corrective to the conspiracy thesis, yet she merely concludes that Northerners brought the missionary impulse to a policy that essentially constituted "social control" of blacks.[14] In his study of the founding of black colleges in the late nineteenth century by northern white religious liberals, James McPherson calls this motive "educational colonialism." He qualifies his critique by pointing out that without liberal interest, "there would have been no Howard, no Fisk, no Lincoln, no Morehouse, no Spelman, no Atlanta University."[15] Indeed, W. E. B. Du Bois thought that these church-sponsored schools provided nearly all the college education and much high school training for southern blacks and were "the finest thing in American history." These colleges spurred social work and community improvement and amounted, he said, to "social settlements."[16] While Du Bois and others contrasted these colleges with the Hampton-Tuskegee model, the latter nevertheless often resembled a social settlement as well. Like the colleges that were limited by the paternalistic, colonialist approach of their benefactors, the industrial schools had to contend with the conservatism of their guardians. The simple conspiracy or social control interpretations, however, fail to explain the participation of local blacks, the involvement of black students and teachers in an enterprise of oppression, or the efforts of whites who dedicated their lives to a cause they genuinely embraced.

An examination of some of the results of education at these institutions suggests that accommodationist rhetoric often veiled significant attempts at local reform. While the leaders of the major institutions of industrial training acquiesced to the paternalism of their donors, their students had greater leeway in their interpretations of the relative emphasis on manual training and other aspects of the program. Several case studies reveal that in practice, the Hampton idea could mean nothing short of attempted community change. Many female Hampton and Tuskegee graduates and ex-teachers went on to found social centers under the title "industrial schools" throughout the South. Like black men, they were largely shut out of the usual methods of wielding power through established channels of administration in existing educational institutions or political office. Like many nineteenth-century female teachers and missionaries before them, they set out into unknown parts to carve out lives and careers. Many of these women founded and headed schools. Perhaps their very experience as women, while in some ways limiting, allowed them to expand their own horizons and the Hampton ideology to the point where calling their work manual training would be a gross misrepresentation.

Margaret Murray Washington, the wife of Booker T. Washington, attended Fisk University but went on to support her husband's industrial school. She established a settlement house on the grounds of Tuskegee Institute called Plantation or Elizabeth Russell Settlement. The settlement had a Mother's Club that provided the organizing structure for social service and reform activities. Hundreds of women gathered weekly for meetings, walking or riding from miles around in the Alabama countryside. The work was divided into departments or committees, each devoted to particular projects such as temperance work, community work, Sunday schools, and Mother's meetings. The women also ran a night school with courses in cooking, sewing, writing, arithmetic, carpentry, reading, and history with special emphasis on black history. Projects entailed courses of study on a topic such as Sex Hygiene, basically a euphemism for birth control. A 1913 Woman's Club report read that "we have not only informed ourselves on this question but have had the opportunity of instructing many women outside of the club." Other programs included Current News and a Music Department. A department in Social Service, raising money by making and selling candy and other food, paid the dentist bill for 100 children one year, provided medical services, built a playground and park, and constructed a Reading Room and a Boys' Social and Literary Club. Members of the Woman's Club, an early supporter of woman suffrage, saw themselves as following in the tradition of the settlement house movement, as symbolized by their vote for the ten greatest living Americans. They chose Jane Addams second, after Thomas Edison, and listed Booker T. Washington sixth.[17]

The specific cases of women strongly influenced by Hampton or Tuskegee thus reveal much broader plans than suggested by the term "industrial school."[18] Indeed, the work of the founders, leaders, and teachers at schools such as the Calhoun Colored School and Social Settlement in Lowndes County, Alabama, the Penn Normal and Agricultural Industrial School on St. Helena Island, South Carolina, and the People's Village School at Mt. Meigs, Alabama, illustrated a lifelong devotion to certain industrial and academic programs only as a part of "total education." In some ways, their programs resembled the full range of activities offered by black colleges at the time. Their activities comprised part of a larger rural education movement to which they were fiercely committed. They sought the education of individual students as part of community regeneration, which in turn pointed to the higher goal of long-term, permanent change in the economic and social facts of black life and race relations. In many ways, their efforts resembled the work of settlement workers.

Calhoun Colored School and Social Settlement, "the Lighthouse on the Hill." Calhoun, Lowndes County, Alabama. (Courtesy of Hampton University Archives)

The Calhoun School

In response to questions about the state of Alabama's educational provisions, Booker T. Washington succinctly described black schooling in a letter to George Washington Cable as something "that is left to the people, and the result is that the schools among the colored people especially are usually taught in church houses."[19] This was indeed the case in 1892 when two white women from the North arrived in an impoverished rural community of blacks in Lowndes County, Alabama, about 100 miles from Tuskegee. The only building they found was a dilapidated one-room shack called Lee Plantation Church that served as a school with a term that lasted less than three months a year and was furnished only with pews made of rough logs.[20]

Mabel Wilhelmina Dillingham from Boston and Charlotte R. Thorn from New Haven, Connecticut, had taught at Hampton Institute, where in 1892 they heard Booker T. Washington talk about the desperation among blacks in rural regions of the Deep South.[21] In the 1890s, Washington often spoke about work among blacks in the gulf states as a vital mission. "The problem is vast and serious; the work is not done," he announced. To young people concerned with current social problems, his description of the deprivations ahead was undaunting in light of the great rewards to be reaped: "There is nothing to invite you there but hard work for our people. . . . But I believe that if you go with the Hampton spirit and the ideas and methods General Armstrong has taught us, you can revolutionize the communities where you go. One point is encouraging; the people want light; they will live and die for such a teacher."[22] The next morning the women presented themselves to Washington and expressed their desire "to go out into some country district and start a school for Negroes that would give a chance for the young people to receive a good common-school

education" and that would "touch the home life of the people so that whole families would be raised to a higher standard of living." Washington decided to send them to the small town of Calhoun because Lowndes County had the highest proportion of blacks to whites of any county in Alabama. In 1891 he visited the area and wrote to Mabel Dillingham that he "found the out-look even more promising than I had dared hope for." Besides destitution, the main problem he observed was that "the people are more than anxious for the school. . . . All day long people were arriving. Some on mules, some in buggies and some in ox carts. All were eager to know what the prospects of 'their school' were." [23]

The new teachers expressed similar excitement about the project. In fact, Hollis Burke Frissell, Vice President of Hampton who became President in 1893 after Armstrong's death, warned that Mabel Dillingham's "scheme for work in Alabama" would require "some one who will look at things more coolly than she is likely to do." Frissell noted her great enthusiasm but feared that the project would demand more "patient endurance" than she usually showed. The conditions in Lowndes County, however, called on every reserve of enthusiasm. The party of Dillingham, Washington, and Thorn, arrived in Calhoun during a long rainy spell. Finally, after days of rain, Washington wrote, "Miss Dillingham suggested that we provide ourselves in the best way we could against the wet weather and go out and select the spot where they would put the first building. I remember distinctly my feelings, and how gloomy, how dismal and how poverty stricken it seemed; how everything seemed to present the worst appearance possible. . . . She did not seem the least daunted, not the least discouraged, and the place was selected." [24]

Dillingham expressed great enthusiasm for the Hampton ideal in 1893 when she reviewed the Tuskegee Negro Conference for Hampton's organ, *The Southern Workman*. Revealing her own feelings, she wrote that in response to Armstrong's speech, "a wave of love" swept the audience. She held in high esteem the members of the Calhoun community who struggled to repay their debts, to buy land, and to build homes, remarking that "to one who lives among these people, who sees and knows how desperately poor they are—the amount of money raised by them for the school is astonishing." Dillingham especially praised the work conducted through schools that could transform entire communities. About teachers and reformers at the Tuskegee Conference, she asked, "are not these people solving the 'Negro Problem,' while others talk of solving it?" [25] Unfortunately, she did not live to see the implementation of her plans. At her funeral in 1894, Washington summoned up a fond recollection. "I see her now as she stood with an umbrella over her head and with mud up to her ankles, while we decided upon the exact spot and measured off the ground where the first building was to be." [26] Dillingham left her missionary zeal as a legacy to a new institution that would continually draw on her type of enthusiasm for years to come.

Charlotte R. Thorn, whom Frissell had recruited from New Haven high society to teach at Hampton, took over Calhoun as coprincipal with Mabel Dillingham's father, Reverend Pitt Dillingham. Thorn dominated the leadership and in 1909 attained the sole principalship, which she held for the next two decades.[27] Initially, the community had reacted to Charlotte Thorn and Mabel Dillingham with suspicion. Washington noted that the people "could not understand it." "They could not realize how it was that somebody was enough interested in their condition, in their life, to come there on such a day as that desiring to give life itself for their uplifting," he explained. The whites in the neighborhood also suspected that "these white teachers had not come there with the best motives." Washington even had to make a special effort of explaining to the white businessman who sold the first ten acres cheaply to the school that "the school was to be conducted by northern white ladies and something of its character, so that he could not say later that he did not understand about matters." [28] Mabel Dillingham had at least lived to see this suspicion dissipate, for at her funeral, Washington was able to observe that the teachers had gained the confidence of the community. "What a change!" he exclaimed. "For we must remember that this is the 'black belt' of Alabama, where only a few years ago it was a crime punishable with death, to teach a black boy or girl a letter in a book." [29]

The Calhoun plan envisioned and implemented by Charlotte Thorn entailed a unique combination of serious elementary and secondary education, a version of industrial training, and social settlement work. The first step of the pioneers was to build a new schoolhouse. The two founders and four assistants then welcomed 300 pupils whose ages ranged from six to twenty-eight, two-thirds of whom could not read or write. Annual reports of Calhoun revealed an extensive schedule of academic and industrial courses and activities the teachers thought would transform the community. Thorn drew inspiration from progres-

Charlotte R. Thorn. (Courtesy of Hampton University Archives)

sive educators like John Dewey and saw all manual training as directly related to intellectual growth. She quoted Dewey's advice that "All concrete work should lead to the library," and valued the accessibility of books, newspapers, and magazines in a well-stocked library. A traveling library supplied nine bookcases of selected books for three months to schools and individuals throughout the county. Calhoun sought to make the best possible educational facilities available to students who had been accustomed to a school building that did not contain windows and desks let alone books, maps, paper, blackboards, and more than one teacher.[30]

While Calhoun aimed to provide an integration of industrial training and academic education, it by no means resorted to a predominantly vocational curriculum. In 1901, for example, the schedule for seniors included six thirty-five to forty minute periods in manual skills out of a total of thirty-two class periods weekly. A sample outline of work for the senior class read as follows:

> Arithmetic. 4 periods per week. Percentage, ratio, square root enough to enable them to find the length of rafters. Many problems.
> Reading. 3 periods. Ethics for Young People. 2 periods (part of the year).
> Geography and History. (Europe.) 3 periods. (Part of the year.)
> Bible History. 2 periods.
> Citizenship. 2 periods. Dole's American Citizen, Alabama Civil Government, United States Constitution.
> Drawing. 2 periods.
> Methods of Teaching. 2 periods.
> Spelling. 2 periods.
> Language. 3 periods. Study of masterpieces, composition.
> Grammar. 2 periods.
> Science. 2 periods. Agriculture.
> Singing. 2 periods.
> News Items. 1 period.
> Educational Work. 6 periods. Boys in carpentry and farming. Girls in sewing, laundry work, or cooking.[31]

This approach focused on relating education to the daily lives of students in a meaningful way, and encouraging "character-building." Teachers tried to inculcate a "love for biography," for instance, to teach the lives of great people as models of virtue and accomplishment. "A love of good reading" and challenging mental work was also fostered, as the pupils came "from homes where there are no books or papers." Over the years the academic plan grew more rigorous and extensive as students advanced, and by 1920, a Calhoun Circular of Information displayed an impressive and detailed course of study that included applied aspects of academic subjects such as business arithmetic, debating, map making, current events, mechanical drawing, industrial mathematics, agricultural science, nursing, hygiene and sanitation, zoology, botany, ethics, local history and geography, as well as traditional academic subjects such as Latin, English, and history. From kindergarten through the tenth grade, the highest level taught, the academic department sought to instill an understanding of the concrete, daily applications of material purveyed. At the same time, a cosmopolitan awareness pervaded the curriculum. A course in commercial geography dealt with "the interdependence of countries of the world through commerce and industry." Classes in English composition included "exercises in derivation of words and history of the English language." "Negro Literature" appeared in the topics for literature courses whose "special aim [was] the enjoyment of the literature read." Other courses heightened political ken through material on the local, state, and national government. By 1919, students received thirty-six hours a week of academic instruction and only two to six hours of industrial training according to grade.[32]

Industrial work at Calhoun was divided into manual training and agriculture for boys and domestic science for girls. "Girls' industries" included "the three constant needs of home life"—sewing, cooking, and laundering. Students' knowledge of "intelligent, trained methods of work" would then travel into their parents' households and their own when they became adults. Many female graduates left Calhoun equipped with the skills to earn livelihoods as seamstresses and dressmakers or as sewing teachers. "Proficiency in cooking or laundering" had similar practical consequences. Cooking lessons aimed "to meet the home needs and pocket books," focusing on materials and ingredients readily available. Cooking included planning, preparation, and cost estimation. Other classes for both girls and boys taught crafts such as weaving, basketry, chair caning, and the making of other necessary household items such as cushions and mattresses. A home nursing class informed students about the "causes and prevention of disease, first aid, bandages, lifting and bathing patient, care of baby," and other skills necessary for women in charge of their families' health.[33]

Boys' industrial work sought similarly to teach skills necessary for life in the local community. Instruction in blacksmithing and carpentry supplemented a program that prepared boys to run their own farms. A course in cobbling "enables the farmer to keep his own shoes in repair and those of his wife and children, and also to mend his farm harnesses." Agricultural training included vegetable gardening, the study of "plant life, soil formation, texture of soil, air and temperature, plant food, farm manures, and commercial fertilizers" for seventh graders. The eighth grade was devoted to "farm crops, giving attention to rotation of crops, the value of legumes, cultivation, and harvesting" along with "fungus and insect enemies together with the means of fighting them." The ninth grade studied animal husbandry, and "the production and care of milk." The point of this work was to replace single-crop cotton farming and its disastrous effects on the soil and the community with modern techniques and tools of farming. The school farm of nearly 100 acres provided an arena for the experimentation and application of course work. Crop diversification, rotation, and fertilization, combined with livestock raising would allow for the self-sufficiency, prosperity, and persistence of the rural community of Lowndes County.[34]

Like Tuskegee and Hampton, Calhoun considered the training of teachers one its most vital missions. The school had two outpost schools in Lowndes County, Sandy Ridge and Lee Place, and matriculated numerous scholars who went on to positions teaching or preaching in the South, or who attended Hampton, Tuskegee, or another institution of advanced learning, and then became teachers, education administrators, or heads of their own schools.[35]

Calhoun teachers had to strike a balance between keeping in touch with the community and fitting graduates for teaching in the surrounding public schools by enabling them to pass the "somewhat old-fashioned academic examination which Alabama requires its colored teachers to pass." Calhoun tried to remain friendly with county and state officials, and to focus on the coming educational reforms of "Alabama's forward movement." Calhoun annual reports cited a "general awakening of the State that should mean more money even to the backward counties of the Cotton Belt." In Lowndes County, blacks far outnumbered whites and the proportion of county funds devoted to each black child was far less than for a white. As a result, a Calhoun report read, Lowndes "must largely furnish its own teachers." Because "few teachers will come from the normal schools of the State," Calhoun workers took on the burden of supplying the best-trained teachers they could produce.[36] Rather than await reform of the State system, Calhoun ushered it in through forums such as an annual Teachers' County Conference. Teachers heading the forty black schools, seven of them Calhoun graduates, met to discuss teaching methods and subjects, the relation of community and school, and various successes. National leaders in education addressed these conferences, and reform ideas thus spread. In 1915, Rural School Agent James L. Sibley asked Calhoun to be the center of the Lowndes County Teachers' Institute. Thirty teachers volunteered to spend two Saturdays a month at Calhoun learning its methods under the faculty in the teachers' reading circle.[37]

Training teachers, farmers, and artisans constituted part of what Calhoun's leaders deemed a valuable service and sensitive understanding of the needs of the community. A separate sphere of activity called community work, however, embraced many other programs. Calhoun conducted a night school for young people who were not free in the daytime as well as for adults. The community night classes opened in 1911 to teach parents of the schoolchildren English and arithmetic and also to provide instruction in the shop under industrial teachers. An Annual Farmers' Conference drew men from a great distance and

Farmers' conference at Calhoun Colored School, Lowndes County, Alabama. Reprinted from Hartshorn, Era of Progress and Promise. *(Courtesy of Hampton University Archives)*

discussed momentous questions such as the future of cotton in the South. Various State and County representatives attended the conferences, such as the agricultural demonstration workers of Lowndes County and the rest of Alabama and nearby states. The school also opened its grounds to the community for an Annual Agricultural Fair, Graduates' Meetings, numerous Christmas gatherings, Emancipation Day, community sales, quarterly Parents' Meetings, and monthly entertainments for the elderly. A "deposit system" allowed members of the community to deposit money at the school and draw on the funds in times of need. Teachers from Calhoun visited surrounding schools and churches to speak about collective self-improvement and other issues. Calhoun's work also included fighting epidemics, teaching preventive medicine through proper sanitation and diet, holding dental clinics, and providing hospital rooms at the school. In sum, as one annual report pointed out, the school functioned as a "community center," integrating a variety of social services and neighborhood improvement activities with the formal education of adults and young people.[38]

Mothers' meetings and Women's Club meetings took place twice monthly and were supplemented by "home visits" by the teachers. A doctor also met with county women, giving them "inspiration and knowledge" for the improvement of their families' health. Mothers' meetings brought about improved care of the sick, increased attention to the education of girls, "the co-operative buying of groceries to secure lower prices," group canning of fruits and vegetables, and enhanced skills in earning and saving money. Participants saw the goal of their efforts as transcending their practical accomplishments. In a 1907 Mothers' Club meeting, one woman declared that "right now is a critical time, and we as mothers must get together and understand one another." The Club thought that Calhoun should aim to "make neighborhoods in the Black Belt where children can grow up into manhood." They enlisted the help of others in this coopera- tive community building. Another woman said, "I am glad to see the men are waking up. Since they are waking up, we women are willing to help them. . . . The mothers cannot raise their children by themselves. Our children are on the minds of the fathers too." Mothers' Club meetings often ended with a renewal of a mutual vow called the "Neighborhood Covenant." Standing with right hands uplifted, the women said in unison, "We promise, with God's help, to live for our children, to do everything we can to put down all that is unfriendly to the life of a little child, and to try in every way to build up the things which will help the children." [39]

The central aim of all phases of Calhoun's work was to attack the social con- ditions diminishing the quality of life for members of the community. Living under the demoralization of the crop-lien system and southern racism, one of the most powerful ways that Calhoun made its influence felt was through a plan initiated in 1894 that established a Land Company. Following the lead of the Tuskegee Negro Conference, the Company bought 120 acres in 1894 and sold them to three men. Within a few years, the Company secured over one thousand acres and later, over four thousand acres were offered in tracts of forty to sixty acres for men's farms, with ten acre lots for single women. Money donated from northern philanthropists helped provide for loans to the new landowners who paid them back at 8 percent interest. By 1910, at least ninety- two deeds had been distributed and new three- to eight-room houses erected in place of the traditional one-room cabin. As a result, the people basked in "the self-respect which the ownership of property brings," noted a Hampton Institute pamphlet.[40]

In its published reports and other formal publications, Calhoun underempha- sized its land-buying plan. A 1902 appeal for funds suggested that Calhoun's sphere of influence was broad but did have limits. "It is building a neighbor- hood of farms and homes and is stimulating the growth of other neighborhoods in its county," the appeal stated, but assured the reader that "the school as a corporation is in no way involved financially in the selling of small holdings to the Negroes." Significantly, the appeal focused its request for funds on its much more acceptable program of industrial work.[41] An appeal written fourteen years later, however, emphasized that Calhoun was not merely a school, but also "a settlement which specializes in community work." A more favorable climate prevailed after farm demonstration work aimed at the self-sufficiency of farm families was marked as a priority by the federal government under the Smith- Lever Act of 1914. Then Calhoun could announce that it "has by the purchase and sale to the Negroes of over 2,000 acres of land created a community of land-owning, self-respecting farmers who in spite of hard times have all been able to retain their property."[42]

A newspaper article noted that the powerful role of Calhoun as neighborhood center revolved around its active role in procuring land and modern homes: "All these men are learning to raise their food and live at home, avoid the crop mortgage and waive note and the credit prices at the store. They have shown themselves capable of thrift. Man and wife together have learned and are learning to plan and to save, for the sake of the children."[43] Called "The Lighthouse on the Hill" by some and "De Mornin' Star" by others because the white buildings stood in stark contrast to the lush greenery of the Alabama countryside, Calhoun effected a great change in its environment. One historian wrote that before Calhoun existed, "practically all the Negroes were being kept in a state similar to peonage." "The Lighthouse on a Hill," he added, "changed the whole community."[44]

Inevitably, Calhoun faced obstacles on the road to its ambitious goal of community regeneration, including the resistance of "friends"—those Northerners upon whose donations the school depended—and neighbors. The powerful minority of southern whites in Lowndes County provided a constant source of concern. Upon the opening of the school, white farmers blamed the teachers for trying to disrupt their labor force. A neighboring businessman named Bell owned much of the land around the school which he had rented to black farm workers for years. As customary in the crop-lien system, blacks paid rent in crops and were deeply indebted to Bell, who controlled the local store as well. In 1909, Charlotte Thorn heard a rumor that Bell planned to sell 12,000 acres surrounding the school to a northern organization, the Baron Hirsh Fund, that sought the land for a colony of Russian Jewish immigrants. Thorn wrote Hollis Burke Frissell at Hampton, "I don't think Bell wants us to get hold of the land." The sale of surrounding land would inevitably frustrate Calhoun's vital goal of community self-sufficiency and strength. Thorn wrote: "I know the Hirsh Fund People are 'good people' but fear that the carrying out of their colonization scheme for the Russian Jews here at Calhoun would naturally oblige the colored people to give up living on the land they are now renting so largely from Bell. The removal of all the colored people from this tract of land would mean reducing the number of Negroes to such an extent that we would have to become an Institution rather than a Settlement." Thorn envisioned obtaining the land for "our people" instead, probably after Bell's death, along with control over the store and the cotton gin at the railroad station, "building up a little business center that would encourage our graduates to return to Calhoun to find occupations." In the future, she surmised, "we might eventually have Calhoun owned largely by colored people."[45]

Meanwhile, the land sale was in the hands of an attorney who had a contract with the "stipulation that the contract or agreement will be of no effect if it is known by the tenants or other parties at Calhoun that this land is for sale." Another attorney explained to Thorn that Bell wanted to keep the information from the tenants so that his current year's crops would not be in jeopardy. Calhoun considered putting up a bid for the land, but only under an outside party, "as you know his [Bell's] feelings toward us," Thorn wrote in a letter to Frissell. In 1924 a Calhoun trustee and educator, George P. Phenix, suggested to another trustee that Bell had ended up retaining his land out of malice: "It affords but another illustration of the fact that the evil men do in their lives, lives after them. There are 13,000 acres of land entirely surrounding the school's property, and so tied up by the will of the late owner that no portion of the estate may be sold until the grandchildren, now very young, are of age." To the Calhoun community, the Bell name was a source of anxiety, which kept blacks from migrating to Calhoun and buying land.[46]

In 1924, F. Raymond Jenkins, head of a Quaker school in Arkansas called Southland Institute, was under consideration for a position at Calhoun. In response to Jenkins's questions about Calhoun, a Hampton worker wrote, "The attitude of the white neighbors has never been friendly, partly because the school's policy of seating colored and white workers together at table has been quite unyielding, partly because the school has fought an unceasing fight against the practical peonage and other evils of the prevailing system of tenant farming in the county."[47] The broader climate of race relations in Alabama heightened the tension at the school. In 1915, for instance, a bill introduced in the state legislature proposed "to prohibit white persons teaching in schools for Negroes." The bill led to much consternation among southern teachers, forcing H. Margaret Beard, Principal of Montgomery Industrial School, to exclaim: "What a bitter blow it will be to all of us if it passes."[48] Henry W. Farnham, professor of economics at Yale University, wrote that the bill is "most alarming. I very much feel that it will pass, and if so this means the end of Calhoun."[49] Fortunately, he was mistaken and the bill was voted down at the end of the year. Teachers subsequently latched with great hope onto the "emphatic repudiation of any legislation which might tend or even seem to limit the freedom of northern schools and northern white educators in their work for the colored people" as the promise of a new progressive movement for reform of Alabama's educational system.[50]

At the school level, similar tensions arose around the integrated nature of the staff of Calhoun. At times, teachers or staff people were found unfriendly to the aims of the school or to the advancement of blacks themselves. Charlotte Thorn, whose devotion to blacks was a constant topic of remark by many, including trustees and graduates, would not tolerate others who lacked that devotion. In

1913 the school chaplain, Reverend A. Field, had several conflicts with Thorn. She wrote Frissell that Field had made a negative remark about Booker T. Washington to a group of white men at the Calhoun railroad station that was "out of accord with our stand here at the school." When she suggested to Field that he consider leaving Calhoun, he said that "as the community were an emotional people he could go around and 'jolly' them and he would soon be in touch with them." In fairness, she said, Field was likeable enough to the people, outside of his "lack of loyalty, as they felt, to the race and to the school."[51]

In 1924, a much more dramatic display of the tension inherent in the Calhoun situation erupted in an incident that, according to an official notice filed at Hampton Institute, "nearly broke up the school."[52] At the end of the spring term, several students brought to the attention of Charlotte Thorn a "too friendly relationship" that existed between two white female teachers and two black male teachers. In addition, one of the women carried on a flirtation with three students. Another of the school's black male teachers, James Webb, asked the white woman not to flirt with the students. When Charlotte Thorn learned of the situation, she dismissed all four of the teachers and Webb, apparently for taking the matter into his own hands by scolding the teacher and disciplining the students. Several Calhoun workers, including the dismissed Webb, charged Thorn with listening to unruly students and using Webb as a scapegoat.[53]

One man wrote that Webb was "driven from the campus in a most disgraceful way because he reported an immoral act that existed between two of the teachers."[54] James Webb himself wrote to Thorn that her action was "biased and prejudiced" and based on the advice of only one trustee. His letter suggested he was being blamed for disciplining students too harshly. He defended his disciplinary measures as appropriate for boys "who have been spoiled and pampered by teachers whose interest is only surface deep." He told Thorn, "I believe I know my race better than you do, I come into closer contact with them daily," and thus argued that he understood the type of discipline necessary for uplift and for the eradication of "immorality" at Calhoun. Webb concluded that "where the white race and the black become involved in unwise association, every colored man within a hundred miles of the place stands in danger," suggesting that he did not think Thorn understood the gravity of the offenses of the students and teachers involved.[55]

While it is difficult to sort out the details of the incident, the turmoil clearly illustrates that tension about the climate of race relations and taboos about sex and race lay just below the surface of everyday life at Calhoun. The implication that Thorn had used a black man as scapegoat seemed to contradict his very claim that she was not harsh enough in dealing with "immoral" associates and unruly black students. On the other hand, Webb's harsh discipline suggests that perhaps he, better than she, understood the terrifying consequences of inter-racial liaisons in the racist South. He might have merely tried to protect and educate the students. In any case, the event left the school in disarray during the summer of 1924 and Charlotte Thorn in a fit of nerves. Some of Calhoun's trustees even sought to remove Thorn permanently from her position as prin-cipal, citing her loss of control over school affairs. By the beginning of the fall term, Thorn was stripped of her active responsibilities. Naturally, she was "very unhappy over her present position" and thought that the trustees had "acted in a discourteous and most inconsiderate way towards her." [56]

Regardless of the trustees' action, Thorn wanted to take an active role in appointing her own successor as she was greatly concerned that the new prin-cipal be dedicated to blacks and Calhoun.[57] The trustees seemed mainly con-cerned about finding someone "strong enough to run the school but to get the money besides." [58] Replacing Thorn was not as easy as imagined, the trustees found, and they soon realized they had acted too soon. Although the pioneering founder of Calhoun might try to control events too much at times, she per-formed an "impossible load." The trustees discovered it would take three people to replace her, a Principal, a Business Manager, and an Educational Director. Furthermore, Thorn had the school's very well-being in her hands since the primary means of fund raising was her personality itself. One trustee wrote to another that "to replace Miss Thorn at the present time would be a calamity." He thought the trustees had acted too hastily and asked, "Is there some way of undoing what was done?" In another letter, he wrote that he could not under-stand how Thorn could raise money when "her status is really anomalous." He advocated reinstating her as full principal, noting that the trustees were not well informed when they stripped her of her managerial duties, adding that "her devotion to the school is without limit." [59]

Since the time of its founding, Calhoun had relied on the superhuman efforts and unquenchable enthusiasm of its leaders for its very life. Local people con-tributed to its support with an initial sum of over two hundred dollars and a yearly tuition of a dollar per child. But the school depended on outside sources of funding such as the Slater Foundation, the General Education Board, the Rockefeller Foundation, the Westchester Association, the Frothingham Fund, and the New Haven Calhoun Club, along with churches, Sunday school classes, missionary societies, women's clubs, civic groups, and individuals. It was a great asset for any experimental effort like Calhoun to have at its head an "attrac-tive Yankee socialite" like Charlotte Thorn, who traveled easily in the circles of northern philanthropists and whose charisma and knowledge of every de-tail of the workings of Calhoun earned many an eager donation. The trustees showed their ignorance not only of the great amount of power vested in Thorn but in the vital role she played as a bridge between two foreign countries, the local community and the donors. Only as long as both groups placed their trust and allegiance in Thorn could the experiment prosper. Belatedly, the trustees recognized the importance of Thorn's role and reinstated her with all of her former responsibilities. In 1927, a trustee wrote to Thorn that northern support had waned and so winning new "friends" was essential. "Your own ability in this direction and your personality continue to be the chief asset in money-raising," he wrote.[60]

Calhoun rarely enjoyed a feeling of financial stability, but its tenuous position increased as the movement for improved county training schools and other government-sponsored schools got underway and philanthropists' donations slowly dried up. As early as 1916, several trustees mentioned relinquishing control to the Unitarians, much to Thorn's disapproval since she did not think that the denominational backing would mesh well with local religious life. Thorn also mentioned that some advocated making Calhoun primarily a vocational school because of the new dedication at the federal level to that type of industrial work, but she objected to the idea.[61] In 1923, several teachers formed a committee representing hundreds of Calhoun graduates and ex-students and commented about the great success of Calhoun in transforming the community and spearheading educational reform throughout the county, adding that "the present financial condition, however, threatens the very life of the school." They noted that Thorn, at age sixty-six, was tiring and needed help from the trustees in raising money. "Knowing her struggles and achievements here, it makes us sick at heart to see her noble and animating spirit daunted."[62]

In 1924, trustees again considered relinquishing control either to a religious body such as the American Church Institute, the Unitarian Association, the Society of Friends, or to the state educational system.[63] One trustee described as a probability the notion of the state educational system's assumption of Calhoun: "The school and its community work, during thirty-five years, have now become a necessity, which should be continued. With the lessening of northern support, many colored schools of the South, so maintained, will undoubtedly be taken over under state control, so that it seems of vital importance to conform to state requirements, and for the Calhoun Colored School to go adjust its program as to become an accredited High School."[64] For another decade and a half, Calhoun managed to resist its absorption into the state system or a denominational organization. However, two pivotal events occurred nearly simultaneously that weakened Calhoun's resistance. In 1931, the onset of the Great Depression dried up donations further, and the school had to halt payment of the teachers' salaries. "Without some large help in the immediate future, the northern members of our Trustee Board are going to be wholly in sympathy with the closing down of the work," Thorn feared.[65] Early the next year, Joseph Loud, president of the Calhoun Board of Trustees, wrote an article for the *Boston Transcript* entitled "Calhoun's Urgent Need of Funds" soliciting contributions for the very "continuance" of Calhoun.[66] Three months later, Loud noted that the Carnegie Corporation had adopted a resolution offering Calhoun five thousand dollars as an "emergency grant" and the General Education Board had donated ten thousand with another five thousand earmarked in matching funds.[67]

In another two months, however, the second momentous event occurred. The administrative Board of Hampton Institute sent a telegram on August 29, 1932, stating that "the Hampton Family sympathize with . . . all the Calhoun Family in the death of Miss Thorn."[68] The night before, the school had lost the great personality that had helped give it its life and its vision.

Charlotte Thorn's contribution to educational and community reform, however, received unprecedented acclaim with the advent of the New Deal. Calhoun had received recognition before that from a variety of sources. Like other schools that had white leadership well after many black colleges had black presidents, the situation at Calhoun requires further analysis. Surely Calhoun could not have lacked a share of the paternalism plaguing other institutions supported and run by white liberals in the early twentieth century. Because of the racist climate, Calhoun's success must be attributed partly to the fact that Charlotte Thorn was white.

It is essential to keep in mind that Calhoun did not transcend all the paternalism and subtle racism of its time. It had the laudable aim of making a model community based on black self-sufficiency, but its success was restricted by the reality of white supremacy. For its time, however, Calhoun represented a serious attempt to alter social conditions. One observer described Calhoun's value as a model for agricultural extension work in the 1910s. Mary White Ovington also commented that work conducted by Charlotte Thorn set the stage for government involvement in agricultural extension work.[69] Jackson Davis, General Education Board field agent from Virginia, thought that Calhoun did some things better than Tuskegee and Hampton. Calhoun, "one of the best schools in the South," he wrote, "is a small school imbued with the ideal of community service and it is exerting a very great influence in shaping the home ideals of the colored people." He went on to say that the broader significance of the school was that it "is keenly alive to the awakened interest in Alabama, not only in the matter of school improvement, but in the great agricultural revolution which is underway."[70]

Another observer noted that Calhoun was "unique of the institutions of the kind existing anywhere," and received visits from prominent educators from

Belgium, France, Japan, China, and India.[71] Those associated with the school praised everything from the beautiful buildings and setting, and the extreme devotion of Charlotte Thorn, to the tremendous effect the school had on the community. In 1924, a trustee observed: "When one visits a school and finds an unusually intelligent teacher, or meets a prosperous farmer, the owner of an attractive home, and discovers that they are graduates of Calhoun School, after a number of such experiences, the fact is effectively driven home that this school has tangible results to show for what has been put into it. It has certainly accomplished a great deal, and its possibilities for future usefulness are unlimited."[72]

The Great Depression had the unexpected benefit of publicizing the poverty of areas like Lowndes County and making it clear that the federal government would have to take a role in relief and reconstruction.[73] Thorn Dickinson, Charlotte Thorn's nephew, had taken over her work at Calhoun after her death and at first saw the New Deal as "wasteful and demoralizing, and a reckless infringement upon the prerogatives of the States." Within a year, however, he headed the Subsistence Homestead Project in Lowndes County, which he called the "most promising" such program in Alabama. As county engineer for the Civil Works Administration, he secured a grant from the federal government of $75,000 for black farmers in Lowndes County and $25,000 from the General Education Board for improving the roads near Calhoun. Thomas Jesse Jones, then Educational Director of the Phelps-Stokes Fund and president of the Calhoun Board of Trustees, saw the Homestead project as a direct result of the community activism conducted at Calhoun, "an impressive continuation of Miss Thorn's land and homestead activities during the last twenty years." Homestead, funded by $200,000 for projects for blacks in Alabama, supplied $75,000 each to Macon County and Lowndes County, and $50,000 to Montgomery County for a project for industrial workers. The money in Lowndes went to land, buildings, roads, a water supply, and terracing for a relief project. A black architect working for the federal government said that "he had not had anything like the cooperation elsewhere that he has received at Calhoun."[74]

In 1935, Will Alexander, Director of the Commission on Interracial Cooperation and Assistant Administrator of the U.S. Resettlement Association, described his travels to the Deep South to learn the ways in which Calhoun assisted tenants and sharecroppers to become land owners. He said that Calhoun's "program which has been carried on for a number of years is the most successful demonstration that has been made of a thing which the Resettlement Administration is now attempting to do on a nation-wide basis." Alexander cited Calhoun's means of "rehabilitating people" through a plan based on "wise family selection," use of fertile soil, careful planning, and supervision. He stressed the importance of Calhoun as a model for government policy: "Calhoun has demonstrated beyond argument that if the above methods are followed a great improvement can be made in the whole economic and social situation among the people in the lower economic strata of the South. The whole country is indebted to Calhoun for this demonstration." [75]

Thomas Jesse Jones believed that the key to Calhoun's success was its responsiveness to local conditions and culture. "School activities and community services have been effectively adapted to the health, the agriculture, the homes, the recreations, and the religious life of the people," he said. Thorn Dickinson added that the government workers found Calhoun's techniques "admirably suited to both black and white children," and that the farm demonstration agents in charge of the program (one of them a Calhoun graduate) "accepted the view-point of Calhoun, and shaped their policy in accordance with the following principles, which the school had adopted as a result of long experience." This policy included several tenets: that assistance should be directed at the immediate needs of "desperately poor people, without any of the frills of social service reformers," that a farm program must be tailored to each individual, that "supervision must at first be thorough and on other occasions severe in order to break old habits of shiftlessness and ignorance," then that supervision must be gradually relaxed and the individual encouraged to be "self-respecting and independent" and not rely on outside assistance, and finally that the goal be eventual ownership of a farm. By 1935, this plan allowed 267 families to be "resettled" and Lowndes to boast the best repayment record in the state.[76] Calhoun also served as the center for Red Cross relief efforts during the Depression, the mediator between the government and individual recipients of relief, and the advocate for farmers seeking government seed and feed loans.[77]

In spite of the centrality of Calhoun in government relief programs and its great achievement as a model for government policy, the Depression hobbled Calhoun. The agricultural depression wrought desperate poverty in a community that had already suffered for years from the replacement of farming with industry and migration out of the rural South. In 1935, Thomas Jesse Jones appealed to donors for funds to save an admirable institution "in severe financial straits." In 1937 the minutes of a Calhoun meeting read that there was "a great need for canvassing for large sums in aid of Calhoun." [78] In 1938, expenses at Calhoun were "cut to the bone." [79]

Furthermore, the current president of Calhoun, Jerome F. Kidder, suggested that government resettlement actually hurt Calhoun's land redistribution program by constructing houses and renting them out nearby, thus competing with the model of land ownership.[80] Several possibilities for solving the financial crisis took the form of the usual choice between state or church sponsorship.[81]

Kidder thought that absorption under the state authorities would mark a loss of independence. Calhoun, he thought, was "so far ahead of the average Negro school that to put it under the same management as the average Negro public school would be a distinct step backward."[82] Others thought state assumption would bring mediocrity. The same year, Kidder's reputation was punctured by accusations that he had whipped some black female students, that he professed to prefer white cooks in the teachers' kitchen because they were "cleaner," that he favored whites at the heads of departments, and that he was "a slave-driving type man."[83]

By September of 1939, Kidder had left the school, finances worsened, and the school failed to open. Some "colored people are weeping," observed Thomas Jesse Jones. Two years later, the school had made the decision to become affiliated with the American Church Institute for Negroes, a corporation of the Protestant Episcopal Church. In 1943, the trustees finally deeded the school to the State of Alabama and gave the Lowndes County Board of Education the responsibility of supervising Calhoun as a public school.[84] While Calhoun's pioneers had attempted a model community in an impoverished region of the Deep South, which guided government policy during the tragedy of the Great Depression, this very success contributed to the downfall of its own ideal. The removal of control over land redistribution from Calhoun began the fragmentation of programs and goals, the integration of which had been the genius of the community school-settlement. The adoption of Calhoun by the state school system meant bureaucratization, standardization, and the decline of open experimentation.

Calhoun's decline no doubt resulted partly from the investment of so much power and responsibility in the single person of Charlotte Thorn. After her death, the school had difficulty proceeding without the animus of the mind that could integrate such diverse functions and moderate such opposing factions. Worst of all, the Great Depression swept Calhoun's voluntary contributions out from under it, money that was already waning with the growth of the state educational system and the growing federal assumption of responsibility for extension and vocational work. Perhaps the Depression merely painted the final stroke over a way of life that was increasingly outmoded in American culture. The rural "good life" defined by community, family, self-sufficiency, and plenty was passing as a possibility and as an ideal. The decline of cotton farming and the continuation of virulent racism paved the road from the countryside to the city and made exodus an easy choice for many blacks.

In the 1930s, Thomas Jesse Jones had taken one last stand for Calhoun. The collapse of "cotton tenancy," he said, had been called "*our greatest social humiliation*," because of the desperate living conditions that were revealed; tenant regions were "a miserable panorama of unpainted shacks, rain-gullied fields, straggling fences, rattle trap Fords, dirt, poverty, disease, drudgery, and monotony." He thought that approaches like Calhoun's had potential for all suffering communities. Like nearly all so-called liberals of the early twentieth century, Jones tended to support white leadership of efforts to assist blacks, a tendency that qualifies the sincerity of his concern.[85] In spite of the omnipresence of paternalism, however, Calhoun remains as evidence of a remarkable attempt to alter the desperate living conditions for blacks in Lowndes County. Charlotte Thorn thought that Calhoun was not "just another school," but instead a type of "education for life."

The People's Village School

The story of the People's Village School at Mt. Meigs, Alabama, also represented a genuine attempt at community regeneration. Driven by a similar spirit, People's Village made more modest gains. Its accomplishments were contained less by a conservative philosophy than by concrete limitations such as a lack of funds and a harsh physical environment. Founded by Georgia Washington, a black woman who graduated from Hampton, the school suffered under constant financial strain, climatic crises, and what she considered a fatalistic attitude among community members. "The one great trouble with our people here is they seem to live in the dark most of the time and never seem to see that it is possible to do more in the future than in the past," she wrote to Hollis Burke Frissell.[86]

Georgia Washington graduated from Hampton in 1882, where she stayed for ten years afterward as an assistant in care of Winona, the dormitory for Indian girls attending Hampton, as a Sunday school teacher, and as a temperance worker. She subsequently spent a year under Charlotte Thorn and Mabel Dillingham helping them launch Calhoun Colored School, and then set off to establish a school-settlement of her own at Mt. Meigs, Alabama, a village fifteen miles from Montgomery and twenty-eight miles from Tuskegee.[87] Washington drew her inspiration from General Samuel Armstrong, founder of Hampton, quoting him as saying, "What is commonly called sacrifice is the best, happiest use of one's self and one's resources—the best investment of time, strength, and means." In 1916, looking back upon her work at People's Village, she concluded that Armstrong was a forerunner of progressive reform and that his "lesson of service for others is being taught throughout the world now." She and Booker T. Washington, among others, merely followed Armstrong's plan that aimed at uplift. The work involved "not only Negroes, but the white man and the red, all working with the same end in view—the uplift of humanity through service." To Georgia Washington, service meant the education of her own people by providing schools to impoverished communities and assisting "in lifting the cloud of ignorance and superstition from my brothers and sisters there."[88] The year before she began People's Village, Washington wrote that during her schooling at Hampton, she had envisioned the type of work she desired to undertake. To a Hampton Anniversary gathering in 1892, she said, "My ideal school all along had been where the people were in a very low state of civilization, some out of the way place where no one else cared to go." It appealed to her to work "side by side with another race, different perhaps from ourselves, yet helping us to grow large-hearted, keeping ever before us Hampton's motto, 'Help one another.'" Washington's words shed light on the motivations of other teachers who chose similarly to serve a higher goal than self or career. Washington and others, once apprised of the conditions of desperate poverty and permanent indebtedness facing blacks in the rural South, thought they had no choice but to follow the "mission" laid manifest before them. "I cannot close my ears to this pitiful appeal of the helpless," Washington wrote.[89]

In the next decades, Georgia Washington had to call on this fervent missionary spirit to endure the many crises that faced People's Village. While Washington shared the same tie to Hampton upon which Thorn and Dillingham depended, she lacked their easy access to northern white philanthropists. A southern black woman, she did not move freely in the society of the white liberal elite and therefore relied on indirect connections through administrators at Hampton or Hampton men on her own staff for raising money. The few white Southerners on the board of trustees were apathetic about raising funds. While Washington understood that financial shortages threatened the very existence of the school, she wrote, the trustees "are perfectly contented." "One old man," she went on, "says well I reckon some body will send it [money] to you from the North." Washington's relations with the southern trustees were strained and she spoke of enlisting their help but making sure not to "rouse them to anger."[90] She ended up having to communicate to them through Hampton leaders Hollis Burke Frissell and George Phenix. Charlotte Thorn's ability to move among three circles—the local community, Hampton, and northern philanthropists—contributed to the success of Calhoun; but Georgia Washington's inability to do so left her frustrated, placing People's Village at the mercy of the climate of northern sentiment and the community's own scarce resources as well as southern racism.[91]

People's Village School rested on a shaky financial foundation. As early as 1898, Georgia Washington noted that "my greatest burden is where to get the money to pay teachers, but I am trusting God for it and doing what I can to interest friends." [92] In 1904, Washington's spirits hung by a thread, and she beseeched Frissell: "Please let me hear a word from you soon, just a few words from you would help me, for the work there is very hard to carry at present but I mean to stick to it until my strength has entirely failed." [93] In 1906, she wrote that the money shortage had become desperate. The school had not managed to pay salaries and one teacher had threatened a lawsuit. Washington voiced the need for an outside person to join People's Village in order to enhance fundraising efforts. [94] Three years later the school was again in debt and the teachers without salaries. Saved by contributions from local people and Northerners, the school limped along, but fluctuations in donations forced students to use the benches on which they sat for desks and teachers to go without salaries for three months in 1915. Finally, the school had to close early. So it went throughout the next two decades. [95]

While the financial condition of the school was tenuous, people in the local community had even worse difficulties. The teachers generally endured salary cuts and nonpayment with patience, as did Georgia Washington herself, partly because they perceived the greater need in the community. [96] Students and their families struggled to overcome the obstacles to their education such as lack of the nominal tuition, great distances between their houses and the school, and difficulty doing without the children's labor in the cotton fields. [97] A People's Village School annual report read:

> Our young men and women are struggling as never before to get what the school is trying to give—a start toward better things in a practical way. Young men have come to us from five and ten miles distance, paid in what they could on tuition, and we feel that we must help them at any sacrifice. We can't turn any one away. The school is their only salvation. Eighty dollars in money has been paid in by the scholars since school opened, this is a small sum from so many, but it means a great sacrifice to many of these people. [98]

Families struggled to keep their children in People's Village for eight months a year, especially since the public schools only stayed open for three months and offered very little education. The ability to pay tuition was directly tied to the cotton crop, so it vacillated according to weather and cotton prices. [99] People in the community lived by sharecropping or in debt peonage, a feeble existence at best, and often faced homelessness when a land owner would "break up," or take all the crop produced the last year of tenancy and send away the family with nothing. Even in secure situations, families suffered from perpetual debt. Nevertheless, parents begged the school to take their children, offering potatoes or syrup in place of tuition. At times children could work on school grounds in lieu of payment. In spite of its impoverishment, the community managed to pay \$470 for tuition for an average daily attendance of 200 in 1894.[100] In 1910, an annual report noted that "930 dollars was paid here in this hard pressed community."[101]

As a result of cooperation, the meager resources of the community allowed the school to accomplish some of the goals of other similar school-settlements. Like Calhoun, People's Village offered a practical but challenging program of "industrial work" and academics. Subjects included grammar, geography, history, spelling, nature study, Bible study, writing, drawing, mathematics, algebra, and reading, along with sewing and gardening.[102] The school, perhaps more importantly, provided a community center for the region. The schoolhouse, remarked Washington in 1896, "is at present the wonder of the village, for both white and colored. The children hang around it all day Saturday, and Sunday too. . . . They are happy."[103] The school also ran numerous community events, a twenty-four acre farm, a night school, a YMCA, Sunday schools, a society for the care of the elderly, and a Sick and Burying Society.[104] In spite of financial problems, one article described People's Village as a "little settlement—home, school, farm, and church," "an oasis in the desert."[105]

One of the most remarkable achievements was a land company that evolved into a cooperative Farmers' Union. As land was difficult to obtain in small acreage, each farmer paid a monthly fee to form a treasury that allowed for the purchase of large plantations to be divided into lots for family farms. The Union also helped surrounding farmers to plan their planting. In 1903, seventy-five men also organized a cotton gin company and soon were "not only ginning cotton themselves but . . . for some of their white neighbors."[106] These plans reversed the financial condition of the community, allowing many blacks to climb out of debt and to own land and build their own houses. In 1913, an annual report stated, "Friends, you cannot imagine how happy these people are when they are able to own the land which they have rented for so many years since the [Civil] war."[107]

Community women also operated collectively through People's Village, distributing garments produced by the sewing class for sale to villagers, or marketing vegetables, chickens, eggs, butter, and fruit by wagon in Montgomery to meet bills for groceries and clothing, thereby helping the family to become self-sufficient.[108] Women also organized a Mother's Conference that sent a delegate to the Tuskegee Women's Conference run by Margaret Murray Washington, the wife of Booker T. Washington.[109] The conference met twice monthly "to talk over and suggest plans for the homes and neighborhood work." Projects included traveling out and organizing clubs among "the women on the far away plantations" who could not travel to the schoolhouse, and "looking after and reporting cases of motherless children on the different plantations."[110]

Like other school-settlements, People's Village sought to prepare students

Teachers' Home at People's Village School, Mt. Meigs, Alabama. Founder and principal Georgia Washington stands at left. (Courtesy of Hampton University Archives)

for teaching and community work among blacks. As one annual report pointed out: "Our object is to keep this day school small, but good. Give the boys a common school education, and as much of the industries as we can, then send them to Tuskegee, Hampton or the State Normal School, where they can be better fitted for future work among our people in the South."[111] Many People's Village students went on to higher training at Tuskegee, Talladega, Payne, Spelman, Wilberforce, Hampton, and State Normal School at Montgomery; others received teaching certificates and taught throughout Alabama.[112] Schools like People's were thus important for their preparatory education and elementary and secondary school teacher training, as well as community improvement.[113]

While People's Village functioned as well as possible given its tight financial backing, the simultaneous retirement of Georgia Washington and the eruption of the Great Depression caused a permanent setback. In 1935, Washington wrote with despair about the difficulty procuring funds: "I have been writing letters for forty-two years for the People's Village School, my hands have grown tired, my heart is weary, my heart is worn out, so I hardly know what to say."[114] Later that year, she took a month's vacation to visit a sister in New York City she had not seen since 1929.[115] Upon returning to People's Village, Washington commented, "My people were glad to see me back and I confess that I was glad to see them and the old school ground with weeds over grown and dilapidated buildings all looked good to me."[116] The next year, however, she gave up the principalship and devoted her time to building up the school library.[117]

In 1937, Washington mentioned that the school was in such financial trouble that she was not receiving her salary. She wrote to Hampton that, "I have to take care of myself, food and etc. I need help. I hate to write this to you but it is all I can do. I hope to get some work next term. I can still [work] now though I am old, yet I am still strong and pretty well in health." For a woman who had foregone pay and luxuries for a mission of teaching self-help to the poor, soliciting personal aid must have been nearly as painful as witnessing the decline of her school. She lamented that the campus showed neglect, the farm was in shambles, the ditches needed digging, the barn needed repairs, and the fences were down. "It makes my head ache just to look out and see things going to nothing," she added. Summing up the school's long-term difficulties, she said, "We just haven't the money" to make improvements. As late as 1946, Washington described the basic struggle of running a school in an impoverished community "with hungry boys and girls some of whom have had no breakfast at all."[118]

The shortage of funds in the Great Depression severely curtailed the cooperative programs run successfully for years by People's Village. Georgia Washington's retirement also marked the end of an era characterized by her broad vision and renewable enthusiasm. It also represented the loss of a leader who at once had served as a teacher, farm manager, housekeeper for the teacher's accommodations, and principal.[119] Hollis Burke Frissell delivered an address about her called "Self-Sacrifice," in which he paid homage to her selflessness and love of her people.[120] One man also testified to Washington's importance to both school and community when she was away from People's Village on a visit to Hampton:

I wish you to send Miss Georgy right back hear Miss Georgy have don more good hear than anny body that ever have bin hear She don't know how much good she have don her self I know she have caus the colard people to buy right Round this School about 1600 acres of Land she all so went about 10 miles from this Place into the Churches and maidspeaches and a few Sundays ago I visit in that Naborhood where the Negros did not oan a foot of Land know they have bought a thousand acres and ar Living on it Since Miss Georgy have bin hear she have cause a better fealing betwean the whites and Blacks. . . . She is the instrument of husbands and wivs getting along together better I would say she have speak over a milion words in different churches and Places when she is not able to go she sends her teachers out [sic].[121]

While People's Village School did not have the distinction of influencing government policy, it represented a sincere attempt at community regeneration and collectivism.

The Penn School

The Penn School on St. Helena Island, South Carolina, provides a final example of a school that combined academic and industrial work with an extensive plan for community rejuvenation. As one reporter stated, "The community is the school." Throughout its life, Penn enjoyed wide acclaim and an eventful history. As part of the Port Royal Experiment, abolitionist Laura M. Towne and her friend Ellen Murray, both from Philadelphia, arrived after the federal occupation of the area in 1861 to help ex-slaves adjust to their new freedom. Willie Lee Rose illustrates the tragedy of the Port Royal Experiment as an effort to provide an example to the rest of the country of the possibilities of reconstruction but also shows the positive results of the missionary enterprise. Unlike most black Southerners, Sea Island blacks largely owned their own land and controlled their own local government.[122]

In addition, Towne and Murray founded Penn School, which offered a classical education to the island blacks. In 1905 Rossa B. Cooley, a New Yorker and graduate of Vassar College, arrived to take over the principalship and thereby gave Penn a new lease on life. As one scholar points out, Cooley thought that "the school was not a mere transmitter of knowledge, but a social dynamo in affecting much needed social change."[123]

Cooley and Grace B. House, both former Hampton teachers, sought to translate the Hampton ideal into practice on St. Helena Island. Phasing out the pedagogical methods of Towne and Murray, which focused on rote memorization, these women aimed to make education more applicable to life on the island and eventually to create an "all-island, an all-the-year-round school, merging school and community."[124] Along the lines of Calhoun and People's Village, Penn initiated an ambitious plan that would enlist the participation of the 8,000 islanders in a cooperative movement for community betterment. The school succeeded to such a degree that it attracted visitors from all over the world and caused one American observer, Paul Kellogg, editor of *The Survey*, to call it "our most arresting experiment in community education." "There is something primal in the rediscovery of the power of the school as a social dynamo . . . its release of the organic strength of the community, and its stirring frontage on change."[125]

Like other school-settlements, Penn attempted to provide high quality academic education with stress on relevance and practical training in agriculture, teaching, and other skills. The school aimed "to produce graduates able to solve the problems of the community; furnish teachers for the local schools; and develop a type of leadership which appreciates that truest happiness comes from a life of service."[126] Along with the academic curriculum, Penn offered instruc-

A class in basketry at Penn Normal, Industrial, and Agricultural School, St. Helena Island, South Carolina. (Courtesy of Hampton University Archives)

tion in such "industries" as carpentry, blacksmithing, wheelwrighting, machine repair, cobbling, basketry, dairy and livestock, agriculture, sewing, laundry, cooking, and housekeeping. Cooley insisted that the whole point of the venture was to make the island a community of yeoman farmers who could sustain life independently yet who had a high standard of citizenship and worldliness. A significant part of the plan was to foster rural collectivism and pride, to encourage people "to be rural-wise, community conscious and self-disciplined persons with a profound concern for the continual redemption of self and society." [127]

With a faith that some might see as naive, Cooley promoted the possibilities of a self-sufficient farming community, exhibiting an honest belief in the superiority of rural over urban conditions for black achievement. Many observers called Cooley "the interpreter" of the Sea Islanders. Like a settlement worker, she tried to respond to the needs of her neighbors and encouraged their independent efforts whenever possible. Kellogg wrote that Cooley's participation in Penn was not "a gesture of paternalism" but an attempt "to release nascent forces for self-development." She aimed "to stir things up and build from the bottom democratically." The goal of industrial work was not training for socially subordinate positions, but self-sufficiency of individuals, families, and communities, especially freedom of blacks from reliance on whites for employment. Cooley wrote that "the gauge that freedom set to these Negro women of the southern countryside was not to become housemaids to be had for wages by city dwellers, but to become the home-makers and mothers and farm women for their own rural communities."[128]

Penn School established a school farm to demonstrate new methods of agriculture including crop rotation and diversification. Land that produced eight to ten bushels of corn per acre soon produced twenty to thirty with the teachers' supervision of the students' "home acres." Acres of corn, sweet potatoes, cowpeas, and oats supplemented the planting of cotton.[129] Other programs included a county teachers' organization, a school committee, a Graduates' Club, a midwives' training class, a public health campaign with community nurse and doctor, a credit union, parent-teacher conferences, a YWCA and YMCA, farm demonstration clubs, and better homes committees. The Home-Makers' Clubs had a membership of several hundred and included projects in gardening, canning, improved poultry, beautification of homes and yards, marketing, food and nutrition, child development, clothing, home management, health and sanitation, and handicrafts. A Cooperative Society, in addition, offered an opportunity for farmers to market and purchase goods collectively in quantity. Finally, a Folklore Society formed in order "to preserve the dialect, folk games and songs of the Islands."[130] A newspaper article stressed that the school aimed to "preserve, uncontaminated, much of its original African culture."[131]

Elizabeth Jacoway, historian of Penn School, assesses the efforts of Penn to provide an example for the solution of the "Negro problem" by "Yankee missionaries." She considers Penn a failure and blames the paternalistic tendency of Cooley and Penn's benefactors to impose a northern, accommodationist vision of race relations and the New England values of hard work and moral uplift. At the same time, Jacoway faults Cooley for failing to develop and follow a particular philosophy and for reacting to concrete situations as they arose.[132] Yet this responsiveness to local conditions was exactly the point of Cooley's notion of community regeneration and seems to argue against the portrait of her efforts as driven by a desire for social control, paternalism, or the imposition of an alien culture. Cooley no doubt brought with her precepts from northern life, but she attempted to create an institution that allowed for the maximum participation by community members for their own power.

More important factors constricting the Penn ideal were the calamitous events such as the advent of the boll weevil, inexorable outmigration, agricultural depression, and finally the Great Depression. Along with the national trend toward industrialization and urbanization, these factors rendered the ideal of a vital, self-sufficient island community increasingly difficult to sustain. Blaming individuals like Cooley for the failure of Penn to revolutionize race relations in the United States is to fault reformers for undertaking a life's work that was at once ambitious and selfless. In fact, Cooley responded to such criticism. An editorial in *The Southern Workman* caused her to write Hampton to express "deep concern and disappointment." The editorial lauded the replacement of missionary spirit with professionalism, as the former "somehow always carried with it the idea of superior going out to help uplift inferior." The regular courses now replaced the old plans of a "work school," it read. Cooley was shocked by the misunderstanding of what she considered work dedicated to giving the community a voice, self-sufficiency, and prosperity, and not merely manual training.[133]

Despite the limitations of her race, class, and regional upbringing, Cooley's aim was to provide a community center that would allow for the development of a sense of collectivism in a demoralized, rural region, and release the power of an educated citizenry. Far from custodian of the status quo, Penn's unique program of community activism made St. Helena into what one reporter calls a "training ground for black organizers."[134]

The Calhoun School, the People's Village School, and the Penn School all ultimately faced obstacles that included financial shortages, climatic crises, and uncommonly virulent racism in the country at large. They were undoubtedly limited by their need to fulfill the desire of their benefactors to solve bitter race relations with a long-term plan of industrial education. Yet women like Charlotte Thorn, Margaret Murray Washington, Georgia Washington, Rossa Cooley, and others managed to expand the realm of industrial training to include rural social work and community activism. Hindsight has proven their agrarian ideal of a self-sufficient community in which blacks controlled the local economy and owned the land to be outmoded. At best, however, their school-settlements attempted to create an alternative vision of the future for blacks in this country. It was a vision based on the belief that blacks should not be forced to move away from southern soil and that they deserved help in finding the means of gaining power over their own labor, families, and communities. The failure of these efforts to provide community regeneration that would revolutionize race relations in this country originated not so much out of a crisis of vision or lack of genuine dedication but as a result of the profound forces standing in their way. The lack of financial support, the agricultural depression, industrialization, and virulent racism constituted major forces of destruction of the ideal of local community regeneration represented by the school-settlements. These community centers, however, did have their successes, which should be measured in the temporary rejuvenation of the psyche of individuals and communities, the provision of essential social and educational services, and the introduction of training grounds for blacks and whites dedicated to community activism.

Four

From "Mother Power"
to Civil Rights

Religion and morality were the avenues that led many black and white women
into settlement work in African American communities. They also provided crucial links between women's experiences in community work and the emergence
of their broader interest in social justice, interracial organization, and even, for
some, civil rights for black Americans. Jacquelyn Dowd Hall has established, for
example, the roots of the women's interracial movement of the 1920s and 1930s
in the confluence of interests of three main groups—black women of the club
and settlement movement, the white women of the Women's Home Missionary
Society of the Methodist Episcopal Church, South, and black and white women
of the Young Women's Christian Association (YWCA).[1] These groups increasingly fostered interdenominational cooperation, in spite of many women's deep
roots in and continuing loyalties to particular churches. The functions of their
religious community centers often included those of the "bona fide" settlement
houses: delivering social services; strengthening the neighborhood; responding
to community needs; fostering cooperation through club work in small groups;
providing the means to a more fulfilling recreational, educational, and social
life; studying local social conditions as the basis for lobbying for policy changes;
and agitating for broad social reforms.

Those who undertook settlement work among blacks professed to share the
same motivations as those settlement workers and reformers of the late nineteenth and early twentieth centuries who worked among white immigrants.
Black and white middle-class women shared a belief in the fundamental responsibility of women, as mothers or potential mothers, for the welfare of their
own children, and, thus, society's children. In addition, many of them ascribed
to the Victorian notion that women possessed a heightened moral sensitivity
that compelled them to tend to society's unfortunates. For southern women,
the New South idea breathed new life into the idea that women had a special

social role; now, through their feminine touch, they should help to modernize the section. Of course, black and white women interpreted the specifics of this imperative differently. Yet both responded through intense involvement in community work. While many of these reformers, regardless of their color, began with a sense of superiority over those they were trying to help, the work itself often forced them to acknowledge the extent of racial discrimination and the ravages of racism and to begin to understand more fully the communities in which they worked. Settlement work was often a transforming and galvanizing experience. For those who worked among blacks, it could culminate in a realization that the problems of the neighborhood demanded more than activities and services, but also agitation for wider change, which could even mean attempting to tear down the barriers of Jim Crow.

The interdenominational and egalitarian emphasis of this settlement work among blacks brought together women of diverse backgrounds to make important decisions and contributions and discuss and affect policy. This civic apprenticeship yielded the confidence, leadership skills, awareness, and sense of efficacy that led to courageous demands for social justice and equal treatment within their own organizations, and eventually, for some, in society itself. Ironically, the religious dimension of their work provided the ideological basis not only for their work in their communities, in the social gospel tradition, but also for their agitation for sweeping social change, in a radical combination of Christianity and democracy. In the process of their work, they developed a powerful new notion of Christian citizenship. Rooted in the most local unit of neighborhood, they managed to develop a truly cosmopolitan religious outlook that, at its best, stressed unity across the bounds of race, culture, nation, and class and opened the door to a philosophy of universal human rights. Their outlook, while based on the religious principles from which the settlement movement sought so diligently to distance itself, gave them a surprisingly pluralistic outlook, considering their intense loyalties to particular communities and deep roots in often segregated constituencies.

An exploration of this type of settlement work among blacks reveals the seeds of interracialism in the development, at the community level, of a sense of injustice combined with a belief in citizens' power of redress. This chapter will explore the nature and significance of the settlement house work conducted by black women associated with the settlement and club movement, white women of the Women's Home Missionary Association of the Methodist Episcopal Church, South, and white and black women of the YWCA. Beginning with a brief review of the important role that scholars have attributed to the convergence of these three groups in bringing about the early twentieth century women's interracial movement, this chapter will go on to explore specific examples of settlement-type activity conducted under their auspices. It will seek to show the role of this settlement work in the transition from the Victorian legacy of motherhood as an imperative for reform to a notion of Christian citizenship and human rights as an international and moral issue.

The first illustration, the case of Lugenia Burns Hope and Atlanta's Neighborhood Union, shows how this settlement work grew out of an expanded notion of women's sphere that included any activity bearing upon the welfare of black children. While some historians have found this notion of activist womanhood prevalent among nineteenth- and early twentieth-century white middle-class women, others have noted that this theme varied slightly in the case of black women. Because of their unique burden, according to Jacqueline Jones, Paula Giddings, and other historians of black women, black female reformers tended to see women's role as going beyond mother and moral guide to provider for the family and soldier in the "uplift" of their race. This understanding of women as more than wives and mothers underpinned a particularly active version of settlement work. In turn, this community organizing gave workers the clout, skills, and knowledge to demand social justice and equal treatment in organizations such as the YWCA, and even from the government.

A second example of women whose ideas were transformed by their involvement in settlement activity were the white women of the Women's Home Missionary Society of the Methodist Episcopal Church, South. While this organization was often disturbingly ambivalent on the issue of race over the course of its history, its community work often energized its members and set the grounding for their embrace of interracial activity. The home missions movement included the establishment of numerous Bethlehem Houses, as settlement houses in black neighborhoods were called, at a time when few other facilities existed. Although these settlements were nearly always segregated, their staffs were often integrated, and they played a significant role in edging the South toward change.

Finally, the YWCA's settlement house activities, conducted by both black and white women in YWCA "homes," "hostess houses," and separate black branches such as the Southwest Belmont Branch in Philadelphia, were a crucial element not only in the interracial movement but, for many women, in the fruition of a human rights philosophy that led to involvement in the civil rights movement of the 1950s and 1960s. The agitation of Hope and other black reformers, a story already told by historians of black women, helped transform the YWCA into a base for working for state as well as community intervention on behalf of civil rights and welfare. They also influenced the direction of the YWCA's philosophy. The specific example of African Americans tested the humanitarian principles of the YWCA's philosophy of Christian democracy.

As the YWCA began to enact a program directed against racism, it articulated a credo of moralist womanhood. But the Y's ideology increasingly stressed a special humanitarianism belonging to women that demanded their participation in community life not only as mothers and neighbors but also as providers and citizens of the nation and the world.

The Women's Interracial Movement

Historian Jacquelyn Hall has related how, in 1920, a set of unusual events led to the cooperation of white and black women interested in the unique problems facing African Americans. Lugenia Burns Hope, founder of the powerful Atlanta settlement Neighborhood Union, held a caucus of black women in her home. Wife of Morehouse College and later Atlanta University President John Hope, Lugenia Hope had agitated for equal treatment of blacks in the YWCA, supervising its work for black soldiers during World War I. Stirred by encounters with racism in organizations and in American life in general, the black women's caucus announced that "the time was ripe [to] go beyond the YWCA and any other organization and reach a few outstanding White and Negro women, Christian and with well-balanced judgement and not afraid [sic]." This move coincided with the white Methodist Women's Missionary Council's convention, which called upon southern women to use their newly won right to vote for the encouragement of interracial cooperation. President Belle Bennett and special guest speaker Will Alexander, head of the Atlanta Commission on Interracial Cooperation, urged a new departure toward greater cooperation with black women at all levels.[2]

Subsequently, Lugenia Hope invited two white Methodist leaders, Sara Estelle Haskin and Carrie Parks Johnson, to the biennial conference of the National Association of Colored Women at Tuskegee Institute. Afterward there was a special meeting in the home of Margaret Murray Washington, founder of Elizabeth Russell Settlement and the Tuskegee Woman's Club as well as wife of Booker T. Washington and head of Women's Work at Tuskegee. The unorthodox meeting initially stumbled on mutual apprehension but ended in a spirit of unity. The meeting led to a landmark in the history of race relations—the interracial women's conference in Memphis, Tennessee, in October of 1920, with ninety-one women from the major Protestant denominations, women's clubs, and the YWCA. The conference opened with the Methodist women's accounts of their trip to Tuskegee and proceeded with four powerful addresses by black female organization leaders, including Margaret Murray Washington. Charlotte Hawkins Brown, founder of a preparatory school for blacks called Palmer

Memorial Institute located near Sedalia, North Carolina, called the conference "the greatest step forward . . . taken since emancipation." The conference
successfully recommended the founding of a Commission on Interracial Cooperation's women's committee that later served as the springboard for Jessie
Daniel Ames's antilynching crusade.[3]

The interracial women's conference in Memphis combined three major
groups of women: black women in the club and settlement movements; white
Methodist women in the home missions movement; and white and black women
in the YWCA. While white and black women came from vastly different social
and cultural backgrounds, and while the organizations they erected differed
markedly, their common experiences allowed for a new level of cooperation.
Significantly, each of these groups had conducted extensive work in black neighborhoods in the settlement house tradition.

Black Club Women and Settlement Workers

Black women intent on progress toward civil rights and the welfare of their
neighborhoods and experienced in organizations for social change found a way
to bridge differences and elicit the cooperation of white women. They not only
succeeded by articulating the imperative of motherhood but brought their own
views of the female sphere to bear on reform organizations. In their positions
as community leaders, black women influenced wider reforms and helped contribute to changing notions of woman's sphere. In addition, black women's own
notions of motherhood and womanhood lay at the root of their involvement in
reform.

Black and white women who united in the interracial movement, albeit errati-
cally, viewed their interests as entwined because of their interpretation of the
important social role of southern women. From the 1890s on, southern leaders
sought to rejuvenate the region by addressing the social problems that caused
the South to seem to lag behind the North both in culture and economic development. Booker T. Washington's Tuskegee idea, W. E. B. Du Bois's Atlanta
University Conferences, and the Southern Sociological Congress exemplified
the various attempts to uncover social problems in order to bring about progress
through reform. These efforts both inspired and were inspired by a multitude of
local reformers and community organizers. Many southern women saw themselves as having an eminent role in revitalizing the South. In 1906, a report of
the Conference for Education in the South, meeting in Lexington, Kentucky,
outlined three projects facing those interested in improving social conditions in
the South: "the rehabilitation of rural life; meeting efficiently a great industrial

movement; and the living together of two races in complete harmony." A representative of the Women's Education Aid Societies stated that "the work of focusing public opinion rests largely with the women." "The destiny of the women of the South," she went on, "[is] to train their children to adapt themselves to these new conditions." "Training their children" meant not only guiding their own families but also embarking on careers in education. The conference called on women to build schoolhouses, to form educational societies, and even to lead educational reform movements.[4]

Much of women's turn-of-the-century club and organizational activity also drew on middle-class Victorian ideals of female behavior for legitimacy. Historians have outlined at length the ideology that held women responsible for nurturing the family, managing the household, acting as moral guide, and rearing children to be good citizens. Scholars have also shown how women used this doctrine of female domesticity to justify their involvement in a range of social reforms, especially those related to educating or nurturing the young, all falling well within the code of respectability. Women merely extended supposedly feminine virtues and prerogatives from the family into the public realm, serving as collective rearers of society's children and as the moral stronghold for the entire country.[5] While much work has addressed the uses of the doctrine of separate male and female spheres in legitimizing the expansion of women's role, its influence in race relations has gone largely unnoticed. In addition, the nature of the change wrought by the twentieth century in that ideology requires further elaboration, as does the role of race in that transformation. In the early twentieth century, the notion of women's exceptionalism combined with the New South idea to make many women, both white and black, conclude that they had a special responsibility for improving living conditions for blacks. At a time when their reform organizations had amassed a national membership, black women successfully seized this opportunity to break new ground in enhancing civil rights through improved race relations. While white female reformers for the most part failed to challenge the South's entrenched segregation, they did at times prove receptive to change. Black women agitated powerfully by appealing effectively to the sense of female morality so highly touted by white middle-class women.

It is essential to point out, however, that commonalities appeared in the views of some white and black middle-class women only despite vastly different social, cultural, economic, and organizational backgrounds. Historians have pointed out that the "cult of true womanhood," when taken to its extreme, could hardly represent the reality of the lives of black women and other working women. For one thing, the assumption that women had the leisure to devote their lives to the glorified domestic sphere did not apply to most black American women, who had a long tradition of working to support themselves and their families. Scholar Toinette Eugene states that black women had a set of values that stressed social activism, self-sacrifice, and a sense of themselves as "moral agents"; she and other writers call this a doctrine of moral "womanism."[6] Besides suggesting that notions of womanhood differed according to ethnicity, class, and race, scholars have shown how the clubs and organizations formed by black middle-class women differed from those created by whites. For one thing, black women had unique concerns with issues affecting their communities in particular, such as discrimination and lynching.[7] Some scholars also argue that African American women much more commonly united their efforts with those of their poor or working-class sisters and with those of black men.[8] Deborah Gray White, on the other hand, states that black women actually found themselves in conflict with men of their race for control over the realm of community work, since the men so often found themselves shut out of the traditional spheres of male power, employment, and politics.[9]

In spite of the essential differences between black and white women's social experience and vision, a major focus of black women's organizations of the 1890s and afterward paved the way for a rapprochement with white women's associations. Anne Firor Scott describes what she considers the "collective ambivalence" running through most black women's associations: "On the one hand members felt a desperate need to establish the elusive respectability that was supposed to bring acceptance from the dominant culture; on the other hand there was the equally desperate need to change the whole structure of race relations, to demand an end to lynching and to job discrimination, to demand civil rights and the right to vote."[10]

Black women's efforts to project "respectability" were part of a conscious plan to fight white racism by teaching blacks to appear and behave in a way that would disprove the stereotypes characterizing African Americans as uncivilized, dependent, amoral, and victimized. Scholars Hazel Carby and Darlene Clark Hine view African American women's adoption of the creed of female moral superiority and sexual purity as a response to this degrading stereotype. Carby finds a different response among black female blues singers who, unlike intellectuals who translated "female desire to female duty," celebrated an alternative vision of women's sexuality and sensuality. Hine believes that the black women's club movement "embodied the shaping and honing" of a "culture of resistance" or "dissemblance" that hid their true identity behind a veil of secrecy and exaggerated morality. Evelyn Brooks suggests that this focus on individual behavior "privatized racial discrimination and rendered it less subject to . . . the authority of the public realm."[11]

In a number of cases, however, middle-class black women appealed to notions of women's role in promoting respectability and morality in an attempt to advance civil rights. By obliterating the debilitating image of black women as promiscuous and ignorant, reformers sought to provide role models for other black women and to enlist the aid of educated, middle-class white women in their cause. Historian Mary Frederickson shows that white and black Methodist Episcopal women "developed relationships that were based not on collaboration or enmity, but on mutual dependence." "Ritualized interactions" allowed black women to enact programs that aided their communities within the acceptable context of white women's ostensible leadership, while white women received education and assistance in their interracial efforts.[12] In scholar Paula Giddings's words, black women "believed that the contribution of women, both Black and White, was essential to racial harmony." As Charlotte Hawkins Brown pointed out, "One of the chief causes of unrest in the South today is the attitude of the women of both races towards each other."[13] As well as making significant inroads toward their stated goals, these women helped broaden the meaning of womanhood, a redefinition that inspired a generation of women to participate actively in the better-known civil rights movement.[14]

Along with men, African American women had a long history of voluntary, organizational activity. Partly because of their exclusion from organizations in a white-dominated culture and partly as an expression of strong ethnic identity and local collectivism, organizations such as churches, lodges, and mutual aid societies helped provide social services, entertainment, and solidarity to black communities.[15] According to one scholar, "benevolent, burial and secret societies existed even under slavery," and abolition societies—many of them female—proliferated with the approach of the Civil War and continued during the conflict to provide assistance to the black regiments and freedmen and women. Scholars have recently tapped a rich vein in their discovery and articulation of a thriving spiritual tradition in black women's activism.[16] Even ostensibly nonreligious organizations among black women seemed to share a network of activists and a high level of religiosity. Beginning after the Civil War, these women's clubs formed to address the needs of the poor and of blacks migrating to the cities. The clubs often met weekly or monthly and devoted themselves to welfare and education through specific projects such as orphanages, schools, and churches. In the 1890s, Ida B. Wells-Barnett's speaking tours against lynching launched an antilynching movement in Britain and the United States. The issue of violence as well as the broader racism of American life spurred the formation in 1896 of the National Association of Colored Women with Mary Church Terrell as president, which united Terrell's National League of Colored Women, Margaret Murray Washington's National Federation of Colored Women, and over a hundred other local organizations.[17]

Josephine St. Pierre Ruffin, president of the New Era Club of black women in Boston in 1895, and later vice president of the NACW, organized the first National Conference of Colored Women in 1895. She discussed the particular goals of black women's organizations that needed to revolve, she believed, around "our peculiar questions":

> We need to talk over not only those things which are of vital importance to us as women, but also the things that are of especial interest to us as *colored* women, the training of our children, openings for our boys and girls, how they can be prepared for occupations and occupations may be found or opened for them, what *we* especially can do in the moral education of the race with which we are identified, our mental elevation and physical development, the home training it is necessary to give our children in order to prepare them to meet the peculiar conditions in which they shall find themselves, how to make the most of our own, to some extent, limited opportunities.[18]

Besides addressing the problems unique to black children, many middle-class black women also felt the need to counteract the negative stereotypes about blacks and especially about black women as ignorant and immoral.[19] This portrayal inhibited the self-expression and achievements of "a large and growing class of earnest, intelligent, progressive colored women" who sought the opportunity "to *be* more." Josephine Ruffin thought that black women needed to organize a movement in order to prove their worth, not with angry denials of stereotypes, but with "a dignified showing of what we are" that would provide "an object lesson to the world." She thought that molding public opinion constituted the special responsibility of "the *women* of the race" who could prove their adherence to universal standards of womanhood: "For the sake of our own dignity, the dignity of our race, and the future good name of our children, it is 'mete, right and our bounden duty' to stand forth and declare ourselves and principles, to teach an ignorant and suspicious world that our aims and interests are identical with those of all good aspiring women."[20] Ruffin concluded that "our woman's movement is woman's movement in that it is led and directed by women for the good of women and men, for the benefit of *all* humanity." Likewise, Margaret Murray Washington noted that the concerns of the National Association of Colored Women should include improving schools, campaigning for woman suffrage, and antilynching, which she considered "women's work now as always."[21]

Five years after the conference's call for unity, Ruffin was excluded from participation in the General Federation of Women's Clubs, an almost entirely white organization founded in 1890. While many black women were outraged by the decision of the General Federation, they drew inspiration from the many who opposed the decision. Black club woman and settlement worker Fannie Barrier Williams wrote that thousands of women "committed to a more liberal view on the admission of colored clubs to the National Federation are [as] equally tenacious of their position [as the exclusionists]." These women "believe that the white women of the country should not be unwilling to aid in every way colored women who are struggling to work out their own salvation." Williams went on to point out that these white women "are not disturbed by the cry of social equality. They stand for progress and for the broadest sympathy and for womankind."[22]

While the General Federation sustained its segregationist policies for decades, black women continued to organize separately, establishing settlement houses, fostering the kindergarten movement, establishing day nurseries for working mothers, and raising money to establish industrial homes, night schools, homes for the aged, literary clubs, Mothers' Clubs, and orphanages. While conducting specific social services and general social work, these women increasingly encountered great obstacles—the attitudes and behavior of racist whites—but managed to use their notion of womanhood as common ground to enlist the empathetic cooperation of white women. The experiences of black women in settlement work often gave them the knowledge, the community backing, and the impetus to agitate for greater change at the city, state, or national level. This expansion of their realm of interest necessitated encounters with whites that often led to attempts at interracial cooperation.

Lugenia Burns Hope's experience as a black woman pioneering in settlement work provided the base from which she helped launch an attack on racism in the YWCA as well as a foundation stone of the interracial movement that began with the Tuskegee and Nashville conferences of 1920. While other scholars have traced Hope's activities, special attention should go to her black settlement, the Neighborhood Union in Atlanta; it is an eloquent example of the transition from a maternalist philosophy of activism toward one based on the rights of citizenship, a metamorphosis caused by direct involvement in settlement work. The Union started as a club of neighbors and faculty wives at Spelman and Atlanta Baptist College (renamed Morehouse in 1913) who gathered to discuss the desperate lack of recreational facilities for their own children. Neighborhood Union became a powerful citywide organization of black neighborhoods and by the 1930s attained acclaim as "a national and international role model for community organization."[23] This example illustrates the emergence of settlement work from an ideology of activist motherhood, the interpretation and contributions of black women to this imperative, and the development of a new emphasis on women's duty as active citizens to demand social justice for blacks.

Jacqueline Anne Rouse, biographer of Lugenia Hope, illustrates that Hope's

Lugenia Burns Hope. (Bethune Museum and Archives, Washington, D.C.)

early experience in social reform in Chicago (including a brief contact with Hull House methods), combined with her sense of the responsibilities of educated black women to their race, laid the grounding for her involvement in community work in Atlanta. The direct inspiration for such work was her concern for children, her own included—an interest she held in common with other black female reformers. Upon moving to Atlanta, Hope received an invitation from W. E. B. Du Bois to participate in one of the Atlanta University conferences entitled "The Welfare of the Negro Child." Out of this conference grew the Gate City Free Kindergarten Association, which developed into a full-time day nursery in 1918. Members of the association received no compensation for their work, and conceived of their efforts as dedicated to "the children of the less fortunate mothers who would have become the wayward and criminal element of our city had it not been for the assistance the organization was privileged to give them." [24]

The kindergarten association's nucleus of middle-class black women proceeded to attack other problems threatening the safe upbringing of children. Rouse writes that "this protectiveness arose out of [Hope's] desire to provide the best possible environment for her own sons." [25] The association sought to remake schools into social centers to encourage "lives of decency and usefulness" by providing baths, wholesome food, information, and other assistance. This plan's appeal rested on a sense of the importance of motherly concern. The imperatives of motherhood, Hope and others argued, necessitated an appeal to humanitarian values that would bridge differences for the sake of the children. An association flyer read: "We believe that the work which we are doing for these children is second to none in the city, and we need the interest and sympathy of every humanity-loving man and woman. . . . In behalf of thousands of little people who need our help, we ask for your cooperation." [26] As a result of her participation in the association, Hope instigated in 1908 the establishment of Neighborhood Union. Its declared goal was "to raise the standard of living in the community and to make the West Side of Atlanta a better place to rear our children." [27]

At the first meeting of the Neighborhood Union on July 8, 1908, eight women met at Hope's home to determine whether settlement work was needed. Each woman was charged with the duty of finding out the names and ages of the neighbors, "especially the girls between eight and 22," in the usual settlement manner of making "friendly visits," but with a special emphasis on youth.[28] One of the settlement's first steps was a successful appeal to the administration of Morehouse College to allow part of its campus to serve as a playground for neighborhood children supervised by Neighborhood Union volunteers. The Union also initiated neighborhood celebrations, improvement efforts, community gardens, clean-up drives, summer vacation Bible schools, antituberculosis campaigns, and participation in Associated Charities.[29]

In 1912, black Neighborhood Union women organized a Social Improvement Committee to investigate and improve the appalling conditions of Atlanta's black public schools. Weekly meetings structured an investigation of every school in the city and the study concluded that unsanitary conditions were universal. In addition, the poor light and ventilation caused children eye strain and sickness, and overcrowding in double sessions rendered the teachers exhausted and students severely undereducated.[30] The Union proceeded to appeal to "every influential white woman in Atlanta to solicit her support," since real educational change would require the attention of other sectors of Atlanta society. At the urging of the black women, many white women of Atlanta visited the schools to witness the deplorable conditions. Social Improvement Committee members also visited the mayor, city council members, and white pastors. Armed with precise information from their study, these women made significant strides toward the improvement of education for blacks. As an immediate result of their efforts, black teachers' salaries rose, South Atlanta built a schoolhouse, and black men and women began to cooperate in the drive for better schools.[31] By 1923, the publicity of poor educational services achieved great results when the city voted to provide twelve public school buildings for blacks, bringing the total to fourteen—an increase of 600 percent. Neighborhood Union organizers continued their efforts in spite of the invidious racism that kept Atlanta's schools segregated and unequal for decades.[32]

The revelations of the school survey led the Neighborhood Union to concentrate on health problems that were exacerbated by inferior or nonexistent hospital facilities, poor nutrition caused by poverty, and ignorance about the importance of hygiene in disease prevention. In 1915, the Union established a health center, which provided a clinic, nursing services, and health education. In 1924, one committee on health reported making 196 visits, organizing a baby clinic, securing playgrounds, giving instruction in home care and home economics, arranging out-patient clinics, leading a vaccination campaign, and distributing literature. In 1927, the Union reported examining 999 children. Under the direction of the Red Cross, workers taught courses in health and hygiene in homes, churches, lodges, and social centers. In 1929, the Union sponsored National Negro Health Week. In addition, the Union added a dental clinic and mothers' clinics in the 1930s and arranged for over 4,000 patients to use the facilities yearly.[33]

The Neighborhood Union was highly organized. It separated the city into different zones and neighborhoods that could be studied and assisted on the local level by workers intimately knowledgeable about conditions. These smaller units often mobilized effectively for citywide projects, thus uniting more people in a more powerful coalition than the typical settlement house. Operating neighborhood centers, the Union provided the usual settlement functions and more. Children and young adults took courses in such skills as needlework, dramatics, basketry, and budgeting and participated in the Little Mother Club, the Little Housekeeper Club, playground activities, girls' social clubs, boys' social clubs, concerts, sewing, lectures, domestic science and good citizenship programs, better home campaigns, legal aid workshops, and projects to further interracial understanding. This varied menu of activities also included courses in business administration, musical and literary programs, and lectures on child welfare and the care of the home, all aimed at community betterment.[34]

The Union's observation of local conditions kindled reform campaigns. From 1917 to 1921, a Home Investigation Committee revealed sorely substandard housing conditions, which included lack of street lights and pavements, insufficient trash removal, contaminated water, and inadequate plumbing and toilet facilities. The publication of this information prodded the city to make improvements.[35]

The Neighborhood Union thus attempted to fill the huge gaps caused by the deficiencies of the public school system, as well as to provide much-needed facilities for public recreation and crucial social services. Union workers conceived of their work as a combination of protection—of women and the young—and uplift. A Wednesday afternoon club of women set a tone of "cultivation" exemplified by the Union's declared aim to "promote culture in communities." Its program included readings from *Hamlet* and other Shakespeare plays, music, prayers, quotations, book reviews, commentary on "the Negro stage," and lectures on topics like "the Meaning of Evolution." Other lecture topics included "International Public Health," "Our Daily Bread and Vitamines [sic]," "Deforestation," and "Louis Pasteur." The Union also hosted talks on civics, the care of children, and interracial goodwill. The staff's concept of cultivation was undeniably middle class, but had a worldly reach.[36]

In addition, the structure of Neighborhood Union caused it to remain responsive to the needs of the community. For instance, its investigations and home visits led to an interest in combating unemployment and providing direct relief, especially after the depression of 1907, during the First World War, and throughout the Great Depression. In its early years, the leaders of Neighborhood Union stressed that its relief efforts constituted emergency measures. It hoped that organized social work and the government would eventually take over these functions. The Union's Social Service Institute held at Morehouse College taught nearly 100 students in 1918 and assisted in the founding of the Atlanta School of Social Work in 1920.[37]

Meanwhile, the Union could not ignore immediate need. It collected and re-distributed food, helped find work for destitute families, raised money to keep people out of the bread lines, and supplied milk and cod liver oil to children as well as clothes so they could stay in school. During the Great Depression, Hope also fought for equitable treatment of blacks by other relief agencies. In 1932, the Neighborhood Union petitioned the Mayor and General Council of Atlanta asking for financial aid. The Union noted that in the previous year, more than 1,100 families had received aid from the Union, thus relieving the city and other agencies, with the result that the medical clinic and the cost of distributing medicine at no charge had depleted its resources. The petition used the usual maternalist logic: "We must improve the health of these thousands of under-nourished children, for should an epidemic break out among them, no child in the city of Atlanta would be safe."[38]

The ethic of maternal care thus contributed to the founding of the Neighbor-hood Union and underpinned its protective and morally and culturally uplifting programs. In addition, maternalism often guarded against patronizing reforms. For example, in 1933, the Union made an effort to provide a bountiful Christ-mas for needy families. The Union's Social Welfare Council asked better-off Atlantans, "What would you want for Christmas if illness or unemployment had left you too poor to plan a Christmas for your children?" Rather than a basket left by a stranger, the women asked, would a proud mother not prefer "the pleasure of planning [her] own Christmas" and privacy in receiving aid? Union leaders urged people to offer aid through a central Christmas Bureau to mothers in need, to help them with stockings, presents, and dinners, as friends and not as charity workers. This type of assistance preserved the poor mother's role as provider for her family and helped "to rebuild family unity" instead of eroding her children's respect. The notion of the mother's vast responsibilities, as keeper of family unity, respect, and morality, guided the relief efforts of the Neighborhood Union.[39]

Hope and her coworkers articulated an imperative for reform based on the enlarged notion of female responsibilities that included protection of and pro-vision for all of society's children. This ideology led to their involvement in any activities bearing even remotely upon the welfare of the young, from schooling to health and from recreation to refinement. As early as 1908, these women realized that their organization filled a void they hoped would prove temporary, before the city, state, and federal government would become involved in ensur-ing equal facilities for the relief of poverty in African American communities. Besides participating in the long-term agitation for federal relief of poverty, these women inaugurated the women's interracial movement. Experienced in methods of activism that included exposing inequities and organizing communities for change, Hope and others were ready by 1920 to hold white women accountable for their claims of motherly protection and care. The pressure of black women combined with the social reform experience of white women and their common understanding of the implications of motherhood caused significant numbers of each group to realize that women could play a vital role in improving race relations.

Bethlehem Houses

The white Methodist women, though part of the triad in the women's interracial movement, took an ambivalent approach toward blacks. While they fought within their own denomination for the right to establish settlement houses in black communities, their segregated facilities did not threaten the premise of Jim Crow. In 1910 *Our Homes*, the organ of the Women's Home Mission Society of the Methodist Episcopal Church, South, devoted an entire issue to "Our Duty to the Negro." While the journal attributed the alienation of blacks and whites to the failure of the southern church to address the problems of the freedmen and women, it also claimed that blacks required the assistance of whites in order to develop their very character. Since this task fell within the province of women, Methodist women believed they were well suited to instruct black women on the elementary lesson of how to be women:

> We believe that no nation or race can develop the highest qualities of truth, honor and uprightness that does not set for itself a high standard of womanhood. What of our standard of negro womanhood? Do we expect and demand of her purity and nobility of character? How can their homes be fit places for developing young lives when wifehood and motherhood are not held sacred, when impurity, dishonesty, and falsehood are at a premium? We are not making these as broad statements, but we know that that in hundreds of negro homes in our rural districts and city slums this is the case.[40]

Despite this condescension, white Methodist women advocated training black women as Methodist deaconesses, social workers, and city missionaries through institutions such as Paine College in Augusta. In addition, Methodist women showed an early interest in local interracial congregating for increased cooperation in the fight against discrimination and prejudice. In 1917, they called for "the protection of the childhood and womanhood of Georgia without regard for race."[41]

Methodist women had pioneered in settlement house work in the South, establishing houses in Nashville in 1901 and in Dallas and Atlanta in 1902. They encountered difficulties gaining acceptance as long as they titled their community centers "settlement houses," which had "nonevangelical and even non-Christian connotations." Women's Home Missionary Society President Belle Bennett recommended a new name: "The Presbyterians do their settlement work in the downtown Church House, the Episcopalians in the Parish House. We are in the infancy of our city mission work. Let us take a distinctive name. Epworth Community House, Wesley Community House, or Methodist Community House." The women soon referred to their settlement houses for whites as Wesley Houses and those for blacks as Bethlehem Houses, Centers, or Community Centers. Numerous settlement houses took root throughout the country in white, black, and racially mixed neighborhoods. Bethlehem Houses formed throughout the South, in cities such as Chattanooga and Nashville, Tennessee, Birmingham, Alabama, and Winston-Salem, North Carolina. By 1952, sixteen Bethlehem Centers were in existence.[42]

The first settlement for blacks run by these Methodist women, the Bethlehem Community Center in Augusta, Georgia, began in an abandoned saloon in 1912 under the supervision of Mary De Bardeleben, a young woman from Alabama who later headed the house. Initially called Galloway Hall, it ran a kindergarten, a Girls' Club, a Boys' Club, a Mothers' Club, a Sunday school, a branch of the National Urban League, and three playgrounds. The settlement soon added sewing and cooking classes, family visiting, a well-baby clinic, and a Bible school. Through these and other activities, it tried to "promote interracial good will in Augusta." The Center also provided a "Social Work Laboratory" for training Paine College students and other cooperative programs that connected the settlement and the college. An integrated staff and advisory board managed the facilities, which included club rooms, a library, an apartment, a kitchen, a dining room, a gymnasium, shower rooms, a work shop, and a playground. In addition, the house ran extension programs in the black neighborhoods in other parts of the city.[43]

The Center moved in 1916, and again in 1929, both times expanding its facilities. In 1936, in response to the dire situation of a downtown area plagued by juvenile delinquency, it opened another site called Springfield Branch, where it hosted playgrounds, classes, and clubs. Under the Center's auspices, the George N. Stoney Clinic opened, with the help of black physicians as well as nurses from the Public Health Department, and later staff from the University Hospital and Health Department. During the Depression, the Center also purchased forty-five acres of land and an old schoolhouse in order to start a "Rural Center" about ten miles from Augusta. This facility provided city children with a summer camp and surrounding rural families with an opportunity for socializing and recreation. Weekly "Family Nights" offered programs of drama, folk dancing, and games, all aimed to counteract rural isolation.[44]

Thelma Stevens, who served as headworker from 1928 to 1939, left a valuable record of her experiences at Bethlehem Community Center in an extensive oral history interview. Her account not only underscores the bold range of activities undertaken at the Center, but describes the extraordinary degree of interdenominational and interracial cooperation that marked its vision for social change as well as its daily existence.

Stevens was born near Huntsville, Mississippi. She attended Hattiesburg State Teachers College in 1922, where she became active in the student YWCA. Because of the Y's open discussion of race at its training conferences, "the whole world opened up" for her. In turn, she initiated interracial organizing at her college by inviting black female school teachers from Hattiesburg for "Wednesday Evening Discussion Meetings" to talk and associate with the college students. Approximately one hundred college women gathered for the meetings, sitting on the floor of a dormitory lobby. The black teachers, Stevens related, "spoke to us about black people and what their problems were and what their needs were and we had questions." This kind of honest communication launched Stevens on a course dictated by her awareness of the extreme hardships faced by African Americans. To the college, however, this kind of eye-opening experience posed a threat, and the president barred the presence of blacks on campus.[45]

When Stevens graduated from college, she intended to go into race relations work in the YWCA, since she had doubts about the possibilities for working for social change through the church. When she received an offer of a scholarship for further study at Scarritt College from the Methodist Board of Missions at Nashville, she agonized: "I didn't want to work for the church, because I didn't think the church would give me a chance to do what I wanted to do. . . . The church was isolated from life. It was a place where you go on Sunday morning and listen to the sermon that didn't mean a thing to you," Stevens recalled. She was particularly impressed by the difference between the church's weak concern for racial equality and what she considered the YWCA's strong stance, which, she said, "just hit me right in the eye." Finally, though, Stevens did decide to attend Scarritt, thinking that women's mission work might allow her some opportunity to pursue her interest. There she came under the influence of an inspiring and dedicated activist and professor, Louise Young, and a worldview in which religiosity and social reform were not only compatible, but inextricable.[46] As a result, she accepted a job as Director of the Augusta Bethlehem Community Center when she graduated from Scarritt. After eleven years at that post, she became superintendent of Christian Social Relations of the Methodist Women's Missionary Council and then Executive Director of Christian Social

Relations of the Women's Division of the Board of Missions, continuing her efforts on behalf of civil rights for blacks.[47]

Stevens's comments about her job as headworker at Bethlehem Community Center reveal the difficulties as well as remarkable strengths of the Center's approach. As director of an interracial staff, she initially planned to live with the other workers in the Center's main building. She and her coworker, Dorothy Weber, who hailed from Louisiana, heard that they could not live with blacks: "Negroes and whites living together in those days would not be wise in the minds of people in the city and would destroy our chance to develop a community center." Despite these community strictures, the white and black workers did socialize together, along with community folk, although, as Stevens put it, "It was something unheard of . . . that we would bring our Negro friends to our home!" The lives of these settlement workers took place nearly entirely in the black community, and this contact seemed to break down any remaining barriers. When Stevens asked one of the black physicians to accept her as a regular patient, he had to remind her that he could not, as it would undoubtedly incur the wrath of the white community. He added that he would naturally treat her in case of an emergency.[48]

Stevens's description of the Bethlehem Center's "three pronged plan" showed an awareness of the limits of her role as well as the roles of the other staff members. The Center aimed above all to promote indigenous leadership and to strengthen that leadership by fostering relationships with other groups throughout the city. With this goal in mind, the Center welcomed people of any creed, ran Saturday religion classes and an active Sunday school, held classes in sermon writing, opened their facilities to church groups, and established ties with local churches in a variety of other ways. A majority of the Center's members, as a result, were Baptists. But the Center, fondly called "the Open Door," sought to fulfill its reputation of welcoming "children from all churches and all parts of town, of every age and circumstance." The attempt to encourage local leadership, to build ties to the community, and to respond to neighborhood needs, clearly led the Center away from denominational narrowness.[49]

The second "prong" of the Center's plan entailed the provision of vital facilities, both educational and recreational. The club and class work, in the context of the impoverishment and deprivation wrought by segregation and discrimination, meant more than mere diversion. It provided materials, space, and teachers who could demonstrate skills, serve as models, and purvey knowledge. Perhaps most importantly, it allowed the community a place to meet, discuss, plan, build ties, foster hope, and express pride and confidence, all in the face of the overwhelming odds against it.[50]

Finally, the Center aspired to provide leadership on the issue of race relations.

It sought to promote interracial contacts among leaders as well as community members. Its advisory board was both interracial and interdenominational. The Center hosted interracial events in the South at a time when such activities not only received harsh criticism from the majority of whites, but often had violent repercussions and constituted violations of the law. In the attempt both to build and to provide leadership, the Center trained from sixty-five to eighty Paine College students at any given time, giving them experience in community work as well as interracial organization. These students returned to their own communities, which often shared many of the same problems with the black neighborhoods in Augusta, and "where they didn't have a community center, they could make a community center at their local churches." Thus, the Center aimed to develop leadership in others, provide a model for leadership, and, at times, serve as a leader itself. In its capacity as leader in race relations, the Center at times found itself involved in the resolution of conflict. A potentially explosive situation arose, for instance, when a white medical intern slapped a black nurse in training at the local hospital. According to Stevens's account, the black nurses went on strike, and immediately telephoned the Center. Stevens listened sympathetically to the group of some fifteen furious nurses, then confronted the hospital administration. Along with an Episcopal minister, she helped the black women receive a satisfactory public apology.[51]

Interestingly, while the Bethlehem Center clearly fulfilled all of the functions of a traditional settlement house, Stevens stressed that the staff considered it a community center and not a settlement house. This distinction is particularly striking, considering settlement workers' recurrent judgment of religious work as susceptible to paternalism and evangelicalism. Stevens illuminated her own distinction between community work and settlement work:

> My concept of what we did was not like my concept of what people used to do in settlement houses. . . . I always thought of settlement houses, the ones I read about and studied about, as more or less a charity operation to a great degree. By charity I mean you had just a bunch of poverty ridden people, for whom you're providing some of the necessities of life and some of the activities that were important. But you didn't have a long term leadership development process. It was not my concept of development, of community development. I'm talking about community development, not just community organization.

However, Stevens did not think that all Methodist women shared this criticism of paternalistic intervention. She saw the same dichotomy that distanced the settlement house from the community center as separating Methodists who believed in missionary work from those who advocated community development: "Unfortunately, when you talked about a community center to the mission minded people, you talked about something you were going to do *for* the Negroes . . . [versus] something you were going to do . . . with the people in the communities."[52]

A belief in community independence, however, could sometimes translate into suspicion of all whites and all outsiders, regardless of their motives or their capacity to assist. Some Methodist Episcopal settlement workers at times viewed their work as a struggle against those black leaders who resisted the idea of receiving any kind of help from whites. But the primary obstacle remained the majority of the white community, which did not support the house's activities or vision. In spite of discouragements, "the future looks bright," settlement house reports stated. In 1945, the Augusta Bethlehem Community Center flourished, turning away as many kindergartners as it could accept, enrolling members in Girl Scouts, Boy Scouts, and other clubs, and hosting basketball tournaments and other recreational programs. It ran the only gymnasium in the city available to blacks, a camping program, and a pediatric clinic. The staff and advisory board sought to improve local conditions for both blacks and whites, not through vague policy statements, but through specific group activities. The house also conducted a Socio-Religious Conference and a Goodwill Christmas Program, both of which had open seating and drew both whites and blacks. Summarizing these events, one headworker wrote that "surely no one can join with a thousand others in singing the beautiful Christmas carols without experiencing a feeling of unity."[53]

The Young Women's Christian Association

In the early twentieth century, locals of the Young Women's Christian Association (YWCA) often carried out programs that resembled those of settlement houses. While the International Institutes of the YWCA actually were settlement houses, mostly serving European immigrants, regular central and black branches also carried out settlement work.[54] Their emphasis on Christianity and their focus on young working women differentiated YWCA workers from settlement workers, while their integration of services and reform made them similar.

The YWCA became involved in a wide range of reform activities, including race relations. The maternalist imperative provided much of the rationale for expanding in the early twentieth century. But over time, the emphasis shifted to a broad and often bold conception of the mandates of Christian democratic citizenship. Early activity concentrated on helping "the restless, surging army of women" that industrialization lured to the "great metropolis." Like other Progressive Era reformers, YWCA workers believed that the young single women who migrated to cities required special protection. At the turn of the century, YWCA "homes" sprouted up in most major cities to provide temporary shelter for migrants seeking work or for young women working for low wages. Besides providing food and lodgings, the association often cooperated with the Travelers' Aid Society or protective associations, which met women at ports or stations and helped with the mechanics of relocation. Like settlements, YWCA homes sought to recreate the structure of a family's home complete with a well-appointed parlor, a piano, and a kitchen for the residents. Resident secretaries often acted as mother-figures. In a study of the Cincinnati YWCA residence, M. Christine Anderson shows that these arrangements had the trappings of a middle-class family. Their lack of father figures, however, provided for the development of an egalitarian community of women.[55]

According to YWCA policy, blacks organized separate branches, often called Phyllis Wheatley homes. These branches offered "shelter, aid, and a home" to young women as well as clubs, reading rooms, music rooms, and other facilities for recreation, gardening, and education. The exclusion of blacks from public facilities placed a much greater burden on these branches to solicit the participation of black women and girls from all over the city "in order to meet the specific needs of the group and community."[56]

In 1912, the construction of recreational facilities at a Phyllis Wheatley branch in St. Louis, for example, gave "the older girls a pleasure which the city itself denied to its Negro inhabitants." The home also offered lessons in sewing, dressmaking, lacemaking, embroidery, china painting, choral study, English, and Bible and mission study. In addition, it held Mothers' Club meetings and entertainments. Far from merely a recreational center, the YWCA saw its ultimate goal as social change. One worker implied that working in segregated branches was only temporary remedial work when she wrote that "we hope the day is not long off when there will be the necessary means available for doing this work on the grand scale upon which it should be done[,] for St. Louis is the best situated city in the country for such a work."[57]

Even before the National Board of Young Women's Christian Association organized in 1906, some work had begun among blacks in southern schools and cities such as Washington, D.C., Baltimore, Philadelphia, and New York City. Black men, in addition, had organized the first YMCA as early as 1853. Strong community leaders like William Alpheus Hunton and Channing H. Tobias had emerged in the men's movement.[58]

Among women, two rival organizations, the International Board and the American Committee, merged in 1906 as the National Board of the YWCA.

Grace Dodge, social welfare worker, proved an essential mediator in the union and served as president of the central organization until her death in 1914.[59] Upon her death, *The Crisis*, the periodical organ of the National Association for the Advancement of Colored People, called her a "friend to the American Negro" and lauded her attempts to eliminate segregation and racial discrimination in the organization. Comparing the records of the YWCA and the YMCA, the article stated that "it was due to her more than any other person that the YWCA, while gravely deficient in some respects, still is so much more Christian and decent than the YMCA." Because of Dodge, white and black women ate together at summer conferences. Even when the segregation of associations occurred in the rigidly Jim Crow South, the rights of black associations were "to be guarded just as carefully and unflinchingly as those of the whites." During Dodge's tenure, Elizabeth Ross Haynes, wife of Urban League founder George Edmund Haynes, became the first student secretary among black students in 1908. The author expressed the fear that Grace Dodge's death would spell "the gradual encroachment of Negro-hating tendencies in this association." [60]

A remarkable example of a Phyllis Wheatley association, not yet connected with the YWCA but conducting similar work, was a home that functioned as a settlement house. Founded in 1913 in Cleveland by Jane Edna Hunter, its "home" housed working girls or those seeking work and held clubs and classes in a nine-story building. Subjects for classes included domestic science, sewing, art, music, and dramatics. The center also housed a nurses' registry and an Employment Department. Living quarters included a dining room, dormitories, parlors, club rooms, a summer camp, and a playground. Three Mothers' Clubs met to support and encourage the work and to emphasize "character building." Attendance for house activities in 1929 was a notable 9,738. Clearly a success in the black community, the house saw itself as "a monument to Negro womanhood" on three counts. First, it had the "ability to endure and to bear with dignity and courage, poverty and insult and discrimination." In addition, the house symbolized "the generosity of American white folk." Third, however, it attested to "American Prejudice; to its inability to rise above alms-giving, into human brotherhood and a desire for the full and free development of every human being to its greatest capacity." [61]

Jane Hunter's Phillis Wheatley House owed its existence partly to segregation even though it was a vibrant social and educational center in its own right. While similar "homes" offered services such as employment bureaus, vocational training, and shelter for the homeless, the Y's set their sights on social change. Mary Sims, chronicler of the YWCA, described the organization's aim as acceptance of diversity, racial and social harmony, application of the spiritual to the social sphere, and humanization of the industrial world: "This is a person by person undertaking, laboriously built over years and through a devotion to a common cause, a cause rooted in the Christian faith in the value of personality—all personalities—and committed to the method of love, a cause committed also to a 'divine discontent' that refuses to put its efforts primarily into fitting women and girls to their environment but rather has the long look, putting its greatest endeavor into the effort to make that environment one in which personality can grow, in which life can and does have satisfactions." [62] This drive to alter the social environment resulted from daily involvement in the problems of individual women and the subsequent realization of the community pressures on their lives. The experiences of women in YWCA homes transformed them from incarnations of the motherly duty to protect the moral purity of the nation's female children to community bases for much broader public concern. [63]

World War I precipitated the expansion of YWCA work in general and especially work among blacks, as large numbers of people relocated to army bases or migrated to cities seeking jobs opened up by the war. With the assistance of the federal government, the YWCA's War Work Council allocated funds for work in black neighborhoods to go toward emergency housing, increased staff and traveling expenses, the Junior War Work Council and Patriotic League, club and recreation work, community housing, publicity, and education. Emergency conditions led to new levels of participation. For example, workers in Columbia, South Carolina, and Richmond, Virginia, equipped soup kitchens for families affected by epidemics, and in Petersburg, Virginia, YWCA workers staffed a hospital during the severe influenza epidemic of 1919. [64]

A new institution, the hostess house, sprung up to attend to black soldiers and their families as well as the communities surrounding army camps. Originally intended mainly to "protect" girls from the soldiers and to prevent the perimeter of the camp from becoming a vice district, the hostess house expanded into a true community center. It started out as a place where wives, mothers, and friends of the soldiers could stay when visiting, as well as a motherly influence on single women in the community. Workers in Newport News, Virginia, sought to curb vice through a citizens' watch organization: "The problem of girls and soldiers was so alarming that some hundred thoughtful colored women organized into 'block patrol'—each woman taking responsibility for girls seen in her block." This work led to a survey of the town, enlistment of the aid of the well-off women, and the beginning of club work and organizational structure. [65]

The hostess house typically included a large room divided in two by a fireplace, a rest room, and a nursery. Simple, elegant, and cheerful, the houses provided "music, gaiety, and cordiality." They responded to the needs of mushrooming army camp communities that severely lacked recreational facilities,

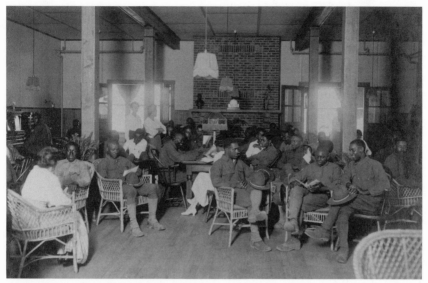

Living room of the YWCA Hostess House at Camp Dix, New Jersey. (YWCA of the U.S.A. National Board Archives)

housing, and many essential services. In Richmond, Virginia, the YWCA welcomed soldiers from Camp Lee and their visitors, functioning as a hostess house. Its work included sewing and knitting for the Red Cross, a choral club, hikes, picnics, basketball, outdoor sports, as well as a soup kitchen, prayer services, lectures, Travelers' Aid, and the Girl Reserves. An average of a thousand people used the facilities monthly.[66]

Eva Bowles described such hostess houses as a tremendous opportunity for black women to demonstrate their management capabilities and praised the courage it took "to stand together for the same ideal for the Negro girl as for the white." She suggested that organizing separately as women allowed them "a chance to show the world what they are capable of doing": "Besides the general educational and religious influences that come through living in a progressive land, the women themselves have developed agencies of their own. Whence would their leadership among the race have developed had not the Federation of Colored Women's Clubs been able to give the means of expression to its members." Caught up in the new opportunities opened by the war, Bowles showed that black women's huge contributions on the home front were only made possible by years of their own organizational efforts, which had prepared them for erecting hostess houses and other settlements. She argued that wartime social work was a boon to the building of a Christian democracy because the black woman, for the first time, finds "no door shut in her face." Her ideas implied that the vital service of black women to the country would only continue if they received equal treatment and education. Their organizations contributed to the well-being of the nation as much as any other group's efforts, Bowles concluded, because they enlist Americans "to stand behind the country's girlhood because it is the hope of the world." [67]

Numerous groups put these ideals into practice. The Phyllis Wheatley branch in Columbia, South Carolina, organized under the War Work Council with 125 women pledging their time and energy. A new center provided recreation rooms, a library, a restroom, offices, and a kitchen and was used regularly by other welfare organizations. During the war, the Red Cross opened a soup kitchen in the Center—and became housed there afterward—and workers visited over 250 families during the epidemic. One observer called it "the civic home of the colored people of Columbia." She also mentioned that in Augusta, Georgia, girls from the surrounding countryside were "interested enough to walk three or four miles" to attend the activities of their new Blue Triangle Center, the YWCA center's common alias. [68]

Adele Ruffin, who became field supervisor of work among blacks for the South Atlantic states in 1917, wrote to Eva Bowles that women in her field "are doing pioneer work which is heroic." Despite the constant frustration of Jim Crow, the dangers of southern prejudice, and privations of food and fuel, YWCA workers in the South Atlantic field supervised an enrollment of over 4,000 girls. In many cases, their buildings offered the only facilities in the city for recreation and other activities. The South Central region witnessed the opening of similar centers: a Phyllis Wheatley branch in Louisville; a camp at Harrod's Creek, Kentucky; a center in Chattanooga; a Blue Triangle Center in Little Rock; and others in Kansas City and St. Joseph, Missouri, and Nashville. Surveys in Montgomery, New Orleans, and Memphis resulted in government investigations of living conditions. The region's headworkers summed up the surveys as revealing "1. a lack of educational opportunity, 2. low wages and the accompanying low standard of living, 3. unwholesome and commercial recreation, 4. improper and unsanitary housing conditions." The YWCA seized the war-era focus on national strength to promote their cause: "Sane thinkers of both races are beginning to realize in a remarkable way that such conditions destroy the morale of girls of any race and make them a liability rather than an asset to the country in which they live." [69]

All over the country, existing YWCA branches and new hostess houses mobilized for the special exigencies of the war and tumultuous domestic conditions. The migration of blacks to cities swelled YWCA membership. In addition, the temporary movement of young black women from domestic work into industry and other jobs bred a feeling of excitement and hope. All over the country African American women joined the YWCA's industrial clubs in unprecedented numbers. In the Northeast and Midwest particularly, the YWCA became involved in issues concerning labor and industry. A black YWCA branch extant since 1905 expanded its membership and observed living and working conditions among black women. It found that black women, more than other workers, had to accept less than a living wage, which undercut white workers and thus aggravated racial tension. Black women, "the marginal workers of industry during the war," usually could not avoid unskilled positions and nearly always labored for white superiors. The YWCA learned of the need for education in collective bargaining and skilled work, as well as publicity aimed at employers and the public that would encourage "an appreciation and acceptance of colored women in industry." [70]

Other activities of black branches of the YWCA included Fresh Air committees, which operated camps for black girls, and room registries. Employment bureaus aimed not only at placing women in jobs, but at setting up training programs to make women suited for the available jobs and to teach them "to cope with industrial problems in industrial life." Numerous new centers formed, and established ones redirected their efforts to meet the industrial situation in Brooklyn and Montclair, New Jersey, where the YWCA became "the clearing house for social problems." YWCA branches often cooperated with churches and settlement houses, as in the case of a Burlington County, New Jersey, center.[71]

Work undertaken during the war united YWCA workers who had otherwise managed activities separately, and spurred a drive toward recruiting members for the organization. In Washington, D.C., Cordella A. Winn began in 1918 as special war worker. A graduate of Columbus Normal and Ohio State University who also attended a summer course at Columbia University, she had conducted social work at home in Columbus. In Washington, Winn encountered a Book Lovers' Club of sixty women who began work "with earnest hearts and empty pocketbooks." The club had provided an employment bureau and Travelers' Aid Society, and during the war cooperated with the government's employment service, the Housing Bureau, and the Red Cross. Winn observed other groups that had enrolled in Patriotic Leagues in schools and the YWCA, but found many young women "had not been reached." All the groups united their efforts in a membership campaign that succeeded in recruiting 1,500 new women and girls. Instructors offered classes in typing, stenography, and music, and workers' efforts secured an adequate building. White and black women cooperated in Germantown, Pennsylvania, to build a black association home in honor of "the highest ideals of Christian womanhood." [72] Workers in city after city faced similar conditions that stirred further activism. The residential segregation, exorbitant rents, lack of any public recreational facilities, poor sanitation, congestion, lack of "decent places to eat," and a general desire for a higher standard of living generated supporters. Workers and members answered the call in Pittsburgh, Williamsport, and Philadelphia, Pennsylvania; Columbus, Dayton, Youngstown, Cincinnati, and Springfield, Ohio; Charleston, West Virginia; as well as Baltimore, St. Paul, Des Moines, Indianapolis, and East St. Louis.[73]

YWCA workers conducted investigations that confirmed their belief that black women faced a peculiar set of obstacles to a manageable existence. In Detroit, for example, workers found that black female migrants seeking work outnumbered black males and that the churches and other organizations often "had no concerted plan for the social welfare of their people." In addition, "the housing conditions were acute." Buildings needed repair and lacked plumbing altogether. Girls earned too little to rent decent rooms and the "one respectable hotel" allowing black guests had "prohibitive rates for the average working woman." Families taking in boarders usually preferred couples or single men. Securing food and other necessities was also a struggle, as many restaurants disallowed the patronage of blacks. In sum, "the segregation in Detroit was almost as marked as in Southern cities." YWCA workers often faulted public employment agencies for encouraging black women to secure employment as domestics, "no matter what their training, experience, or education." As a result of these conditions and because of the glimpse of light provided by wartime opportunities, black women flocked to the YWCA. As one observer put it, "they were doing their share in war industries and got little or nothing in return. It seemed imperative to organize the work immediately." They proceeded boldly by visiting factories to secure industrial opportunities for women, especially trying to influence employers who did not hire blacks, and agitated against unfair wages and poor working conditions.[74]

The work undertaken during the war continued after the armistice. Black women realized that their gains could be rolled back if they did not harness the energy seething during the war. In addition, the successes in securing employment for both black and white women as well as local and national cooperation in YWCA work led to a new awareness of their mutual interests. Eva Bowles wrote that the first steps of black women into the city and industry were opportunities "beset with dangers." The black girl had entered "a new world of thought and feeling," learning that when she has a problem, it "not only affects her, but the white girl who has been fighting for standards; and together, they must understand their own interrelationships." Bowles pointed out that the YWCA's commitment to the working girl necessarily included the black girl, since, for "more than two centuries the Colored woman gave this country an unrecognized contribution of love, loyalty, and unrequited labor."[75]

Even after the war had wrought a great change in the American Victorian worldview, and after woman suffrage took the heart out of declarations of true womanhood and separate male and female spheres, YWCA workers often continued to evoke images of women's uniqueness to support agitation on social issues. In a movement segregated by sex, any issues that touched the lives of young women technically fell within its reach. As women entered the work force in increasing numbers, issues such as industrial conditions, wages, unemployment, and protective labor legislation became valid concerns. Women could also legitimately discuss legislative matters "affecting primarily women and girls," which included prohibition and law enforcement. Other public issues particularly of interest to women's supposedly superior moral nature were peace and international affairs, for "all of these subjects relate themselves directly to making this world a more satisfactory place to live in." These issues could also provide common ground for interracial cooperation, some women realized, for "they are of common interest to white and Negro women alike." [76] The maternalist ethos thus pulled women into new worlds of public activity. Their experience there, combined with concrete experiences in settlement work, changed that ideology drastically. New conceptions of women as providers and citizens muted the age-old cry of domesticity.

The Southwest Belmont Branch of the YWCA, the black branch in Philadelphia, illustrates the rising sights and growing sense of power, civic awareness, and efficacy that resulted from the community work during and after the Great Migration. Southwest's Annual Report of 1926 glowed with a sense of past achievements and future possibilities for women. "This is a new age for women . . . all over the world. Everywhere the womanhood of the world is awakening, one by one, a group here, a group there emerges and stretches itself in its new-found liberty." The report differentiated between traditional reform work emerging from women's imperative as nurturers and the new demands put on women as active citizens to do more than nurture:

> Up until now the work done by women's organizations may be described as salutary and salvaging. Through the influences of home, school, and church, woman [sic] have tried to place wholesome environment and helpful institutions in reach of the children. And for those unfortunates who were declared delinquents before the courts, salvaging institutions have been provided. . . . But, friends this is not enough. . . . Why build institutions to house delinquents and then by our customs, both of the community, church, school and home, keep right on making delinquents?

The wartime efforts augured well for the greater contributions all women could make in the world: "The late war showed as never before the great reserve force stored away in the hands and hearts of women." Thus, the community organizations of women had provided a civic apprenticeship, teaching skills and heightened expectations for new kinds of actions.[77]

Throughout the next decades, this branch carried on many of the activities of a typical settlement house, combining community service and reform. In its own view, it was "in its *expression* a social service organization for women and girls, providing for them those things which they most need—in many cases housing, a place to eat, a chance to get a job, opportunities for friendships, for educational classes, and for recreation. It is in addition a *fellowship* of women committed to the belief that it is possible to make Christian standards and ideals of life come true in our cities today." The branch offered classes in French, Spanish, and Public Speaking; recreational activities such as badminton, skating, and swimming; musical instruction in piano, vocal skills, and instrumental techniques; arts and crafts such as dressmaking and knitting; and a worker's education program (including writing, English, arithmetic, and spelling). It featured art exhibits, Camp Arcola, and permanent and temporary lodgings for hundreds of young women each year. It also served as everything from social service referral agency and public lecture hall to meeting grounds for antiwar rallies.[78]

In 1936, topics for discussion at Southwest included "Why Are We Prejudiced?; Household Employment and Its Organization; Household Employment and the Minimum Wage Law; The Ethiopian Situation; Books." Classes included "What's in the News and Why?; How to Run a Meeting; Social Hygiene; Knitting; and Typing." Special activities included an exhibit of the work of African American artists, cooperation with the World Fellowship committee, and Negro Health Week, which featured discussions on "Sex, Love and Marriage"; social insurance; "What I Know about My Daughter's Health"; and "Are You Bodily Wise?"[79]

True to the settlement movement's philosophy of responding to the needs of the neighbors, the branch sought "to guide and not dominate."[80] In order to glean the desires of its members, it sent out periodic questionnaires. One survey listed thirty-three possible courses, including Sunday School Teacher Training, Negro History and Literature, Current Events/Citizenship, Know Your City, as well as Charm School, The Home Beautiful, and Folk and Aesthetic Dancing. A range of courses in basic academic subjects, arts and crafts, religious education, and health education rounded out the list. The questionnaire ended with an open-ended invitation to "list here other subjects you desire."[81]

Another questionnaire sought to reach the "unattached ladies," those association members who belonged to the association but did not participate in its programs. The flyer urged members to suggest their own ideas for "sound ways by which Christian principles can be carried out in this day and age in individual lives and in society." It asked how often members wanted groups to meet, at what

Girls enter Y Building at Southwest Belmont YWCA, Philadelphia, Pennsylvania. (Urban Archives, Temple University, Philadelphia, Pennsylvania)

time of day, on what subjects, where (at the YWCA or in individuals' homes or other places in the neighborhood), and whether refreshments should be served. It also solicited ideas for directed reading courses for groups or individuals, and concluded, "Have you a different suggestion?" [82]

Not all those who used YWCA facilities thus belonged to a group or engaged in settlement work. Many of the residents, who in 1936 included students in beauty schools, commercial schools, and senior high schools, as well as beauticians, factory workers, and waitresses, merely resided there; others used the facilities such as the swimming pool. Some, however, became actively involved either in the committees that ran the branch, classes and clubs, or social service activities.[83] In addition, the leaders of the clubs and classes were urged not to teach in a traditional manner, but instead, consistent with the tenets of progressive education, to help foster girls' own initiative, leadership skills, self-esteem, and character development. The "rating sheet" for employees used in 1932 manifests this philosophy. The form asked evaluators a variety of questions about desirable leadership qualities, such as "To what extent does she lead without dominating?" and "Does she develop leadership in others?"[84]

This receptiveness to the ideas and concerns of the members led to a heightened awareness of the problems of the female worker. One of the problems cited by Y members was a feeling of powerlessness they experienced on their jobs, and even in their labor unions, which "are formed to do something about their work conditions" yet frequently left out their female members: "[Union groups] are often formed under high pressure and the leaders are men. The girls feel that they are not listened to seriously in the meetings and they have no experience in expressing themselves on their problems. Through the industrial department, the YWCA undertakes to help these girls participate in their union groups by giving them knowledge, self-confidence in group situations, and a more wholesome point of view."[85] This "wholesome point of view" entailed a recognition of their strength as individuals and as members of groups such that, when armed with skills and knowledge, they could effect change. This outlook was fostered by numerous social activities designed to build alliances among working women as well as by workers' educational programs. The Southwest Belmont Branch participated in vocational guidance conferences, ran an employment bureau, held classes to teach secretarial and other vocational skills, and participated in citywide monthly parties for "industrial girls." Parties, picnics, and "industrial conferences" for working women were interracial, and no doubt added to a sense of strength in numbers and in collective action.[86]

The activities of the YWCA, according to its leaders, aimed to realize individuals' true potential in the only way they deemed possible—through participation in the group. Drawing on the tradition of "group work," a staple of settlement house work, the YWCA's proponents believed that small group experience provided the link between individual self-development and large-scale social change. Only by developing oneself at the group level would one become fully aware of one's skills as well as the interdependent nature of human existence. One could only achieve fulfillment as a contributing member to an entity larger than oneself; without small group experience or active involvement in

Industrial Club picnic, Kensington YWCA, Philadelphia, Pennsylvania. (Urban Archives, Temple University, Philadelphia, Pennsylvania)

one's community, one would possess neither skills and awareness nor appreciation and tolerance of other people. The ability to live in harmony with other individuals and groups unlike one's own constituted an essential element of the YWCA's ideal—the attainment of both a moral society and the fulfillment of the needs of the individual through community belonging, meaningful work, constructive leisure, and harmonious family life.

YWCA branches often conducted "group work" along the same lines as the settlement houses. They believed, along with settlement worker Mary Simkhovitch, author of *The Settlement Primer*, that "the object of clubs is training in self-government and in the art of group accomplishment," or to learn "by doing," to be an active citizen. Group work would develop not only good citizens, but a more democratic society.[87]

Group work developed into a school of thought in social work as a response to twentieth-century living conditions. Its adherents pointed out that migration, industrialization, urbanization, and other changes threatened "primary neighborhood contacts and community feelings." The minutes of a 1935 conference on group work stated, "The individual loses his self-esteem in a city civilization dominated by the subway and elevated where impersonal relations predominate." The mechanization of life inhibited the individual's expression of the cre-

Employed girls at Southwest Belmont YWCA, Philadelphia, Pennsylvania. (Urban Archives, Temple University, Philadelphia, Pennsylvania)

ative aspects of personality. As this conference illustrated, group workers, who ranged from social workers and settlement workers to leaders of the Boy Scouts, disagreed about the purpose of group work. One group thought it could allow for "a wholesome release of energy, creative or otherwise." Another thought it could "create types of personality desirable in society" by teaching people to get along with others and contribute constructively to the community and nation. The third group thought the purpose was education, both for leaders and members: "Groups are organized to affect the fundamental social conditions in which people live their work [sic]; to make modifications and in transformations of the social order." [88]

Branches like Southwest sought to combine all three functions in its group work. The YWCA added to the notion of group work an emphasis on fellowship and friendship. Its goal was not merely a society in which all individuals had an equal voice and a meaningful vote, or a society of individuals who had adjusted to their civic responsibilities, but one that fulfilled more fundamental, less political needs and desires. Group work in YWCA branches could thus fill a perceived void created by the forces of modern American life—migration, industrialism, urbanization, and other agencies that fragmented and destroyed community. Its members recognized the need to humanize the industrial order, to foster community in an increasingly impersonal world, and to help people build self-confidence and develop their civic identities. The YWCA went even further; it sought to build networks of people interested in the ideal of a world fellowship. [89]

A strong emphasis on fellowship added a spiritual and universal dimension to the quest for community. This goal led members to establish ties with organizations throughout the world. In the fall of 1935, the YWCA sent a black delegation to India to meet with other Christian student groups. Earlier that year, the National Student Council of the YWCA mimeographed and distributed materials it recommended for use in the branches' observation of "Race Relations Sunday," a ritual of the interracial movement. The document made explicit the parallel between the caste system in India and Jim Crow. It juxtaposed songs and poems by African Americans with those of Indians. YWCA members read Langston Hughes's "The Negro Speaks of Rivers": "I heard the singing of the Mississippi when / Abe Lincoln went down to New Orleans / And I've seen its muddy bosom turn all golden in the sunset." They read James Weldon Johnson's "The Creation," the spiritual "Lift Every Voice and Sing," and James Edward McCall's "The New Negro": "He scans the world with calm and fearless eyes, / Conscious within of powers long since forgot; / At every step, new man-made barriers rise / To bar his progress—but he heeds them not." Indian writers' expressions of protest and unity followed, including a poem entitled "For Social Emancipation," which asked the "Lord of all nations" that "There be none, high or low, whatever his race or caste, / Who is bound by the shackles of ancient contempt, / And is barred from his right of free manhood." [90] The similarities between American and Indian oppression and the call to Americans to follow in the footsteps of Gandhi's movement were unmistakable.

The international experience of many of YWCA members provided a stepping stone from world Christian fellowship to human rights. Just as women's community work educated them in the realities of the black experience of racism, their international work taught them about similar conditions endured by other groups. The YWCA encouraged and made possible travel abroad for many of its workers, and hosted women and girls from other countries. This led to a sense of belonging to a group much larger than one's personal circle and, for some, to an understanding of human rights as an issue transcending particular community customs and boundaries. At the same time, the national and international ties fostered a sense of efficacy and strength in numbers. As early as 1928, the YWCA publicized its interest in "girls of every race, every creed, every occupation, the wide world round." It sought members not as mere contributors, but as full partners in the project, since the "democracy of a common faith" theoretically made all participants equal. It was the power of an agglomeration of people dedicated to a shared moral vision that could lead to social change: "Membership means sharing. Sharing means giving. Combined giving means power. One can influence the development of China. One can speak a message that will be heard in South America. One can send a message of good will to Europe. One can cease to be a spectator and become a working partner in building the kingdom of God."[91]

The stress on group work as a source of community and citizenship, combined with the ideal of a Christian democracy and an inclusive fellowship based on an ethical worldview, translated, for many members, into an imperative for change. The YWCA's efforts on behalf of working women are well known, and some scholars have written of the early interracial work of the YWCA.[92] The black branches played a vital role in rendering these ideals into an increasing receptiveness on the part of the YWCA to the idea of breaking down racial barriers. The belief in fellowship as part of the purpose of a true participatory democracy made the YWCA more vulnerable than many other organizations to blacks' demands for equal treatment in the organization and for civil rights more generally.

The local work of the YWCA branches, then, provided the concrete small group experience that gave many women, both white and black, an opportunity to build confidence and leadership skills and to speak out against the discrimination they saw as a major part of the problems of the people they organized. The YWCA's appeal to universal sisterhood, as the source of a purer democracy and more fulfilling individual lives, combined with concrete settlement activity to lead many members to embrace interracial organizing, to believe that change was possible, and to have the skills to help bring it about.

One YWCA worker, Dorothy Height, especially exemplifies this dynamic fusion of religious principles, dedication to service, and experience in community development. These traits eventually led her, along with many other women whose ideas were forged in YWCA settlement-type work, into civil rights.[93] Born in Richmond, Virginia, on March 24, 1912, her family moved to Rankin, Pennsylvania, a small town near Pittsburgh. Active Baptists, they helped black people who migrated to the area to work in the steel mills. Height was active in the club movement from the age of fourteen, when she became president of the Pennsylvania State Federation of Girls' Clubs. She attended New York University for a bachelor's degree and a master's degree in educational psychology. She played a leadership role in the United Christian Movement in the 1930s, and began her long association with the YWCA, where she became head of the Department of Racial Justice in 1963. Also a member and leader of the National Council of Negro Women, Height was a powerful participant in the civil rights movement.[94]

Height described the religious orientation of her first settlement work as a high school student. Her family lived across the street from the Rankin Christian Center, which only permitted blacks to attend on Thursdays. She made an

Dorothy I. Height. (Bethune Museum and Archives, Washington, D.C.)

offer to the Center's director to teach Bible stories to small groups of children: "I knew how to tell Bible stories. I asked her if she'd like me to come and tell Bible stories. . . . And, I said I'd come on Thursdays, but I noticed that they had these classes for little children going along, so she said if I'd like to, sure, just come in. So I went in and I started telling Bible stories to these little classes. And one day, some people came who had funded the Rankin Christian Center, and they were quite intrigued. I really was the only black person around there." Some of these observers were also Baptists, and one of them later helped her obtain a field work position in religious social work during her graduate work at Brownsville Community Center in Brooklyn in a predominantly Jewish neighborhood, where she soon became Assistant to the Director. In the mid-1930s, she participated in the world Christian movement during the evenings and weekends and served as an investigator, during the days, in the Department of Welfare for New York City, where she was the first black personnel supervisor in the department. In 1937, she decided to work for the YWCA in an effort to combine these two sides of her life: "I discovered that my interests were not just in doing things, but that I had a keen desire to see the relation between faith and action." [95]

In 1937, Height attended a world conference on the "Life and Work of the Church" in Oxford, England, as the representative from the United Christian Youth Movement (she was then president of the Christian Youth Council of New York State and leader of the Harlem Christian Youth Council, which coordinated over eighty youth groups). The only African American woman present, she participated along with young people from thirty-five countries and then took a seminar in International Affairs. Cecilia Cabaniss Saunders, Executive of the Harlem Branch YWCA, offered Height a job as her assistant. Height felt it was an agonizing decision, but decided that the YWCA would offer her a "broader base" for action than either the "strictly church-related agencies" she had worked for or the bureaucratic Department of Welfare. She worked as Assistant Director and then Director of Emma Ransom House, the Harlem YWCA. In Harlem, in the 1930s, she met many other activists and radicals, but she cited as especially transformative her concrete experiences in community work. Here the vague YWCA creed translated into a specific guide for action, as she encountered conditions daily that demanded redress. Working with the young girls who flocked to New York City for jobs, she became familiar with the "slave market corners" to which black women resorted out of desperation in order to take nearly any kind of work available. "I found myself constantly dealing with the problems of young people who were just plain exploited," Height recollects.[96]

In 1939, Height took a job as Executive at the Phillis Wheatley YWCA in Washington, D.C., which at that time was not even counted as a branch. During World War II, she witnessed the dramatic migration of people to the city. Young black women often found themselves with no place to reside, and the YWCA had the huge burden of finding them housing, training them for jobs, and locating work for them. During the war, Height left to participate in an interracial team working with the college students' associations in the South and became Secretary for Interracial Education of the National Board. In this position, she wrote her pamphlet *Step by Step with Interracial Groups*, which spelled out her theories and codified the YWCA's attempts to promote interracial understanding through small groups. At this time, the YWCA underwent a serious self-evaluation. Many members challenged segregation. Height was to "help give professional direction of the efforts the YWCA was making" by writing a "primer on how to work with groups of different races." Agonizing over the task, she revealed her background in settlement work when she reached this simple formula: "Well, there are different steps that you take. You have to understand different places where people are; to choose what kinds of activities help people who are of different races come together more easily than others; what kinds of activities are people most fearful of doing with people that they have some ideas about; how do such things as myths about health and disease and all that—how do these things affect the way people react in groups?"[97]

This small group experience became the basis for radical social change in *Step by Step with Interracial Groups*, a document that not only showed how far the YWCA's principles could extend, but also indicated the direction Height, and many others inspired by the powerful combination of religious work and settlement work, would take them. Height's book judged the treatment of blacks as an issue of human rights, and the problem of racial justice as not only a matter for blacks to undertake, but for both blacks and whites to confront together. The guidelines for interracial workers entailed the application of the earlier YWCA's group work methods to interracial matters.[98]

Height spoke for many women, both black and white, when she summed up the role religion had played in bringing to maturation this human rights philosophy so many years before the civil rights movement emerged. "I grew up in the church, and so I saw the church as having a role to play in bringing about change. And if you look at it, every organization that I have been related to itself was involved in dealing with some of the social issues. . . . Service and action, somehow or other, have been the two kinds of strands—some kind of public service, some kind of social action."[99]

In conclusion, black women and men at the turn of the twentieth century faced a hostile society. Lynching, Jim Crow, economic exploitation, employment discrimination, and residential segregation all constituted the harsh reality endured daily by African Americans. Through the exhaustive efforts of black women, local communities established social centers that provided essential services, neighborhood forums, and bases where women could develop confidence and leadership skills. They also organized successfully a national organization of black women's organizations that became a powerful voice for change. Black women's local work was the catalyst for the southern women's interracial move-ment that, albeit limited by the racist opposition of the time, helped begin to sway sentiment in favor of desegregation and civil rights.

Particularly in the late nineteenth century to the 1910s, black women suc-ceeded in urging interracial cooperation partly by articulating the ideals of activist motherhood and moralist womanhood, which they held in common with white evangelical middle-class reformers. In holding white women account-able for their professed ideals, black women helped transform the definition of women's imperative. Black women's experiences—both as members of the African American community and as reformers—led to a broader notion of women's responsibilities that included supporting or helping to support the family and providing for the welfare of the entire community. Black women's concrete experiences with the realities of racism and the obstacles to their own activities gave them a deep understanding of the great necessity for human rights. By agitating strongly for change through cooperation, they successfully held white women to their often nebulous, even patronizing urge to help the poor. At the same time, both black and white women's focus began to change. Organizations stressing the application of Christianity to everyday life—the Women's Home Missionary Society of the Methodist Episcopal Church, South, and the YWCA—began to envision a new channel for social change: the united force of black and white women working toward a moral society. Those women, enlightened by their actual experiences in community work and inspired by the ambitions of an idealistic movement, managed to redefine their imperative for reform. No longer was community work merely a maternalistic duty, but a calling for the moral citizen. Confrontation with the living conditions of black Americans and with the demands of black women tested the professions and ideals of white women and, in some cases, succeeded in transforming the ideol-ogy of moralist womanhood into a summons for women to struggle for human rights in the public arena.

Conclusion

The Promise and Tragedy
of the Settlement Movement

In 1934, an incident occurred that symbolized the failure of the National Federation of Settlements (NFS) to welcome blacks into the movement as equals. Settlement house workers and other neighborhood reformers in Kansas City, Missouri, scheduled a regional conference to meet prior to the National Conference of Social Work's gathering in May of 1934. The planners of the conference arranged for overnight accommodations at the farm of the Unity School of Christianity. Unity Farm's racial policy, although excluding blacks from housing, was otherwise the least objectionable they could find in the area. Three black delegates were sent word of this policy, but did not receive it before their departure for the conference. At a luncheon meeting, W. Gertrude Brown, who headed the Phyllis Wheatley House for blacks in Minneapolis, jettisoned her prepared speech and criticized the managers of the farm. "We must make this organization one hundred percent for everybody or let it go. . . . If Christianity is not big enough to span the chasm of prejudice then certainly it must fail," she declared.[1]

The president of the National Federation, Lea Taylor, explained its usual policy of meeting only in places that did not discriminate. She apologized to the black delegates and tried to secure lodgings for them in her own room. The management of Unity Farm, however, refused to permit any alternative arrangement, and the black delegates withdrew from the conference. Only after Twin Cities settlement houses threatened to leave the Federation altogether, and the National Conference of Social Work registered an official complaint, did the Federation formally apologize. A month later, the NFS resolved that it would hold conferences only "where there is no discrimination against any delegates because of their race or creed," and that in the future all arrangements for regional conferences would be made in consultation with the national office to insure no "future infringement of such national policy."[2]

Some individuals in the mainstream settlement movement clearly believed in accepting blacks as equals into the organization. These mavericks rejected segregation both in the NFS and in society. Yet the cherished creed of responsiveness to one's neighbors and the view differentiating blacks from white immigrants prohibited the settlement movement from confronting the issue directly. The mainstream workers provided tremendous leadership concerning the influx of huge numbers of European immigrants into the country, but faltered when it came to blacks. When the movement witnessed a major transformation during and after World War I, it underwent continual self-evaluation. The replacement of white immigrants by blacks in many settlement house environs presented a chance for a reorientation of the movement. True responsiveness to the community might have given the movement a new lease on life.

Instead, the movement's failure to adapt its plans for drastic community change to blacks hastened the migration of social service and civil rights activities into other organizations dedicated only to aspects of the integrated, ambitious settlement work programs. It made the problems faced by African Americans seem like issues pertaining only to special organizations dedicated to the promotion of black interests, instead of concerns for whole communities, neighborhoods, and settlement houses.

The 1920s and 1930s continued this fragmentation of social welfare services and reform work which, combined with the settlement movement's failure to redirect its efforts toward its new clientele, contributed to its long-term decline. The innovation of psychiatric social work threatened to break apart the marriage between social service and reform, the union that distinguished the settlement. During the 1920s, settlement workers began to describe two facets of their activity, group work and casework. Group work entailed education in attitudes toward other groups and individuals as well as the development of character and civic consciousness. Its premise was that no one should be an outsider. Thus, this type of social work best describes the work conducted by Progressive Era reformers like Jane Addams, who thought smoother relations among classes, ethnic groups, and the sexes would democratize access to resources and power. Group workers believed that clubs and classes could mitigate prejudice at the most local level. Headworkers attempted to learn about individual and group problems in order to help them effect social and political change. From their privileged positions, settlement workers would bridge differences and "interpret" the needs of the poor to the upper and middle class, who would provide sorely needed resources and support.[3]

Casework, on the other hand, dealt with individuals and their families and sought to assess private needs and provide direct services.[4] Mary Simkhovitch answered the question, "For what is casework?": "Simply individual treatment to satisfy a given need." In other words, she said, it entails "understanding and bringing out the best there is of resourcefulness in the patient in response to treatment." While caseworkers went to great lengths to differentiate themselves from paternalistic charity workers, they put themselves in a similarly powerful and superior position when they redefined their former "neighbors" as "clients" or "patients." Though not without merit, when it was the sole method employed, casework certified settlement workers as custodians of normality instead of catalysts for change. Even Simkhovitch, a pioneer in the group work techniques of Progressive Era settlement work, eventually believed that settlement work and psychology were inextricable. In the early 1930s she wrote, "Just as no settlement of the future can conceive of a program of social education and recreation without the aid of a psychologist, so the caseworker must be attached to a program of community development."[5]

While the settlement had always needed to balance group work and casework because of its dual identity as an agency of reform and service, the triumph of psychiatry stressed the individual's deviance from an imagined norm. It also emphasized individual health at the expense of the group and wrenched individual fulfillment out of context, thus denying the interdependence between group and individual well-being. Abraham Lincoln Centre, one of the few early integrated settlements, ran a child guidance center that focused on helping "children to adjust with some degree of satisfaction to home, school, and playmates" and "to conform to community demands." Rather than observing neighbors to "interpret" their needs as a guide for social change, clinicians would teach mothers to help children "develop their own talents to the best of their ability within the social framework." This meant educating mothers in the symptoms of abnormal child behavior and in proper motherhood itself. This type of program abbreviated the settlement's former commitment to altering the social structure to accommodate the individual. Instead, it stressed the need to alter the individual to fit the environment. It comes as no surprise to find that two-thirds of the "patient" families in need of "guidance" were black.[6]

Focusing on individual abnormality in some ways resurrected nineteenth-century practices of charity that the settlement movement had aimed to overthrow. Those conventions presumed the moral weakness of families who needed material assistance. Blacks began to move into settlement neighborhoods in great numbers during and after World War I, just when psychiatric social work began to take hold of some American settlements. Considering the views of blacks held by many mainstream settlement leaders delineated earlier, this convergence is suggestive. Blacks had never benefited from the reorientation in early twentieth-century reform ideology that blamed the environment and not heredity for social inequality. The belief that culture, morality, and the apparatus of civilization itself had disappeared in blacks because of the harsh environment of slavery emphasized the need for black individuals to turn to organizations of self-help for rudimentary moral instruction and the creation of culture. Black migration into settlement neighborhoods, along with other factors, hastened the replacement of group work by casework. The reactionary wind of the post-war years and the aftershock of the urban race riots also sapped the settlement movement of much of its emphasis on reform, while migration, segregation, and demobilization and its social implications accelerated the need for social services.[7]

Allen Davis points out that settlements also began to suffer in the 1920s as a result of "their own success." Their agitation for services contributed to the erection of public libraries, baths, and parks, city museums, and other improvements that rendered crucial aspects of their program obsolete. During and after the war, institutions like schools, recreation centers, and community councils assumed many of the settlements' functions. While numerous members of these organizations had received training in settlements, the fragmentation of settlement functions depleted much vitality from the early movement. Institutionalization of separate functions destroyed the sense of avant-garde experimentation. As a result, many settlements continued only their cultural programs in art, music, and drama. In an ironic analogy, considering the National Federation of Settlement's perennial attempt to distinguish the settlement from the religious mission, Paul Kellogg, editor of *The Survey*, warned in 1926 that settlements "might become more like abbeys and monasteries than like missionary posts." Another worker concurred that "there is a strong tendency toward research and specialization rather than toward common action."[8]

The revolution in social welfare precipitated by the Great Depression and the New Deal both exacerbated the fragmentation of the settlement's integrated program and prolonged the life of the house itself. The cataclysmic change represented by the New Deal's premise that the federal government had responsibility for individual welfare fulfilled many settlement workers' dreams. Long-term efforts of reformers culminated in provisions for public housing, social security, collective bargaining, job training, and relief.[9] Many settlement workers held offices in New Deal programs or operated centers that were revived by the desperate need of the Depression and the influx of paid Works Progress Administration and National Youth Administration workers who increased settlement staffs tenfold.[10]

While the New Deal validated the goals for which settlement workers had long labored, its adoption of responsibility for relief ate away at the justification for the settlement's existence. In many ways, too, the government programs that operated through particular houses during the 1930s altered the identity of the settlement. During World War II, the withdrawal of government workers hurt settlements, though the exigencies of war mitigated the most damaging effects. The Lanham Act provided government funding to expand day-care programs substantially so that women with children could contribute their labor to the war effort, but those funds were cut in 1946. The New Deal made settlements vulnerable to governmental policies and the changing political climate.[11] The assumption of public welfare by state and federal authorities also contributed to the proliferation of agencies, the professionalization of social services, and continued fragmentation of services.

Settlements missed their chance to prevent their own decline by redirecting their efforts to a group struggling for the same integration of economic betterment, social welfare services, and social change. The Great Migration of blacks and the decline of European immigration after the triumph of restrictionism in the 1920s provided a perfect opportunity for settlements to turn their efforts to the new group whose vitality and eagerness for change was obvious. The Garvey movement, the Harlem Renaissance, the public school campaigns, the community school-settlements in the rural South, the NAACP, the Urban League, black settlements, religious community centers, and the Y's all testified to the organizing fervor of African Americans during the early twentieth century. Settlement workers' attempt at cosmopolitanism had a vision limited by its northern, urban, secular bias that coupled with a negative view of black culture to make the National Federation of Settlements head a restricted movement. The NFS left it up to the local settlements to respond to the influx of blacks. Houses either shut down, ran segregated activities or separate facilities, or followed their white neighbors to better neighborhoods, but only rarely tried wholeheartedly to integrate.[12]

During the second great wave of black migration from the rural South to the city that occurred during World War II, the settlement movement made a sudden but long overdue realization of the importance of race in settlement work. As many historians have shown, the war years brought civil rights into the nation's eye. The rise of fascism in Europe and the clear links between oppression abroad and at home placed the reality of American democracy under examination. Wartime job opportunities also gave blacks another ray of hope and raised expectations. Urban neighborhoods in flux witnessed serious and numerous confrontations. The Detroit riot of 1943, for example, pointed out the great importance of addressing racial tensions. As a consequence of the riot, Detroit settlements proposed a plan of racial cooperation that the city enacted. The "Interracial Code of Metropolitan Detroit," formulated by the Board of Directors of the Council of Social Agencies, stated that the Council permitted no segregation in any of its programs. It recommended that member agencies reevaluate their interracial practices, including client, staff, board, and community relationships.[13]

In the 1940s, the leaders of the National Federation of Settlements realized that the settlement's future was in question. They concluded that race was the main issue facing the movement and that its program had to change to reflect this perception. In addition, settlement workers began to question the common policies of closing down houses after the desertion of traditional neighbors and of following immigrants to better neighborhoods. Workers discussed the meaning of the notion of "neighborhood," concluding that a settlement that followed its old neighbors was an interest group devoted to a group of people and not a settlement dedicated to a certain locale.[14] In 1942, the Committee of Race Relations in Cleveland recommended to its member settlements "checking the racial and national composition of your neighborhood and comparing it against your total numbers." The proportion of each group in the house should mirror the proportion in the neighborhood. In order to remedy any imbalance, settlement workers should conduct programs in interracial education, set examples through nondiscriminatory practices, and recruit new members. This document symbolized a serious new commitment to integration by the mainstream settlement movement.[15]

In the early 1940s, under the aegis of the NFS, Albert Kennedy, former NFS secretary, conducted a study of race and the settlement movement. The responses he received revealed that religious settlements had long worked among blacks, as had the YWCA, school-settlements in the South, and settlements run by blacks. The evidence showed that in the late 1930s and early 1940s, a significant number of settlements opened in black communities, such as the Booker T. Washington Community Center in Macon, Georgia. In October 1939, this settlement originated as a demonstration in community organization under the WPA. The center provided well-baby clinics, a citywide health and cleanup campaign, nutrition classes, cooking demonstrations, Red Cross first-aid and nursing classes, a nursery, a branch of the city library, recreational activities, crafts, gardening, and a camp. An interracial board and staff supervised the center's all-black clientele.[16] Along with the new centers, many preexisting settlements undertook new programs designed to accommodate both whites and blacks. By 1944, at least twenty-five houses served blacks primarily; many other houses began to admit African Americans in the 1940s and 1950s. The NFS encouraged integration in settlement houses by offering only "provisional membership" until they allowed blacks on an equal basis. Finally even the segregated Bethlehem and Wesley Houses founded by the Methodist Episcopal Church, South, struggled to integrate, but achieved only limited success in the 1960s.[17]

Some of the settlement movement's efforts to recognize the concerns of blacks hinted at an ambivalence that would mature in the 1960s. The construction of facilities for blacks under the guise of progress was often reminiscent of the provision of "separate but equal" facilities, the fallacy underpinning Jim Crow. During World War II, Neighborhood Association, a St. Louis settlement house, received government funding for "negro work." In 1941, the settlement's headworker, J. A. Wolf, observed the influx of blacks into the neighborhood, caused partly by the opening of a low-cost housing project for African Americans adjacent to the settlement house. Wolf planned to move the settlement, following the older white neighbors out of the locale, but then to turn the original building over to blacks. In 1942, Wolf made an appeal for support. He declared that, although the initial program aimed at European immigrants, the facilities should go to the "poor, needy, uncomplaining negroes who are part of our city and whose welfare is essential to the well-being of us all." By 1945, the original house had an all-black staff and membership. While providing essential services and facilities, the process bolstered a sense that segregation was a natural and desirable end.[18]

In the past, settlements had often acquiesced to the racism of their white neighbors and failed to integrate with the partially valid excuse that they would lose their clientele if they did. In the 1940s, the NFS and certain local settlements realized that they had a responsibility to lead and not to follow community attitudes.[19] By then, settlement workers had begun to acknowledge that the "Negro problem" did not only involve assisting blacks to help themselves but also finding a way to eradicate invidious white racism.[20]

Urged to carry out the Federation's new mission of integration, individual settlement houses often found themselves treading a thin line between fostering better relations and aggravating tensions inherent in the community. Neighborhood stress sometimes erupted into violence over the settlement houses themselves. In overcrowded residential areas, recreational facilities held great significance, as symbols of territorial boundaries, possession, power, and freedom.[21] In an urban context, where space was at a premium, limits on the use of facilities could provoke violent confrontation between the "owners" and the "outsiders." For settlements trying to integrate in the 1940s, these sensitivities often exploded over the issue of interracial dancing, which epitomized fears and taboos surrounding race and sex.

In Buffalo, New York, neighbors living near a settlement called Neighborhood House included Irish Catholics, Jews, Germans, Greeks, and African Americans. A "Beverly Road Property Owners" organization opposed the movement of blacks into the area and the Parent-Teacher Association disbanded because members had to meet in each other's houses and whites refused to host blacks. Local dances, however, attracted both black and white youths. A brawl broke out after one dance when a white girl accepted an invitation to dance from a black boy. Other black boys misinterpreted the girl's intentions and tried to force her into a car with them. As a consequence of a supposed attack on their "property," white boys began to try to force her into their car. Finally, a group of white girls saved the victim but afterward ostracized her.[22] The incident suggests that interracial dancing stirred animosities kindled by a combination of racist and sexist reactions.

At Soho Community House in Pittsburgh, headworker John McDowell and other workers began a program of interracial dancing in the early 1940s. Since 1921, blacks and whites had participated equally in the settlement, but mingled only in the children's story hours and the library. All other activities were segregated. In the 1920s, some progress occurred; the staff included some blacks, and black girls obtained swimming privileges. During the 1930s, black membership declined in response to a hostile administration, and black women protested when they were barred from a community party. In 1936, an Advisory Committee resolved to find a way to say to black neighbors, "This settlement house and its facilities are for your use and enjoyment." One administrator wrote in 1938 that Soho's "greatest contribution can be to open its doors to Negroes along with their white neighbors." It should "welcome them, give them friendship and an opportunity to develop the best that is in them." "Most important of all," he concluded, it should "allow Negro and white to learn that they have much to give each other and many problems to solve in common."[23]

In 1941, the house began an interracial dancing program that immediately induced distress. A group of white boys refused to participate in one dance, apparently out of competitiveness. The group work leader wrote that the whites feared that the black boys' superior dancing ability "will make them look that much worse when they do try to dance." In a house meeting, the black boys subsequently objected to mixed dances. The head of the Friday Mothers' Club said that she could not understand the disapproval of blacks and threatened to keep her children at home if they continued to oppose open dances. One young black member of the settlement, Sam Corbin, stated that since blacks entered the army through the draft and fought side by side with whites, blacks and whites could certainly dance together. White and black girls both expressed a friendly desire to welcome everyone. But the group worker thought that the black youths in general "thoroughly accepted the unwritten law on segregation" and refrained from initiating a conflict "with boys and girls in the neighborhood whom they knew well." Given the historical virulence of American racism, their reluctance to integrate is understandable. But again Corbin spoke out, eloquently connecting segregation at the settlement house with general social inequality:

Soho Community House, Pittsburgh, Pennsylvania. (Archives of Industrial Society, University of Pittsburgh)

Before we make a decision about this, I think we ought to examine the reasons why the white people—some of them—don't want us there. I think it's because they think we aren't as good as they are. Now are you fellows going to admit they're right and put yourselves off in a corner? I can't see that. We behaved better than almost anyone there last week and they've got no reason to say we can't dance on the same floor with them if House policy says we can and we act right. Once you start doing this, you know where you end up? Taking whatever the white people who have pushed you aside feel like leaving over for you and you're glad to get it.

Roused by this speech, the black youths walked into a white dance. White boys stormed into the office of headworker John McDowell, who defended the house's democratic policy. The boys claimed that their mothers would not allow them to attend the house if it held mixed dances.[24]

Two months later, at a Mothers' Club Bingo Night, the issue of interracial dancing again came up. "We know that this is a Community House, but we don't have to socialize with the Negro," the white women announced, and prepared a petition calling for a return to segregated activities. A long discussion ensued, revealing that the real issue of concern was that a black boy might ask a white girl to dance. In a grisly reincarnation of the belief in the special imperatives of motherhood, the mothers stressed that their role as nurturers and protectors directed them to withdraw their children from the settlement if interracial dancing recurred. In another meeting, a black mother said she would not allow her children to attend the settlement house if dances were segregated. Another pointed out that white girls, if threatened by the prospect of interracial dancing, could always refuse to dance with any boy, white or black. Then one night, a mixed dance did take place. From other rooms in the house, clubs let out and black and white mothers poured into the dance hall and stood on the sidelines arguing. The hostilities continued, but John McDowell refused to give in, and house policy shifted accordingly. From then on, any house-sponsored gathering or dance would be integrated. McDowell told the NFS that all settlements should share the goal of sticking "to our policy of non-segregation in spite of unpleasantness." [25] The settlement went on to encounter other incidents of racial conflict among neighbors as well as outside obstacles to their interracial efforts. But under the remarkable leadership of McDowell, and then Soho worker Margaret Berry, the settlement stood firm on its policy of integration. It conducted numerous interracial activities, resolved community tensions, and attempted to provide a model of cooperation, justice, and sanity.[26]

The situation at Soho evokes the anxiousness plaguing numerous neighborhoods throughout the country in the early 1940s. Changes wrought by World War II transformed many communities into powder kegs, several of which did ignite in the subsequent decades.[27] The civil rights movement, triggered by the kind of thinking expressed by Sam Corbin at Soho, as well as by similar tensions over public accommodations, questioned the practice of American democracy at every level. The resistance of local communities hindered the attempt by the NFS to encourage integration until the civil rights movement gained momentum.

The intriguing story of the settlement house and community center in the modern period has yet to be fully explored. Judith Trolander shows that by the 1960s a new situation prevailed in the settlements. Black men possessing master's degrees in social work had replaced white middle-class volunteers as headworkers and inner-city neighborhoods had become predominantly black. In addition to changed social and political conditions, reform styles themselves transformed in response to the civil rights movement. The community activism of Saul Alinsky and other agents of grass-roots reform led to a sharp critique of settlements. Along with sociologists like Herbert Gans, Alinsky faulted the middle-class white staff of the settlement house for disguising its urge toward social control beneath an ideology that stressed moderating class antagonism.

The new activists promoted indigenous leadership to the exclusion of sympa-
thizers. The War on Poverty also pushed for locally recruited staffs, implying
that middle-class whites no longer had a place in the settlement movement. At
this time, residency became outmoded, and larger institutional edifices replaced
the former settlements, which had sought to provide hospitable buildings re-
sembling actual houses. As professional black men replaced women, much of
the settlement style also altered. Trolander describes the vanishing of a reform
style associated with early twentieth-century women that combined a maternalist impulse with a commitment to reform, immense idealism, self-sacrifice,
and an "emphasis on 'bridging' among conflicting groups." In contrast, men
inspired by Alinsky and others tended to emphasize competition, confrontation,
and professionalism.[28]

The advent of blacks into leadership roles in the settlement movement marked
a significant advance, especially considering the movement's prior failure to
embrace blacks to the same extent as white immigrants. The redirection of
settlement work toward black communities and their revitalization by government funding in the 1960s were also welcome changes. Tragically, the loss of
valuable aspects of the settlement house occurred simultaneously. Margaret
Berry, NFS director in the 1960s, feared that to transform the settlement into
a "protest agency for the poor" would further separate blacks and cut off access to opportunities only available through a bridging of class and racial lines.
When the national political climate shifted again after the twilight of the 1960s,
settlements suffered permanently from the loss of funding. By then, separatism had alienated former supporters and workers. "In emphasizing 'maximum
feasible participation of the poor,' settlements may have forgone much of their
opportunity to build social class bridges and lost a certain kind of influence in
the process," writes Trolander.[29]

The story of blacks and the settlement house—a unique consolidation of
social services, educational and recreational facilities, and a dedication to social
reform—seems best described as a tragic tale of missed opportunities, untimely
exclusion, and unfulfilled promise. While settlement work for blacks did thrive
in some instances, it was usually not welcomed and recognized by the formal
settlement house movement. As previous examples have illustrated, blacks and
a few interested whites organized instead through separate black settlement
houses, local affiliates of the Urban League, the YWCA, school-settlements,
religious settlements, community centers, and church missions.

In the 1960s, sociologist St. Clair Drake conducted a study of settlement
houses that portrayed them as the best way to revitalize American democracy.
Through the organization of local communities to address the needs of all
classes, settlements could be the agents of enormous positive social change.

The united cross-class efforts of whites and blacks, embodied in strong local coalitions, would increase access to the power and resources in this country. Settlements, Drake thought, should welcome outside "initiative" in "breaking ghetto walls." Not just funding and political power but cultural contacts constituted the building blocks of a fully integrated democracy. Drake's ideas seemed fated to remain unheard by settlement leaders, as they entered public discourse during an era that emphasized militant separatism at the expense of other aspects of reform. While the civil rights movement's shift from nonviolent resistance to revolution "by any means necessary" had a variety of valid causes, its interpretation within the settlement movement was ultimately damaging.[30] Drake's views hold new significance now that the Reagan and Bush years have sapped the lifeblood from settlements. The withdrawal of funding for community centers since the 1960s cemented their transition to fragmented single-service agencies aimed only at isolated aspects of recreation, psychiatry, or welfare.

St. Clair Drake supported the drive of African Americans for pride, consciousness, identity, and power. He also believed that blacks had to transcend their historical separation from the sources of power and resources. He opposed any measures he thought would perpetuate the "ghettoization" that caused alienation and powerlessness. Emphasizing that the civil rights movement had a history of interracial participation, he thought that the issues concerning minorities in a democracy had implications for the lives of every citizen. Neither blacks nor whites could confront the issues of housing, jobs, and citizenship in a vacuum. Drake thought that settlements could play a vital role in social transformation, striving "to provide meaningful interracial participation to offset the isolation imposed by ghettoization." Cross-class, interracial alliances would end psychic, physical, political, economic, social, in sum, total isolation. Drake concluded that the settlement could revitalize all neighborhoods by educating Americans in black history, by participating in the struggle for civil rights, by developing a maximum degree of integration at every level, and by promoting interracial cooperation for the solution of shared social problems.[31]

St. Clair Drake understood the urgency of blacks' drive for psychic and social power. Yet like Martin Luther King, Jr., and also like the noblest idealists of the settlement house movement, Drake did not favor adopting the tools—such as segregation—and committing the crimes—such as violence—of the oppressor. "In a multiracial society, no group can make it alone," King wrote, adding that "to succeed in a pluralistic society, and an often hostile one at that, the Negro obviously needs organized strength, but that strength will only be effective when it is consolidated through constructive alliances with the majority group." Drake belonged to that cadre of reformers who, like King, realistically discussed a future for this country that differed from the segregated past. As symbolized by the failure of the settlement movement—one of the most pluralistic twentieth-century social movements—to welcome blacks, American society had caused blacks and a few concerned whites to address on their own the basic problems of community survival. Like Martin Luther King, Jr., Drake understood that separatism had been the best response available under hostile fire, but did not picture further isolation as a desirable future for either blacks or whites.[32] Our mutual interest in democracy makes the public concerns of every other American our own.

Notes

Introduction

1. Addams, "Social Control," p. 22.

2. For a survey of migration, see Henri, *Black Migration*. Literature on the formation of the ghetto includes Kusmer, *A Ghetto Takes Shape*; Osofsky, *Harlem*; Clark, *Dark Ghetto*; and Spear, *Black Chicago*.

3. The most important treatments of the mainstream settlement movement include Davis, *Spearheads for Reform*; Higham, *Strangers in the Land*; Trolander, *Settlement Houses and Professionalism and Social Change*; Chambers, *Seedtime of Reform*; and Lubove, *Professional Altruist*.

4. Addams, *Twenty Years at Hull-House*, p. 217.

5. Woods and Kennedy, *Handbook of Settlements*, p. v.

6. Taylor, *Chicago Commons*, plate. These words, which Taylor called "the keynote of

the whole adventure," were printed on a Gutenberg hand press at the Chicago Century of Progress Exposition in 1934.

7. See Davis, *Spearheads for Reform*; Chambers, *Seedtime of Reform*; Lubove, *Professional Altruist*; Boyer, *Urban Masses and Moral Order*; Bremner, *From the Depths*; and Sklar, "Hull House in the 1890s." That the very working definition of the American settlement house was linked with immigration is also evident in the entries on settlement workers in James, James, and Boyer, *Notable American Women*; and Sicherman et al., *Notable American Women*.

8. Trolander, *Settlement Houses*, pp. 137–40.

9. Philpott, *Slum and the Ghetto*; Karger, "Phyllis Wheatley House" and *Sentinels of Order*; Crocker, *Social Work and Social Order*; and Lissak, *Pluralism and Progressives*.

10. Higham, *Strangers in the Land*; Davis, *Spearheads for Reform*, p. 96.

11. Trolander, *Settlement Houses* and *Professionalism and Social Change*.

12. A staple for the study of African American women's involvement in social reform and community work is Hine, *Black Women in American History*. Some of the most useful volumes in the series include Salem, *To Better Our World*, vol. 14; Jones, *Jane Edna Hunter*, vol. 12; and *Black Women in American History*, vols. 5–8, which are collections of essays. Also informative are Neverdon-Morton, *Afro-American Women*; and Rouse, *Lugenia Burns Hope*; among many others.

13. Luker, *Social Gospel in Black and White*, pp. 159–90; Salem, *To Better Our World*, pp. 65–100.

14. Trolander, *Settlement Houses*, p. 159.

15. Du Bois, *The Souls of Black Folk*, p. 17.

Chapter 1

1. William Byrd Community House Report, Richmond, Virginia, September 1943, "Interracial Study," Folder 101: "Virginia, 1940–46," Box 9, Kennedy Papers, SWHA.

2. Brandt, "Make-up of Negro City Groups"; Kelsey, "Negro Emigration"; Kellor, "Assisted Emigration"; Daniels, "Industrial Conditions"; Williams, "Social Bonds in the 'Black Belt'"; Waring, "Criminality among Colored People"; Fernandis, "Social Settlement in South Washington"; Jones, "In the Country at Large"; Washington, "Why Should Negro Business Men Go South"; and other articles in *Charities*, 15, 1 (October 7, 1905).

3. See, for instance, Henri, *Black Migration*; Osofsky, *Harlem*; Foner, *Organized Labor*; Jones, *Labor of Love*.

4. This is only a partial list of some of the most significant works on blacks. Others include Baker, *Following the Color Line*; Wright, *Negro in Pennsylvania*; Haynes, *Negro at Work*; Quillin, *Color Line in Ohio*; and Crossland, *Industrial Conditions*. For others, see Osofsky, *Harlem*, p. 54 and bibliographic essay.

5. For an interpretation of settlement houses as puppets of employers, see Crocker, "Sympathy and Science."

6. See Higham, *Strangers in the Land*, p. 251, for a discussion of Jane Addams's doctrine of "immigrant gifts." On Americanization and restrictionism, see Higham, *Strangers in the Land*; Korman, *Industrialization, Immigrants, and Americanizers*; Hartmann, *Movement to Americanize the Immigrant*; as well as contemporary views such as Kellor, *Neighborhood Americanization*.

7. For the range of histories that assume this dichotomy, see, for example, Franklin and Moss, *From Slavery to Freedom*; Quarles, *Negro in the Making of America*, pp. 166–74; Meier, *Negro Thought in America*, pp. 207–47; Williamson, *Crucible of Race*, pp. 70–78.

8. Some critics believe that the epitome of this thinking was the publication in 1965 of Moynihan's report, *Negro Family: The Case for National Action*. The report suggested that slavery had doomed the black family to a future of pathology. Historians Stanley Elkins, Kenneth Stampp, and E. Franklin Frazier unwittingly fueled this view by emphasizing the psychological devastation wrought by slavery. Their stress on the brutality of the system was a welcome rebuttal of U. B. Phillips's apologist argument that depicted slavery as paternal and civilizing. Nevertheless, a generation of revisionist scholars found that this tale of domination and victimization only furthered the dehumanization of African Americans by failing to note the resilience of African traditions, the creation of an adaptive culture, and attempts at outright rebellion. See, for example, Gutman, *Black Family*; Genovese, *Roll, Jordan, Roll*; Blassingame, *The Slave Community*; Levine, *Black Culture and Black Consciousness*; and Jones, *Labor of Love*. However, the problem with the stress on slavery as destroying culture and character was not only its estimation of the black individual, but also its location of the explanation for blacks' contemporary problems in slavery alone, instead of in the new economic and social order.

9. Addams, "Social Control," pp. 22–23. While Addams spoke from a keen understanding of Americans' participation in "a world-wide yielding to race antagonism," her manner of indicting racism devalued blacks themselves. She rightly attacked slavery, but clearly differentiated between blacks and Italian immigrants when she wrote that "the civilizations in Africa are even older than those in Italy and naturally tribal life everywhere has its own traditions and taboos which control the relations between the sexes and between parents and children. But of course these were broken up during the period of chattel slavery for seldom were family ties permitted to stand in the way of profitable slave sales." Quoted in Diner, "Chicago Social Workers and Blacks in the Progressive Era," p. 399.

10. Addams, *Second Twenty Years*, pp. 400–401; and Bowen, "Colored People of Chicago," pp. 117–20, excerpted in Davis and McCree, *Eighty Years*, p. 122.

11. Diner, "Chicago Social Workers and Blacks in the Progressive Era," pp. 393–410; McCree, "Louise de Koven Bowen," pp. 99–101; Bowen quoted in Davis and McCree, *Eighty Years*, p. 127.

12. Philpott, *Slum and the Ghetto*, pp. 293, 301.

13. Bowen, *Colored People of Chicago*, quoted in Philpott, *Slum and the Ghetto*, p. 301.

14. O'Connell, "Frances Kellor," pp. 393–95; Osofsky, *Harlem*, pp. 57–58; Kellor, "Assisted Emigration," pp. 11–14.

15. Kellor, "Criminal Negro," pp. 60–61.

16. Ibid., pp. 65–68.

17. Ibid., p. 190.

18. Ibid., pp. 308–10.

19. Ibid., pp. 309–11.

20. Newby, *Jim Crow's Defense*; Kogut, "The Negro and the Charity Organization Society," p. 12.

21. Bruère, quoted in Philpott, *Slum and the Ghetto*, p. 296.

22. Contemporary articles like the following exhibit this current of racism even in their titles: "Keeping the New Blood Pure," pp. 219–21; Ross, "Causes of Race Superiority," pp. 85–86; "Race Suicide and Common Sense," pp. 892–900. These are a minute

sample of the vast amount of print devoted to the concern with racial purity and the perils of immigration. Tracts aimed specifically at blacks include Carroll, *Negro a Beast*; and Pemberton, "Barbarization of Civilization."

23. Addams and Wells, "Lynching and Rape: An Exchange of Views."

24. For excellent treatments of forms of racist thought in the early twentieth century, see especially Newby, *Jim Crow's Defense*; Frederickson, *Black Image*; Gossett, *Race*.

25. Woods, Introduction to Daniels, *In Freedom's Birthplace*, pp. ix–xi.

26. Ibid.

27. Woods's stress on self-help bears a superficial resemblance to separatist strategies of Marcus Garvey and others who encouraged blacks to build a strong, independent economic base apart from reliance on whites. It is important to note, however, that the definition and especially the implications of self-help differ substantially according to the speaker and the context. In the views of Woods and Daniels, self-help for blacks implied that blacks needed to "catch up" culturally and economically, to pull themselves up by their bootstraps. This view suggested that blacks were inferior to whites, albeit temporarily. Garvey urged blacks to remain loyal to their own race because whites were not about to assist them in their drive for pride and liberty. Throughout the twentieth century, black separatism sometimes played into the hands of white racists, providing a rationale for ignoring the plight of blacks and recasting segregation as voluntary and expedient. Touching on this point, W. E. B. Du Bois saw Garvey as "the type of dark man whom the white world is making daily, molding, marring, tossing to the air," a person whose identity burst forth from the rage inspired in him by "whites [who] have laughed and sneered at him and torn his soul" and whose extremism furthers white prejudice. Du Bois, "Back to Africa," p. 113.

28. Woods, Introduction to Daniels, *In Freedom's Birthplace*, pp. xii–xiii.

29. Daniels, *In Freedom's Birthplace*, pp. 398–402.

30. Ibid., pp. 400–401.

31. Ibid., pp. 401–2.

32. Ibid., pp. 404–11.

33. Lindenberg and Zittel, "Settlement Scene Changes," pp. 562–64.

34. Trolander, *Settlement Houses*, pp. 137–40; Philpott, *Slum and the Ghetto*, p. 301.

35. Trolander, *Settlement Houses*, pp. 139–40; Philpott, *Slum and the Ghetto*, pp. 315, 332.

36. Peterson, "From Social Settlement to Social Agency," pp. 192–93, 198–99.

37. By 1911, blacks were the second most populous group in the Guild's neighborhood (Irish Americans were the first). Woods and Kennedy, *Handbook of Settlements*, pp. 259–60; Peterson, "From Social Settlement to Social Agency," pp. 207–8.

38. Woods and Kennedy, *Handbook of Settlements*, p. 73; Trolander, *Settlement Movement*, pp. 137–38.

39. Philpott, *Slum and the Ghetto*, pp. 337–41.

40. Ibid., pp. 340–41. The Chicago Commission on Race Relations discussed this tendency of whites to stop using recreational and social service facilities as the number of blacks using them increased, in *Negro in Chicago*, pp. 231–326, and noted the increased use of Lincoln Centre by blacks, p. 150.

41. "Eighth Ward House," and Bartholomew, "A Northern Social Settlement for Negroes," unidentified clippings, Folder 492, Box 46, National Federation of Settlements Papers, SWHA.

42. Hartshorn, *Era of Progress and Promise*, pp. vi–vii.

43. Lattimore, *A Palace of Delight*, p. 12, Janie Porter Barrett Papers, Hampton.

44. "Eighth Ward House," Folder 492, Box 46, National Federation of Settlements Papers, SWHA.

45. Kennedy, "Settlement Contributions to the Understanding of White-Negro Relations in Northern Cities," unpublished mss., p. 3, Kennedy Papers, SWHA.

46. Diner, *In the Almost Promised Land*, pp. 182–84.

47. Cass, interview, conducted by Tahi Lani Mottl, in Hill, BWOHP, 2:310–12, 340–42, 370, and biographical sketch, 2:272–74.

48. Selby, *Beyond Civil Rights*.

49. Sinclair, "I, Too, Sing America," clipping, *Cleveland Common Ground* (Autumn 1942), pp. 99, 106, Folder 464, Box 44, National Federation of Settlements Papers, SWHA.

50. Ibid.; Kennedy to Grayson Kirk, March 30, 1953, seconding a Karamu appeal to the trustees of the Jacob Schiffe Fund, National Federation of Settlements Papers, SWHA.

51. Sinclair, "I, Too, Sing America," pp. 99, 106.

52. Jelliffe and Jelliffe, Report on Karamu House, March 1946, Folder 464, Box 44, National Federation of Settlements Papers, SWHA; Selby, *Beyond Civil Rights*.

53. McDowell, "Field Report on a Visit to Karamu House," March 4, 1946, Folder 464, Box 44, National Federation of Settlements Papers, SWHA.

54. Annual Reports, Whittier Centre Housing Company, Wharton Centre Papers, Temple.

55. Jane P. Rushmore to "Friend," Feb. 5, 1945; untitled typescript, history of Wharton Centre, n.d.; "Activities of the Year 1916," Whittier Centre; and Report, Whittier Centre, 1927, ibid.

56. "Study Regarding Recreation for Colored People in North Philadelphia," Community Department of the Council of Social Agencies of the Welfare Federation of Philadelphia, ibid.

57. "The Wharton Centre"; Charles F. Judson to Mr. and Mrs. David, June 16, 1932; "Appeal for Donations," Whittier Centre; and Annual Report, The Susan Parrish Wharton Settlement of The Whittier Centre, 1931–32, ibid.

58. First Annual Report, Wharton Centre, ibid.

59. Ibid.

60. John N. Doggett, Jr., to Claudia Grant, October 15, 1952, Wharton Centre Papers, Temple.

61. First Annual Report, Wharton Centre; and Mothers' Clubs Group Work Records, 1936–39, ibid.

62. Mothers' Clubs Group Work Records, 1936–39, Wharton Centre Papers; and Annual Report, Wharton Centre, 1942, ibid.

63. Mothers' Clubs Group Work Records, 1936–39, ibid.

64. Annual Report, Wharton Centre, 1949; Claudia Grant, Production Prepared for twenty-fifth anniversary of Wharton Centre, Towncrier Productions, May 5, 1957. In 1952, a staff member who had worked with the Saints wrote to Wharton that he had run into the former leader of the gang; he "was studying at Greeley State College in Colorado and he was loud in his praises of things that he had learned through his association with Wharton Center." W. Miller Barbour to "The Board and Friends of Wharton Center," October 24, 1952. Ibid.

65. See, for example, Annual Report, Wharton Centre, 1944, ibid.

66. Typescript on the history of Whittier Centre, ibid.

67. Claudia Grant, "Ten Years of Experience in Conducting Wharton Settlement House," October 28, 1947, typescript, ibid.

68. Karger, "Phyllis Wheatley House," p. 90.

69. Weiss, *National Urban League*, pp. 40–46.

70. Ibid., pp. 88–89, 110–23, 174.

71. Ibid., pp. 88–89.

72. "A Social Service Achievement: A Four Year Record," Springfield Urban League; Annual Report, Armstrong Association of Philadelphia, 1918; "Twelve Months in the Tampa Urban League," 1927; Report, Toledo Urban League, 1931; Sixth Annual Report, Saint Paul–Minneapolis Urban League; "Important Achievements of Pearl Street Community Center," 1927; "Summary of the Work of the Warren Urban League," 1931; Annual Report, Urban League of Lincoln, Nebraska, 1935; Annual Report, Wheatley Social Center, 1930; Annual Report, Detroit Urban League, 1930; Records of the National Urban League, LC.

73. Report, Frederick Douglass Community Association, Toledo Urban League, 1930, ibid.

74. "A Social Service Achievement: A Four Year Record," Douglas Community Center, Springfield Urban League, 1930, ibid. The Armstrong Association similarly showed its discontent with the limited employment opportunities for blacks when it stopped placing black women in domestic service, with the aim of calling attention to the lack of industrial jobs. In spite of this stance, in 1927 the Association managed to place 356 women and 627 men in employment. Annual Report, Armstrong Association of Philadelphia, 1918, ibid.

75. "Twelve Months in the Tampa Urban League"; "Action on Interracial Frontiers: The National Urban League Comes of Age," 1930, ibid.

76. Williamson, *Crucible of Race*, pp. 77–78, and Davis, *Spearheads for Reform*, pp. 101–2.

77. Cryer, "Mary White Ovington," pp. 517–19.

78. The friendship between Ovington and Du Bois exploded during the 1930s over the argument about whether the NAACP should attempt economic reform or continue its course of legal action. See Cryer, "Mary White Ovington," pp. 518–19. Ovington to Du Bois, June 10, 1904, Du Bois Papers, UMASS.

79. Ovington to Du Bois, June 6, 1904, Du Bois Papers, UMASS.

80. Ibid., January 9, 1905.

81. Ibid., January 25, 1905.

82. Ibid.

83. Ibid., and Cryer, "Ovington and the Rise of the NAACP."

84. Ovington to Du Bois, October 7, 1904, and January 25, 1905, Du Bois Papers, UMASS.

85. Cryer, "Mary White Ovington," pp. 517–19; Ovington, *Walls Came Tumbling Down*, pp. 43–52, and *Half a Man*, p. ii.

86. Du Bois's realization that the NAACP emphasized political power to the exclusion of economic strength led him to resign from the organization he had been so influential in building. Wolters, *Negroes and the Great Depression*, pp. 266–301.

Chapter 2

1. Du Bois, *Philadelphia Negro*, p. 205.

2. Frazier, *Negro Church in America*.

3. Lincoln, "Black Church in the Context of American Religion," pp. 52–75. Scholar Gayrand Wilmore called the Free African Society that laid the cornerstone for the founding in 1816 of the national African Methodist Episcopal Church, "the classic pattern for the black church in the U.S." It combined free worship and mutual welfare programs with the "objective of providing not only for religious needs, but for social service, mutual aid, and solidarity." Quoted in Lincoln, "The Black Church," pp. 54–55.

4. Davis, *Spearheads for Reform*, pp. xii, 23. Davis justifies his examination of sources primarily for Boston, Chicago, and New York, with the claim that "the movement was strongest and most concerned with reform" in those cities. This regional bias, as well as his study of the confined years of 1890 to 1914, merely reinforces the unfounded presupposition that southern settlements were scarce and weak and that religious motives completely undermined the settlement effort.

5. Kennedy, "Types of Settlements, 1930s," Folder 18, Box 3, Kennedy Papers, SWHA.

6. Ibid.

7. Klein, "Settlement Movement," in *From Philanthropy to Social Welfare*. In "Negro and the Charity Organization Society," p. 20, Kogut shows that the COS adapted its Social Darwinist, laissez-faire view of welfare that emphasized individual rather than social shortcomings to the progressive urge toward reform aimed at poor immigrants. Significantly, this organization toed the color line, dropped all talk of assimilation, and continued stressing "character reform rather than social reform" when it came to blacks. Davis, *Spearheads for Reform*, p. 17, writes that "especially annoying to many settlement workers were the people who confused settlements with missions, or those who assumed that settlements and charity organizations were somehow connected, even synonymous. The latter carried special irony because in one sense the settlement movement began as a protest against the very methods and philosophy of organized charity."

8. "'Settlements' or 'Missions,'" in Barnett and Barnett, *Towards Social Reform*, pp. 271–73. In 1883, Reverend Canon Samuel A. Barnett, of St. Jude's Church, Whitechapel, E. London, inspired a group of university students at Cambridge to begin the first settlement, Toynbee Hall in London, by suggesting the "settlement idea." White, "Social Settlement," pp. 47–48.

9. Barnett and Barnett, *Towards Social Reform*, pp. 274, 284–85.

10. Ibid., p. 285.

11. Ibid., pp. 274, 286.

12. White, "Social Settlement," pp. 51–57.

13. Woods and Kennedy, *Handbook of Settlements*, p. v.

14. Hutchinson, "Cultural Strain and Protestant Liberalism." Hutchinson shows that the answer to whether Protestantism was waxing or waning in the late nineteenth century differed drastically according to the observer. Social Gospelers responded to what they perceived as a declining interest in religion and the deteriorating appeal of Protestant churches; in fact, Hutchinson's study of the careers of evangelical reformers concluded that this perception was a main cause of the Social Gospel movement.

15. Woods, *City Wilderness*, pp. 225–30.

16. Davis, *Spearheads for Reform*, p. 15 and p. 262, n. 33. The statistics, based on the

Handbook of Settlements by Woods and Kennedy, are roughly 400 "bona fide" and 167 religious settlements in 1910 (24 Jewish, 31 Methodist, 29 Episcopal, 20 Presbyterian, 10 Congregational). The *Handbook* only mentioned the existence of about twenty Catholic settlements. Apparently, the 2,500 Catholic settlements cited by others as existing in 1915 did not even come close enough to count in the roll of religious settlements. Figures for Catholic settlements come from Abell, *American Catholicism and Social Action*, pp. 155–66. For evidence of a strong Catholic settlement movement, see McGinley, "A New Field," which draws parallels between convent and settlement life; and McGinley, "The Scope of the Catholic Social Settlement."

17. "Social Settlements and the Church," *Nashville Christian Advocate*, p. 3.

18. Taylor, "Southern Social Awakening."

19. Davis, *Spearheads for Reform*, pp. 14–17, acknowledges the influence of the Social Gospel on the settlement movement, but thinks that religious organizations adopted the techniques of settlements rather than vice versa.

20. White, "Social Settlement," p. 70.

21. *Settlement Goals*, pp. 22, 36.

22. Standard texts on the Social Gospel include Abell, *Urban Impact*; May, *Protestant Churches*; Hopkins, *Rise of the Social Gospel*; and Carter, *Decline and Revival of the Social Gospel*. Since the 1960s, several historians have revised the study of the Social Gospel, pointing out that the South partook in the movement within the limits of its regional culture; see, for instance, Eighmy, *Churches in Cultural Captivity*, and Hill, "South's Two Cultures" in a collection of essays he edited, *Religion and the Solid South*. More compelling, however, is Luker, "Social Gospel," who questions the explanation of the Social Gospel as a response to urban industrialism. Instead Luker sees it as an outgrowth of abolition and antebellum voluntary societies and directly related to the reform of race relations in the form of home missions, colonization societies, and post-abolition movements for civil equality. The existence of an antebellum pan-Protestant crusade for better race relations paved the way for missionary efforts that continued until reactionary white Southerners and other forces crushed the movement. My analysis seeks to add the failure of northern, urban reformers to make common cause with religious liberals to the reasons for the failure of racial reform. Another enlightening book, McDowell's *Social Gospel in the South*, highlights schisms within the ranks of Southerners over interpreting the Social Gospel; he finds that church women held a much more activist, reformist theory of religion than the church fathers.

23. For the centrality of religion to southern life, see, for instance, Cash, *Mind of the South*.

24. Conference Report, International Sunday School Association, Field Workers and Superintendent and State Secretaries, 1907, Greensboro, North Carolina, Hampton.

25. Hartshorn, *Era of Progress and Promise*, p. vi.

26. Ibid., p. vii.

27. Du Bois, "Negro Church," in *Atlanta University Publications*, pp. 2–7.

28. Frazier, "Psychological Factors in Negro Health"; about Frazier's contributions to social change, see Platt and Chandler, "Constant Struggle: E. Franklin Frazier and Black Social Work in the 1920s."

29. Cooper to Kennedy, June 9, 1925, Folder 94: "Interracial Study: Pennsylvania, 1925–1944," Box 9, National Federation of Settlements (NFS) Papers, SWHA.

30. Johnson, *Social Work of the Churches*, pp. 56–74.

31. Ibid., p. 164.

32. Elliott, "After Twenty Years," p. 252.

33. Elliott, NFS Settlement Conference, 1916, p. 19.

34. Martin, "Community Church and the Ethical Movement."

35. Young, Director of Carver House Community Center, to Kennedy, August 28, 1945, Folder 79: "Interracial Study: Missouri, 1933–1945," Box 8, Kennedy Papers, SWHA. Further research is needed on the racial policies of Ethical Societies in other cities to determine whether the St. Louis branch was typical.

36. Trolander discusses these factors briefly in her book, *Settlement Houses*. Davis, *Spearheads for Reform*, p. 234, thinks that the decline of the settlement movement in the 1920s resulted partly from its own success.

37. Frank, "An American Looks at His World: Unsettling the Social Settlement."

38. Lewis, *Babbitt*, p. 17.

39. Minutes of NFS Conference, May 24, 1926, Cleveland, NFS Microfilm, SWHA.

40. Trolander's entire book *Settlement Houses* rests on the thesis that Community Chest funding caused the metamorphosis of the settlement from a Progressive Era reform aimed at social change to the more staid New Deal institution that merely delivered services. Trolander cites the loss of financial independence for growing conservatism. "Well-to-do people who controlled the pursestrings of private charity were adamantly opposed to the New Deal. Furthermore, with the rise of the Community Chest, they had extended their control over private charity. Therefore, it is not surprising that settlements were more central to reform in the Progressive Era than in the New Deal" (p. 31). While no doubt partially true, this argument is incomplete because it is ahistorical. The huge private donors relied upon in the Progressive Era kept the settlement houses well within the bounds of respectability. Indeed, it was the settlement workers' ability to move within the two worlds of the wealthy and the working class that gave them their unique identity. This view also ignores the political reality of persecution of anyone with supposed Communist leanings during the "Red Scare," such as Jane Addams. Dissension within the movement about the future direction of social activism also remains unaddressed. For Kellogg's comment, see Minutes of NFS Conference, May 24, 1926, Cleveland, NFS Microfilm, SWHA.

41. Minutes of the Executive Committee of the National Federation of Settlements, May 13, 1923, NFS Microfilm, SWHA.

42. Ibid., February 22, 1924.

43. Business Meeting Minutes, January 25, 1924, NFS Microfilm, SWHA.

44. Minutes of NFS Meeting, 1928, Cleveland, ibid.

45. Minutes of the Executive Committee, April 12–15, 1928, Boston, ibid.

46. Ibid.

47. Ibid.

48. Ibid.

49. Cooper made this comment at the Executive Committee Meeting, April 12–15, Boston, p. 27; Simkhovitch expressed her view at a Meeting in Cleveland in 1928, p. 46; both in NFS Microfilm, SWHA.

50. Dinning, "The Jane Addams of the South," unidentified clipping, Box 33, Folder 321: "Louisville, Kentucky, Neighborhood House, 1898–1950"; and Folder 323: "New Orleans, Louisiana, Kingsley House, 1920–1954," Box 33, NFS Papers, SWHA.

51. McDowell, *Social Gospel*, pp. 84–115.

52. Secretary to Louise Young, Field Report, Folder 522: "Nashville, Tennessee, Bethlehem Center, 1933–1952," Box 49, NFS Papers; the minutes of a NFS Board of Directors Meeting, January 26–27, 1935, called it "an interracial experiment of long standing" but even so, questioned whether it might be "a missionary group." NFS Microfilm, SWHA.

53. Minutes of Board of Directors Meeting, June 6–8, 1935, Montreal, NFS Microfilm, SWHA.

54. Trolander, *Settlement Houses.*

55. Minutes of Board of Directors Meeting, December 4–5, 1937, summarized in Memoranda dated December 23, 1937, Folder: "Membership Standards and Admissions Committee, 1937–1952," Box 12, NFS Papers, Supplement 2, SWHA.

56. Ibid.

57. Folder: "Membership Standards and Admissions Committee, 1937–1952," Box 12, NFS Papers, Supplement 2, SWHA.

58. Ingram, "The Settlement Movement in the South."

59. Ibid., 38. In a later study, "The Movement of the Settlement House Idea into the South," Speizman echoes the biases of the movement when he writes that houses like Kingsley House in New Orleans were "the only genuine social settlements in their communities." He gives the impression that cultural "lag" caused the South to be far behind the North; the South was still recovering from the Civil War and had homogeneous populations, fewer metropolises, and a smaller number of immigrants. He seeks to redress the way the South has been written out of the history of social reform, yet devotes only a brief paragraph to blacks, Hispanics, and religious activism.

60. Wright to Kennedy, July 14, 1945, Folder 98: "Interracial Study: Tennessee, 1923–1947," Box 9, Kennedy Papers, SWHA.

61. Chicago Commission on Race Relations, *Negro in Chicago,* pp. 142–44.

62. Wright to Kennedy, July 14, 1945, Folder 98: "Interracial Study, Tennessee, 1923–1947," Box 9, Kennedy Papers, SWHA.

63. Graham to Kennedy, January 7, 1946, Folder 99: "Interracial Study, Texas, 1930–1948," Box 9, ibid.

64. Ibid.

65. Longstreth to Miller, June 7, 1945, Folder 55: "Interracial Study: Correspondence and Papers, 1945–1946," Kennedy Papers, SWHA.

66. Ibid.; Lippincott, clipping from *The Friend* (April 26, 1928): 537–38, Folder 95: "Interracial Study, Pennsylvania, 1944–1946," Box 9, Kennedy Papers, SWHA.

67. Tingley to Kennedy, September 11, 1945, Kennedy Papers, SWHA.

68. Ibid.

69. Unsigned letter to McCullough, November 20, 1915, Box 7, Folder 71: "Interracial Study: Kentucky, 1915–1947," Kennedy Papers, SWHA.

70. "Dorchester Data," prepared by the Missions Council of the Congregational Christian Churches, Folder 67: "Interracial Study, Georgia, 1945–1947," Box 7, ibid.

71. Burdick to Kennedy, August 24, 1945, Folder 84: "Interracial Study, New York, 1945–1946," Box 8, ibid.

72. Kennedy to Rosenstein, July 5, 1946, Folder 55: "Interracial Study: Correspondence and Papers, 1945–1946," ibid.

73. Kennedy to Little, December 11, 1945, Folder 71: "Interracial Study, Kentucky, 1915–1947," Box 7; Hope Community Center and Grace Community Center, Annual Report, 1944, Folder 71: "Interracial Study, Kentucky, 1915, 1947," Box 7, ibid.

74. "Faith Presbyterian Church and Service Center," pamphlet, Folder 62: "Interracial Study: California, 1946," Box 7, ibid.

75. Meeker, *Six Decades of Service.*

76. Bennett, quoted in McDowell, *Social Gospel,* p. 84.

77. See, for example, Women's Missionary Society leader Lily Hammond's works advocating social change, *In Black and White* and *Southern Women and Race Adjustment,* both published during the zenith of white racism in the South.

78. The women of the Methodist Episcopal Church, South, were inspired by the northern settlement movement and tried to carry out its ideals. R. W. MacDonell, "Wesley Houses and the Social Work of the Women's Home Mission Society."

79. Report on a Meeting of Representatives of Religious Organizations Sponsoring Neighborhood Centers and the NFSNC, May, 1952, p. 4, NFS Papers, SWHA.

80. Adler, "The Question of an Ethical Creed."

81. Ibid., p. 161.

Chapter 3

1. Ovington, "Negro in America: Today and Tomorrow."

2. Armstrong, *Education for Life,* pp. 18–43. For Booker T. Washington's interpretation and promotion of industrial training, see his "Fruits of Industrial Training."

3. Washington, "Speech at the Memorial Service for Samuel Chapman Armstrong," May 25, 1893, in Harlan, Kaufman, and Smock, *Booker T. Washington Papers,* 3:317.

4. Ibid., 3:319–20. The "mortgage system," in contemporary usage, connoted the crop-lien or sharecropping sytem that replaced slavery as the main economic relation between the races in the South at the end of Reconstruction. In other forums, Washington told this same story with language only slightly altered. See, for instance, his "Speech before the New York Congregational Club," January 16, 1893, ibid., pp. 284–85.

5. Washington, "Speech at the Memorial Service for Samuel Chapman Armstrong," ibid., p. 320.

6. Washington, "Speech before the New York Congregational Club," January 16, 1893, ibid., p. 285.

7. Washington quoted in Ludlow, "An Account of the Tuskegee Negro Conference," February 20–21, 1895, ibid., p. 523.

8. For the extent of community and educational work undertaken by Hampton graduates, see, for instance, Williams, "Hampton Graduates as Teachers."

9. Anderson, "Hampton Model," p. 61. Donald Spivey gives a similar rendition of industrial education in *Schooling for the New Slavery.* While his criticisms of the education offered at Tuskegee are well founded, he underemphasizes the importance of one aspect of the Hampton model, which he acknowledges as "the school-community movement." Other works that discuss the debate over industrial education include Hawkins, *Booker T. Washington and His Critics,* a collection of writings by Washington's contemporary critics; Sherer, *Subordination or Liberation?*; Aptheker, *Education of Black People*; Bond, *Education of the Negro.*

10. Anderson, "The Hampton Model," p. 62. On innovations in American education, see Cremin, *Transformation of the School*; and Curti, *Social Ideas of American Educators.*

11. On the replacement of slavery with a new type of bondage in sharecropping or the crop-lien system, see Ransom and Sutch, *One Kind of Freedom*; Shlomowitz, "Ori-

gins of Southern Sharecropping"; Mandle, *Roots of Black Poverty*; Foner, *Nothing but Freedom*; and Wiener, *Social Origins of the New South*. On urban living conditions for blacks, see Rabinowitz, *Race Relations in the Urban South*; Harris, *Harder We Run*; Osofsky, *Harlem*; Spear, *Black Chicago*; and other studies of particular ghettos. A number of excellent studies have described the emergence of a new set of social relations in the late nineteenth and early twentieth centuries and the racial ideologies underpinning the renewed subordination of blacks, such as Newby's *Jim Crow's Defense*; and Gaston, *New South Creed*. Tindall writes that "the whole country was drifting closer to the white South's racial attitudes" with the popularity of Social Darwinism and imperialism at the turn of the century that helped bring about an "increasing respectability of racism." See Chapter 4 on "The Central Theme Revisited" in his *Ethnic Southerners*, especially p. 70.

12. Photos of Tuskegee Institute students in agricultural classes, Carrie Burton Overton Collection, ALUA. Stanfield describes the relation between the racial thinking of American social scientists and the foundations that funded their research. While his interpretation offers many brilliant observations, it smacks of determinism and thus ignores the ability and tendency of people to retain agency even within an intellectually oppressive situation. See his *Philanthropy and Jim Crow*.

13. Jacoway, *Yankee Missionaries in the South*, pp. 4–6; Jones is quoted on p. 6. See Chapter 1, "Industrial Education Myth," for an excellent discussion of the clashing interpretations of industrial education.

14. Ibid., pp. 252–67.

15. McPherson, "White Liberals and Black Power in Negro Education."

16. Du Bois, *Souls of Black Folk*, p. 100, quoted in McPherson, ibid., p. 1358.

17. Washington, "The Tuskegee Woman's Club."

18. See the remarkable work conducted by women described in Neverdon-Morton's *Afro-American Women*.

19. Washington to Cable, January 9, 1891, in Harlan et al., *Washington Papers*, pp. 120–21.

20. From a slide of the interior of Lee Plantation Church, Calhoun Colored School and Social Settlement, Slides, Hampton.

21. Washington, "Address at the Funeral of Dillingham," October 17, 1894, in Harlan et al., *Washington Papers*, pp. 481–82.

22. Washington, "Key Note," quoted in "Proceedings of the Triennial Reunion of the Hampton Alumni Association," May 28, 1893, ibid., p. 324.

23. Washington to Dillingham, August 15, 1891, in Harlan, *Washington Papers*, pp. 163–64.

24. Washington, "Address at the Funeral of Dillingham," ibid., p. 482.

25. Dillingham, "Account of the Tuskegee Negro Conference," February 21, 1893, ibid., pp. 295–96.

26. Washington, "Address at the Funeral of Dillingham," ibid., p. 482.

27. Footnote 1 for a letter from Frissell to Washington, July 24, 1891, ibid., p. 162; and Ellis, "The Calhoun School, Miss Charlotte Thorn's 'Lighthouse on the Hill.'"

28. Washington, "Address at the Funeral of Dillingham," p. 482; and Washington to Dillingham, August 15, 1891, pp. 163–64, both in Harlan et al., *Washington Papers*.

29. Washington, "An Address at the Funeral of Dillingham," ibid., p. 483.

30. Hartshorn, *Era of Progress and Promise*, p. 335. In the *Twentieth Annual Report of the Principal of the Calhoun Colored School*, teachers compared the academic program of Calhoun to progressive schools of the North, p. 21. The traveling library is described in

the *Ninth Annual Report of the Principal of the Calhoun Colored School*, p. 43; this report also shows pictures of the old school building beside the new, a dramatic contrast, on p. 20.

31. *Ninth Annual Report, Calhoun*, pp. 24–25.

32. *Circular of Information for Students and Applicants*, pp. 3, 8–14.

33. Ibid., pp. 9, 23–25.

34. *Twentieth Annual Report, Calhoun*, pp. 26–31. See Dabney, *Universal Education in the South*, 1:488, for a brief account of this plan.

35. *Twentieth Annual Report, Calhoun*, p. 15.

36. *Sixteenth Annual Report, Calhoun*, pp. 9–10; *Thirteenth Annual Report, Calhoun*, pp. 8–10.

37. Sibley to Dickinson, September 29, 1915, Calhoun School Papers, Hampton.

38. *Twentieth Annual Report, Calhoun*, pp. 9, 18; *Ninth Annual Report, Calhoun*, p. 9; *Sixteenth Annual Report, Calhoun*, pp. 11–13; *Nineteenth Annual Report, Calhoun*, pp. 47–50, 60.

39. *Thirteenth Annual Report, Calhoun*, pp. 11–13. "Home visiting" was a common activity of early settlement workers in the cities of the Northeast and Midwest. Lillian Wald, for instance, used this technique as the basis for a whole program of trained "visiting nurses" at Henry Street Settlement in New York City, as she discussed in her *House on Henry Street*. Mothers' Club information was culled from the *Sixteenth Annual Report, Calhoun*, pp. 17–18.

40. Hartshorn, *Era of Progress*, p. 337; *What Hampton Graduates Are Doing*.

41. Calhoun School Report from 1902, pp. 3–4, Calhoun-General Education Board Folder, Hampton Archives.

42. On Smith-Lever and the beginning of a favorable national attitude toward agricultural experimentation that had struggled at the grass-roots level for years, see Brunner and Yang, *Rural America*, pp. 13–16; Bliss et al., *Spirit and Philosophy of Extension Work*, pp. 112–15; Blauch, *Federal Cooperation*, pp. 86–94. Also cited, Trustees of Calhoun Colored School to Gates, Chairman of the General Education Board, January 7, 1916, Calhoun-General Education Board Folder, Hampton. This letter asked for a renewal of the previous year's appropriation of $5,000 from the General Education Board.

43. "Plantations Paid For," unidentified clipping (probably 1904), Calhoun School Papers, Hampton.

44. Dabney, *Universal Education*, pp. 487–88.

45. Ibid., p. 487; Thorn to Frissell, January 21, 1909; Thorn to Frissell, January 26, 1909. The Hirsh land scheme was also mentioned in Thorn to Frissell, February 22, 1909, Calhoun Papers, Hampton.

46. Thorn to Frissell; Phenix to Hallowell, November 17, 1924, ibid.

47. Jenkins to Gregg, August 28, 1924; the quote is from an unsigned letter to Jenkins, September 2, 1924, ibid.

48. Beard to Frissell, May 13, 1915; Dickinson, Guernsey, and Hallowell to the Trustees of Calhoun Colored School, October 14, 1915, ibid.

49. Farnham to Scoville, May 19, 1915, ibid.

50. Beard to Frissell, May 13, 1915; Dickinson, Guernsey, and Hallowell to the Trustees of Calhoun Colored School, October 14, 1915, ibid.

51. Thorn to Frissell, January 1, 1913. Thorn wrote Frissell about Field at another point that it was difficult to believe that he could "identify himself with a work that he was not in sympathy with and for a people that he did not believe in thoroughly and entirely as we do." Another teacher, Cornelia Bowen at Mt. Meigs, Alabama, said that she would

quit her position in sympathy if Field did not leave Calhoun, stating that men refuse to work under his supervision. Thorn to Frissell, December 15, 1912, ibid.

52. Record Office Report, Hampton Institute, July 1924, ibid. This report said that one of the black men "became interested in one of the white teachers at Calhoun this year and the young woman was very indiscreet and seemed rather glad to receive his attentions."

53. Kirby to Gregg, July 19, 1924, ibid.

54. Brown to Gregg, July 14, 1924, ibid.

55. Webb to Charlotte Thorn, May 20, 1924, ibid.

56. Hallowell to Gregg, September 17, 1924, ibid.

57. Ibid., September 26, 1924.

58. Ibid., September 17, 1924.

59. Phenix to Hallowell, October 20, 1924, Calhoun Papers, Hampton.

60. President of the Board of Trustees of Calhoun Colored School to Thorn, March 21, 1927, ibid. One trustee wrote that he voted to have Thorn leave the school, but changed his mind because "if we insist on that plan of action, she will go out a broken-hearted woman who will consider that she had been very badly treated, and this will mean, of course, that we will lose the support of a great number of very valuable friends of the school." Unsigned to Frothingham, July 2, 1924, ibid.

61. Thorn to Frissell, October 13, 1916; Thorn to Frissell, November 14, 1916, ibid. Blauch discussed the fomenting interest in the U.S. Congress in vocational education during the years leading up to the passage of the Smith-Hughes Act in January of 1917 in his *Federal Cooperation in Agricultural Extension Work*, pp. 101–8.

62. Brown, Rhetta, and Roper to Hallowell, November 30, 1923, Calhoun Papers, Hampton.

63. Unsigned letter to Frothingham, July 2, 1924, ibid.

64. President of the Board of Trustees to Thorn, March 21, 1927, ibid.

65. Thorn to Howe, November 5, 1931, ibid.

66. Loud, "Calhoun's Urgent Need of Funds," *Boston Transcript*, March 9, 1932, clipping in ibid.

67. Loud to Howe, June 22, 1932, ibid.

68. Telegram from Administrative Board of Hampton Institute to Calhoun Colored School, August 29, 1932, ibid.

69. Ovington, "Woman Who Answered a Prayer," *The Woman Citizen* (March 1927), in ibid.

70. Davis to Frissell, January 12, 1917, ibid.

71. Frothingham, "For Calhoun School," December 11, 1924, unidentified clipping, ibid.

72. Phenix to Hallowell, November 17, 1924, ibid.

73. Harrington, *Other America*.

74. Jones to the Trustees and Friends of the Calhoun Colored School, concerning the Subsistence Homestead Project in Lowndes County, Alabama, n.d., Calhoun Papers, Hampton.

75. Jones, "The Calhoun School: A Successful Demonstration of Rural Reconstruction and Community Education," including a letter from Alexander to Jones, December 23, 1935, ibid.

76. Ibid.

77. *Forty-first Annual Report, Calhoun*.

78. Jones, "Calhoun School"; Minutes of the Corporation Meeting of Calhoun Colored School, February 4, 1937, Calhoun Papers, Hampton.

79. Minutes of the Meeting of the Board of Trustees of Calhoun Colored School, January 14, 1938, ibid.

80. Donald Holley, "Negro in the New Deal Resettlement Program." This fascinating article points out the weaknesses of the resettlement program, particularly the tendencies to create segregated communities, to deny blacks leading administrative positions, and to fall short of projected goals.

81. Minutes of the Meeting of the Board of Trustees of Calhoun Colored School, November 7, 1935, Calhoun Papers, Hampton.

82. Kidder to the Board of Trustees of Calhoun Colored School, May 3, 1938, ibid.

83. Rhetta to the Board of Trustees of Calhoun Colored School, n.d., ibid.

84. Calhoun School Records, Savery Library, Talladega College.

85. For resounding criticism of Jones's tendency to support white over black leadership of projects designed to help blacks, see Du Bois, "Thomas Jesse Jones."

86. Washington to Frissell, February 25, 1905, People's Village School Papers, Hampton.

87. Clipping, *Talks and Thoughts* (June 1895); clipping, *Talks and Thoughts* (September 1892); Washington, "Resident Graduate's Fifteen Years at Hampton," *Southern Workman* (July 1892); "Georgia Washington," clipping, *Southern Workman* (August 1902), ibid. While working under Thorn and Dillingham, Washington wrote, "I never enjoyed anything any more than being here among these people who seem to be just waking up." Washington, clipping, "A Southern Letter," *Talks and Thoughts* (February 1893). She also commented on the beauty of the place, and her surprise that "the colored people are in a better condition than I dreamed of finding them; they are thrifty, as far as they know how to be; most of them are neat and clean in their dress and homes." Washington, clipping, "A Letter from the Calhoun School" (January 1893), ibid.

88. *Third Annual Report of the People's Village School*; Washington, "General Armstrong," *Southern Workman* (August 1916); Washington, "A Well-Spent Life," *Southern Workman* (November 1917); Washington, "A Resident Graduate's Fifteen Years at Hampton," *Southern Workman* (July 1892), clippings, People's Village School Papers, Hampton.

89. Washington, "Resident Graduate's Fifteen Years at Hampton," *Southern Workman* (July 1892), clipping, ibid.

90. Washington to Frissell, February 25, 1905, ibid.

91. Ibid.

92. Ibid., December 2, 1898.

93. Ibid., May 10, 1909, and December 3, 1904.

94. Ibid., June 6, 1906.

95. *Twenty-first Annual Report of People's Village School*, People's Village School Papers, Hampton.

96. Hampton "Principal's Annual Report," *Southern Workman* (May 1907), clipping, ibid. The article noted that Washington "has made an oasis in the desert of ignorance, with the help of her brave little band of workers, some of whom have refused comfortable salaries in city schools in order to make possible this life of self-sacrificing devotion, where salaries are never assured and where the necessities of life are not always forthcoming."

97. In 1894, the tuition varied according to class: seventy-five cents for the highest,

sixty for the middle grades, and fifty cents for the primary grade; in *Southern Workman* (April 1894), clipping. Students often had to walk miles to school. In addition, many boys would wake up at four in the morning and plow until nine, then go to school for a full day. In *Twentieth Annual Report of People's Village School*; both in ibid.

98. Untitled clipping, *Southern Workman* (August 1898), ibid.

99. A clipping in *Southern Workman* (April 1894) read, "None ought to be turned away from school, for that means something worse than despair; this is their only hope, and unless the house goes up during the summer, they will have to be refused. The people ought to pay 350 dollars themselves, but a good deal depends on the success of the cotton crop." Also "News from Mt. Meigs," unidentified clipping. Both in ibid.

100. "A Black Belt Missionary," unidentified clipping, 1899; and unidentified clipping in *Southern Workman* (April 1894), both in ibid.

101. *Seventeenth Annual Report of People's Village School*, ibid.

102. *Outline of Course of Study of People's Village School*, n.d., ibid.

103. Washington, "Dear Friends," *Southern Workman* (May 1896), ibid.

104. Clipping, *Southern Workman* (August 1902); *Third Annual Report of the People's Village School*, both in ibid.

105. Davis, "What Hampton Graduates Are Doing," unidentified clipping, 1905, ibid.
106. Ibid.

107. *Twentieth Annual Report of People's Village School*, People's Village School Papers, Hampton.

108. *Seventeenth Annual Report of People's Village School*, ibid.

109. Unidentified clipping, *Southern Workman* (April 1894); *Third Annual Report of People's Village School*, ibid.

110. *Fourth Annual Report of People's Village School*, ibid.

111. *Third Annual Report of People's Village School*, ibid.

112. *Twenty-first Annual Report of People's Village School*, ibid.

113. *Seventeenth Annual Report of People's Village School*, ibid.

114. Washington to White, June 8, 1935, ibid.

115. Ibid., September 12, 1935; in a letter to George Peabody, July 22, 1935, White arranged for fifty dollars for travel money for Washington's vacation; in People's Village School Papers, Hampton.

116. Washington to White, September 24, 1935, ibid.

117. Washington to Cooper, February 22, 1946, ibid.

118. Ibid.

119. *Ninth Annual Report of People's Village School*, People's Village School Papers, Hampton.

120. Frissell, "Self-Sacrifice," an address to Hampton Institute teachers, *The Institute Journal* (August 1, 1903), ibid.

121. Smothers to Frissell, August 20, 1900, ibid.

122. Rose, *Rehearsal for Reconstruction*, pp. 76–79, 406–7; Woofter, *Black Yeomanry*, p. 35. Woofter wrote that "most of the land at Port Royal was sold for taxes in March, 1863. The government bid in about two-thirds of the amount and loyal citizens of the North the remainder. In September, 1863, the President issued instructions reserving 36 tracts of 160 acres each for school farms, the profits of which were to go to the education of the Negro, and certain tracts for 'heads of families of the African race.' " The portion for black families was divided and sold in ten acre lots, before the redemption act of 1872 allowed land in the government's possession to be reclaimed (pp. 42–44).

123. Woofter, *Black Yeomanry*, p. 193; and Robbins, "Rossa B. Cooley and Penn School," p. 43.

124. Cooley, *School Acres*, pp. 4–5. Cooley said that as she first found the school, education was "plastered on, regardless of the life and needs of the people" (p. 20).

125. Kellogg, Introduction to Cooley, *School Acres*, pp. xi–xii.

126. "Penn School Facts," pamphlet, Penn School Papers, Hampton.

127. *Penn School Catalogue 1945–1946*, ibid.

128. Kellogg, Introduction to Cooley, *School Acres*, pp. xvii–xviii; Cooley, quoted on p. xviii.

129. Cooley, *School Acres*, p. 47.

130. *Historical Handbook of Penn School and St. Helena Island, South Carolina*, pp. 1–20, pamphlet, Penn School Papers, Hampton.

131. Curtis, "Boston to Hear Penn School Singers," *Boston Evening Transcript*, August 21, 1926, clipping in ibid.

132. Jacoway, *Yankee Missionaries in the South*.

133. Cooley to Gregg, March 15, 1929, and clipping, "The New Because of the Old," *Southern Workman*, ibid.

134. David Butwin, "Booked for Travel: Low Country Safari," unidentified clipping, April 22, 1972, ibid.

Chapter 4

1. Hall, *Revolt Against Chivalry*.

2. Ibid., p. 86.

3. For accounts of the Tuskegee meeting and both conferences, see Neverdon-Morton, *Afro-American Women*, pp. 226–33, for black women's point of view; McDowell, *Social Gospel*, pp. 86–92, for Methodist women's point of view; Hall, *Revolt Against Chivalry*, pp. 86–95, 107–91, for the interracial aspect; and Rouse, *Lugenia Burns Hope*, pp. 107–14, for Lugenia Burns Hope's participation. Brown is quoted in Hall, *Revolt Against Chivalry*, p. 94. For biographical information, see "Margaret Murray Washington," in Brown, *Homespun Heroines*, pp. 225–30, and Stewart, "Charlotte Hawkins Brown," pp. 111–13.

4. Brown, "Southern Educational Conference."

5. For the doctrine of separate spheres, its sources and implications for the lives of women, see Welter, "The Cult of True Womanhood: 1820–1860," pp. 313–33; Smith-Rosenberg, *Disorderly Conduct*; Cott, *Bonds of Womanhood*; Degler, *At Odds*; and, for its philosophical implications, Elshtain, *Public Man, Private Woman*. A number of fascinating studies have illustrated how women transformed the restrictive doctrines of "separate spheres" and the "cult of true womanhood" into an expanded realm of activity that overflowed into the public arena. See, for instance, Douglas, *Feminization of American Culture*; Sklar, *Catharine Beecher*; and Epstein, *Politics of Domesticity*. Baker has shown how many women's experience in their separate sphere led to a unique female political culture that provided an alternative to the dominant male political style in "Domestication of Politics." Other scholars have even suggested that a female culture and politics paved the way for the emergence of the welfare state. See Koven and Michel, "Gender and the Origins of the Welfare State," and Gordon, *Heroes of Their Own Lives*.

6. Eugene, "Moral Values and Black Womanists"; Brown, "Womanist Consciousness"; Walker, *In Search of Our Mothers' Gardens*; Jones, *Labor of Love*; and many others.

Collins gives a succinct overview of "womanism" as formulated by a variety of thinkers; she equates the notion with a "humanist vision in Black feminist thought," in *Black Feminist Thought*, pp. 37–39. Scott points out that myths of womanhood differed from the reality of women's responsibilities even in the case of many southern white women in her book, *Southern Lady*, pp. 3–44.

7. Scott, "Most Invisible of All," p. 19.

8. Griffin's "'A Layin' on of Hands'" analyzes the differences between mutual aid activities of working women and benevolent activities of middle-class women aimed at working women. In many cases, Griffin notes, even the latter managed to cross the class barrier. In the 1920s, many middle-class women's organizations, however, began to distance themselves more from their working-class sisters. See also Neverdon-Morton, *Afro-American Women*, pp. 1–9, and Giddings, *When and Where I Enter*, pp. 178–79.

9. White, "The Cost of Club Work."

10. Scott, "Most Invisible of All," p. 12.

11. Giddings, *When and Where I Enter*; Carby, "It Jus Be's Dat Way Sometime"; Hine, "Rape and the Inner Lives of Black Women," pp. 912, 920; Brooks, "Religion, Politics, and Gender," p. 13.

12. Frederickson, "'Each One Is Dependent On the Other.'"

13. Giddings, *When and Where I Enter*, and Brown, quoted in Giddings, p. 173.

14. Terrell, for instance, also believed "that women were the leaders of the struggle for racial betterment," according to Neverdon-Morton, who cites her 1910 statement that "if anyone should ask me what special phase of the colored American's development makes me most hopeful of his ultimate triumph over present obstacles, I should answer unhesitatingly, it is the magnificent work the women are doing to regenerate and elevate the race." Quoted in *Afro-American Women*, p. 3.

15. Du Bois, "Efforts for Social Betterment," in *Atlanta University Publications*. On the essential role of voluntary societies in black communities, see, for instance, Franklin and Moss, *From Slavery to Freedom*; Jacobs, "Benevolent Societies"; and Layng, "Voluntary Associations." For an example of the political significance of one local voluntary association, see Hines and Jones, "A Voice of Black Protest."

16. See, for instance, Brooks, "Religion, Politics, and Gender"; Brown, "Womanist Consciousness"; and the numerous relevant essays in Hine, *Black Women in American History*, such as Gilkes, "'Together in Harness,'" 2:377–98.

17. Lerner, *Black Women in White America*, pp. 435–37. The direct catalyst for the formation of the National Association of Colored Women was a comment by James Jacks, president of the Missouri Press Association, who told the British antilynching society that "the Negroes in this country were wholly devoid of morality, the women were prostitutes and all were natural thieves and liars" (quoted in Lerner, p. 436). For the black women's antilynching movement, see Duster, *Crusade for Justice*. Other essential sources for the black women's club movement include Giddings, *Where and When I Enter*; Davis, "Black Women and the Club Movement," in her *Women, Race, and Class*; Lerner, "Community Work of Black Club Women"; Salem, *To Better Our World*; Dill, "Dialectics of Black Womanhood"; Neverdon-Morton, *Afro-American Women*; Griffin, "'A Layin' on of Hands,'" pp. 23–29; Jones, *Labor of Love*, pp. 190–95; Terborg-Penn and Harley, *Afro-American Women*; Harley, "Beyond the Classroom"; Gordon, "Black and White Visions of Welfare"; and Scott, "Most Invisible of All," pp. 3–22, and *Natural Allies*. Excellent early descriptions of the black women's club work are Williams, "Club Movement among Negro Women," and Davis, *Lifting as They Climb*.

18. Ruffin, address, National Conference of Colored Women, July 29–31, 1895, in Lerner, *Black Women in White America*, pp. 441. For a biographical sketch, see "Josephine St. Pierre Ruffin," in Brown, *Homespun Heroines*, pp. 151–53.

19. Brooks presents a provocative analysis of the campaign to reverse negative stereotypes. She asserts that emphasizing personal attributes such as hygiene and appearance "privatized racial discrimination" because it blamed racial inequality on the personality of the victim. Stressing the need first to change individual behavior, she writes, made racism "less subject to government regulation, to the authority of the public realm." "Religion, Politics, and Gender," p. 13.

20. Ruffin, address, First National Conference of Colored Women, July 29–31, 1895, in Lerner, *Black Women in White America*, p. 442.

21. Washington, "Club Work among Negro Women," excerpted in Lerner, *Black Women in White America*, pp. 443–47.

22. Williams, "Club Movement among Negro Women," in Gibson and Crogman, *Colored American*, pp. 225–26. She gives a thorough account of the "Ruffin Incident" on pp. 218–30. For another account of the affair, see Davis, "Black Women and the Club Movement," in *Women, Race, and Class*, pp. 127–33.

23. Rouse, *Lugenia Burns Hope*, pp. 30, 90; Shivery, "Neighborhood Union," p. 152. On Neighborhood Union, also see Neverdon-Morton, *Afro-American Women*, pp. 145–63; and Lerner, "Community Work of Black Club Women," pp. 88–93. Neighborhood Union is placed in the context of important innovations in social work that took place in Atlanta in Brawley, "Atlanta Striving," and Ross, "Black Heritage in Social Welfare."

24. "Gate City Free Kindergarten," flyer, excerpted in Lerner, *Black Women in White America*, p. 510.

25. Rouse, *Lugenia Burns Hope*, p. 31.

26. "Gate City Free Kindergarten," flyer, excerpted in Lerner, *Black Women in White America*, p. 512.

27. Rouse, *Lugenia Burns Hope*, p. 66.

28. Neverdon-Morton, *Afro-American Women*, p. 145; also "Neighborhood Union," a pamphlet commemorating the twenty-fifth anniversary of the organization, 1933, Hope Papers, UMASS.

29. Lerner, "Neighborhood Union: Summary of Activities," in *Black Women in White America*, p. 505.

30. "Neighborhood Union: Survey of Colored Public Schools," excerpted in Lerner, *Black Women in White America*, pp. 503–5.

31. Neverdon-Morton, *Afro-American Women*, pp. 153–59.

32. Shivery, "Neighborhood Union," p. 158.

33. Lerner, "Neighborhood Union: Summary of Activities," in *Black Women in White America*, pp. 506–8; "Neighborhood Union Program" and "Neighborhood Union—Review of Work 1929," Hope Papers, UMASS.

34. "Neighborhood Union," Hope Papers, UMASS.

35. Lerner, "Neighborhood Union: Summary of Activities," in *Black Women in White America*, p. 506.

36. "Neighborhood Union—Program" and Inquirers' Meeting Program, Hope Papers, UMASS.

37. Shivery, "Neighborhood Union," p. 156; Ross, "Black Heritage in Social Welfare," p. 306.

38. Lerner, "Neighborhood Union: Summary of Activities," in *Black Women in White*

America, pp. 505–9; "Neighborhood Union"; Memorandum of a Conversation of Mrs. John Hope with Mr. Nix of the Relief Center, December 22, 1931; and Petition to the Mayor and General Council of the City of Atlanta, May 23, 1932; in Hope Papers, UMASS.

39. "The Christmas Giver," December 1933, a Neighborhood Union appeal, Hope Papers, UMASS.

40. Mary De Bardeleben, "Training for Christian Negro Workers."

41. Ibid.; Ames and Newell, *"Repairers of the Breach,"* pp. 7–8; and Hammond, *Southern Women*, pp. 9–10. See Frederickson's intriguing work on the dynamics between black and white Methodist Episcopal women, " 'Each One Is Dependent on the Other.' "

42. Bennett, quoted in Letzig, *Expressions of Faith*, p. 28; [Goerner], "A Window and an Open Door," unpublished paper; MacDonell, "Wesley Houses"; *National Program Division Handbook: A Handbook of Programs, Projects, and Relationships.* Other Bethlehem Houses are described in Folder 12: "Fiftieth Anniversary of the Settlement Movement in the U.S., 1936," Box 2, NFS Papers, SWHA. See also Nutt, "Bethlehem Center, Nashville, Tennessee." In 1988, the National Division of Institutional Ministries ran seventy-seven community centers, seven schools, five health and/or aging facilities, ten residential programs, and ten youth homes. "National Division Institutional Ministries Historical Perspective."

43. [Goerner], "A Window and an Open Door"; "Chronological Summary of Bethlehem Community Center's History," Bethlehem Community Center, Augusta, Georgia, and Annual Report, 1944–45, Bethlehem Center, "Interracial Study: Georgia, 1945–1947," Kennedy Papers, SWHA.

44. [Goerner], "A Window and an Open Door," pp. 3–7.

45. Stevens and her college associates continued their interracial activities by meeting away from the campus. Stevens, interview by Hall, SOHP, February 13, 1972, pp. 1–17. See the helpful guide for a brief biography of Stevens and for biographical sketches and a listing of oral history interviews with a number of other women in the home missions movement who combined religious and community concerns in a powerful program for change both within and outside of the boundaries of the movement: Nasstrom, *Women's Voices.*

46. Young, interview by Hall, 1976, and Biographical Sketch, SOHP. The interview elaborates this activist religious worldview and offers another intriguing example of a white woman who devoted her energies to interracial organizing. Young was Chairman of the Committee on Interracial Cooperation of the Methodist Women's Missionary Council, member of the Board of Directors of the Nashville Bethlehem House, and involved in the national YWCA.

47. Stevens, interview, SOHP, pp. 16–22, and biographical sketch by Hall.

48. Ibid., pp. 47–50.

49. Ibid., pp. 53–54; [Goerner], "A Window and an Open Door," p. 2.

50. Stevens, interview, SOHP; [Goerner], "A Window and an Open Door."

51. Stevens, interview, SOHP, pp. 56–61.

52. Ibid., pp. 23–30.

53. Bell, *Missions and Cooperation*, p. 85. The quotation is from Fannie Bame, Director of the Bethlehem Community House in Augusta, Georgia, August 29, 1945, Folder 67: "Interracial Study, Georgia, 1945–1947," Box 7, Kennedy Papers, SWHA.

54. Harper, *Past Is Prelude*, pp. 34–35; Montalto, *International Institute Movement*, pp.

vii–xi; Mohl, "Americanization through Cultural Pluralism," Session 97, American Historical Association Meeting, Dallas, Texas, December 28–30, 1977, in possession of the National Board YWCA Library, New York City.

55. Hunton, "Women's Clubs: Caring for Young Women"; Butler and Barnes to Barnett, January 27, 1940, Claude Barnett/Associated Negro Press Papers, UMASS; and Anderson, "Home and Community."

56. Curtis, "A Girls' Clubhouse," pp. 295–96; Wilson, *Fifty Years of Association Work*, pp. 239, 271–72, 285. "Phillis" was commonly misspelled "Phyllis."

57. Curtis, "A Girls' Clubhouse," pp. 295–96.

58. Tobias, "The Colored YMCA," p. 33. On the work done by black men in the YMCA, see also Tobias, "A Decade of Student YMCA Work"; Hope, "Colored YMCA"; Franklin and Moss, *From Slavery to Freedom*, pp. 290, 302. On the black New York City YMCA, see Osofsky, *Harlem*; Williams, "To Elevate the Race"; other studies of particular cities and YMCA branches; and "Plans for the Celebration of the Fiftieth Anniversary of the Founding of the First Regular YMCA for Colored Men and Boys in the United States," Planning Conference, December 11, 1937, Philadelphia, Claude Barnett/Associated Negro Press Papers, UMASS.

59. Cross, "Grace Hoadley Dodge," in James, James, and Boyer, *Notable American Women*, 1:489–92.

60. "A Lost Friend." Elizabeth Ross Haynes became the first black member of the National Board in 1924. See Bogin, "Elizabeth Ross Haynes," pp. 324–25, and Hunton, "Women's Clubs: Caring for Young Women."

61. "Colored Girls in Cleveland"; Tyler, "Phyllis Wheatley Association," 121–26; and Jones, *Jane Edna Hunter*.

62. Sims, "YWCA at Detroit," pp. 335, 356.

63. Numerous examples of individual biographies indicate that this shift was common. About YWCA worker Daisy Florence Simms, for example, Flexner writes that until Simms became director of the YWCA's Industrial Department in 1909, her "concept of the needs of working women had reflected the conventional evangelical ideas of her Methodist upbringing." At first, she looked down on the working women and said she merely "wanted to give them religion." Concrete involvement in reform and association with other reformers and working women "converted her to the 'social gospel' of Walter Rauschenbusch and others, with its emphasis on economic reform, and she became convinced that no religious work among women in industry could have meaning unless it attempted to improve the bad working conditions which cramped and impoverished their spirits." Eleanor Flexner, "Daisy Florence Simms," in James, James, and Boyer, *Notable American Women*, 3:291–93.

64. Olcott, *Work of Colored Women*, pp. 46–47; "Report of Eva D. Bowles, Secretary for Colored Work: Convention, 1915–1920," Box 42b, Folder 6; and "The Colored Girl—A National Asset," unidentified clipping, January 1919, Box 42a, Folder 1, YWCA Papers, Smith.

65. Olcott, *Work of Colored Women*, pp. 46–49, 52–53, 64.

66. Ibid., pp. 48–49. The Girl Reserve Movement had one of the largest memberships of girls' clubs in the United States, with a membership of 325,000 in 1934. The YWCA devoted this aspect of its program to younger girls. It offered progressive education to supplement the public school, seeking to promote democratic participation in "community, national, and international life," creativity, character, cooperation, self-reliance, and

morality. Blacks and Native Americans also participated in the Girl Reserves, leading to their claim to be interracial. Vance, *Girl Reserve Movement*, pp. 2–4, 51.

67. Bowles, "Negro Women and the War," pp. 425–26.

68. Olcott, *Work of Colored Women*, p. 48.

69. Ibid., pp. 77–78.

70. Ibid., pp. 79–82.

71. Ibid., pp. 83–84.

72. Ibid., pp. 90–94.

73. Ibid., pp. 95–110. Olcott describes how, in East St. Louis, a black women's Phyllis Wheatley Club actually met evenings in the meat packing plant restrooms; women were not willing to travel to the club's headquarters in the evenings because of the strained racial situation that Rudwick elaborated in *Race Riot at East St. Louis*.

74. Olcott, *Work of Colored Women*, pp. 77, 109–11.

75. Report of Bowles, Secretary for Colored Work Convention, 1915–20, Box 42b, Folder 6; on Bowles, see Speer, "Eva D. Bowles," *Woman's Press*, clipping, July 1932, Box 32b, Folder 6, YWCA Papers, Smith.

76. Sims, "YWCA at Detroit," pp. 335, 356.

77. "Forward! We Have the Gas," in Annual Report, Southwest Belmont Branch YWCA, 1926, Temple.

78. Program of Annual Meeting, Southwest Belmont Branch YWCA, December 14, 1939, Temple.

79. Annual Report, Southwest Belmont Branch YWCA, 1935, Temple.

80. Ibid.

81. "Questionnaire—Educational," Southwest Belmont Branch YWCA, 1926–32, Temple.

82. "YWCA" Flyer, Membership Campaign, 1939, Southwest Belmont Branch YWCA, Temple.

83. "Interesting and Significant Gains," p. 6.

84. Rating Sheet, Employee Evaluation Form, 1932, Southwest Belmont Branch YWCA, Temple.

85. "Interesting and Significant Gains," p. 6.

86. Annual Report, 1935, Southwest Belmont Branch YWCA, and Photographs of Industrial Conferences, Temple.

87. Simkhovitch, *Settlement Primer*, pp. 21–22.

88. Minutes, Conference on Group Work, December 5, 1935, Southwest Belmont Branch YWCA, Temple.

89. Wilson, *Fifty Years of Association Work among Young Women*.

90. Poems quoted in "Material for Use in a Service for the Observance of Race Relations Sunday," February 10, 1935, National Student Council, YWCA, Temple. In "On the Edge of Tomorrow," Taylor describes the pioneering interracial efforts of the student YWCA and the adherence of many YWCA leaders to Gandhi's philosophy of nonviolent resistance. See particularly pp. 5–8, 44, 140–41, 159–67, and 217–18.

91. "Suggestions for YWCA Membership," Temple.

92. See, for example, Taylor, "On the Edge of Tomorrow"; Hall, *Revolt Against Chivalry*, pp. 103–4; and Scott, *Natural Allies*, pp. 108–9. Salem, in *To Better Our World*, pp. 240–53, emphasizes the limitations of the YWCA's interracial movement. See also Center for Racial Justice and Services to Student Associations Unit, National Board

YWCA, *Highlights of Steps*; Harper, *Past Is Prelude*; Bell and Wilkins, *Interracial Practices in Community YWCAs*, for information on the interracial organizing of the YWCA.

93. The gold mine of recent oral history interviews conducted by the Black Women Oral History Project and the Southern Oral History Program reveals the astonishing numbers of women, both black and white, who became involved in the YWCA and later moved on into the interracial movement, civil rights, and other movements for social justice. For just a few examples, see Stokes, interview by Watson, 1979, in Hill, BWOHP, 9:123–215; Adams, interview by Banks, 1977, BWOHP, 1:103–21; Williams, interview by Tate, 1977, BWOHP, 10:275–308; and Stone, interview by Gluck, part 2 of a series of interviews, 1975, SOHP.

94. Height, interview by Cowan, 1974–76, in Hill, BWOHP, 5:35–39; and Height, interview by Mosby, 1970, CRDP.

95. Height, interview, BWOHP, 5:35–39, 44, 47, 50.

96. Ibid., pp. 50–53, 63.

97. Ibid., p. 101.

98. Height, *Step by Step with Interracial Groups*.

99. Height, interview, BWOHP, 5:85.

Conclusion

1. Karger, "Phyllis Wheatley House," p. 84.

2. Trolander, *Settlement Houses*, pp. 135–36; Karger, "Phyllis Wheatley House," pp. 83–85; and Minutes of the Executive Committee Board Annual Business Meeting, June 1934 to May 1935, National Federation of Settlements Papers, SWHA.

3. For the idea of settlement work in the Progressive Era, see, for just a few examples, Addams, *Twenty Years at Hull-House*; Barnett and Barnett, *Towards Social Reform*; Taylor, *Pioneering on Social Frontiers*; Wald, *House on Henry Street*; Woods, *City Wilderness*; and Woods and Kennedy, *Handbook of Settlements*.

4. On the shift from group work to casework, see Trolander, *Settlement Houses*, pp. 26–30, 48, 68.

5. Simkhovitch, "Casework as the Settlement Sees It," unidentified clipping [1932?], Folder 40: "Casework, 1922–1932," Box 6, NFS Papers, SWHA.

6. Hansen, "The Child Guidance Clinic of Abraham Lincoln Centre," pp. 49–58.

7. Davis, *Spearheads for Reform*, pp. 229–30.

8. Ibid., p. 234; General Session of the National Federation of Settlements Conference, May 24, 1926, Cleveland, Ohio, NFS Microfilm, SWHA. This conference focused on the negative results of professionalization. Eva Whiting White of Elizabeth Peabody House in Boston observed a period of reaction that, following a time of action, had resulted in "a sort of mechanical organization for social work" that follows "the ABC steps of procedure." Bruno Lasker thought the art of settlement work suffered exceedingly from professionalization. The stress on efficiency and personal success "may have a bad psychological effect upon us—and I believe it has. . . . I can't imagine a real artist in his studio continually being preoccupied with those things pertaining to the most efficient way of putting the color on the canvas, or in selling the canvas after it has been completed."

9. Davis, *Spearheads for Reform*, pp. 242–45; on settlements' support for federally sub-

sidized low-cost housing, federal social insurance, and outright financial aid, as well as their stand against war, in favor of the distribution of birth-control information, and in favor of works projects over relief programs, see Minutes of the Executive Committee Board's Annual Business Meeting, June 1934–May 1935; and Resolutions, Minutes of the Board of Directors and Business Meeting, June 4–7, 1936, Tennessee; Resolution on the Development of Federal WPA Cultural and Educational Projects into a Federal Department of Cultural-Educational Work, Digest of Minutes of Board of Directors and Business Meeting, Appendix, June 1–5, 1938, Pittsburgh, all in NFS Microfilm, SWHA.

10. Trolander, *Professionalism and Social Change*, p. 26.

11. Ibid., p. 28.

12. Trolander, *Settlement Houses*, pp. 137–40.

13. Trolander, *Professionalism and Social Change*, pp. 111–12, and "Interracial Code of Metropolitan Detroit," 1943–44, Folder 47: "Interracial Study," Kennedy Papers, SWHA.

14. Minutes of the Interracial and Intercultural Committee Meeting, January 7, 1942, Folder 47: "Interracial Study, NFS Interracial and Intercultural Commission, 1941–1943," Kennedy Papers, SWHA.

15. Ollendorf to the Headworkers of the Cleveland Settlements and the Members of the Committee on Race Relations, undated [1942–43?], Folder 48, ibid.

16. "Report of the Activities of the Booker T. Washington Community Center," March 14, 1944, Folder 67: "Interracial Study, Georgia, 1945–1947," Box 7, ibid.

17. Trolander, *Professionalism and Social Change*, p. 107.

18. Wolf to Mr. President and Board Members of Neighborhood Association, February 18, 1942; Wolf to Peck, May 28, 1941, Folder 394: "St. Louis, Missouri, Neighborhood Association, 1931–1955," Box 34, NFS Papers; and Wolf to Peck, November 17, 1942, and Peck to Wolf, November 23, 1942; Wolf to Kennedy, July 13, 1945; "Neighborhood Association—Cole St. Branch," flyer; "Historical Sketch of Neighborhood Association," flyer, March 29, 1938, Folder 79: "Interracial Study—Missouri, 1933–1945," Box 8, Kennedy Papers, SWHA. In Peck's letter to Wolf, she suggested a joint venture of whites and blacks that would ensure mutual respect, but apparently her idea never came to fruition.

19. Berry, "Civil Rights and Social Welfare," in *Social Welfare Forum*, pp. 84–96.

20. Kennedy promoted a shift in emphasis from black self-help to "white self-education" in a letter to Mr. Rosenstein, draft, July 2, 1946, Folder 55: "Interracial Study: Correspondence and Papers, 1945–1946," Kennedy Papers, SWHA.

21. Rudwick, *Race Riot in East St. Louis*, p. 219. He remarks upon the relation between the lack of recreational facilities and racial violence, pointing out that urban riots are often triggered when blacks try to enter areas controlled and guarded by whites.

22. Report on Neighborhood House, Buffalo, New York, Folder 79, Box 8, Kennedy Papers, SWHA.

23. Serotkin, quoted in "Racial Policy," manuscript, Soho Community House, Pittsburgh, Folder 94: "Interracial Study: Pennsylvania, 1925–1944," Box 9, ibid.

24. "Summary of Interracial Dancing," Soho Community House, Pittsburgh, Folder 47: "Interracial Dancing, March 15–29, 1940–1941," ibid.

25. "Group Record: Wednesday Night Mother's Club," Folder 47: "Interracial Study: NFS Interracial and Intercultural Commission, 1941–1943," ibid.

26. Annual Reports, 1937–38, 1940–41, 1941–42, 1942–43, 1944–46, 1947–48, 1949–50, 1950–51, Soho Community House, AIS.

27. Tensions reminiscent of the Pittsburgh and Buffalo incidents afflicted the neighborhood surrounding the William Byrd Community House in Richmond, Virginia. "Factual Information of the William Byrd Community House, Richmond, Virginia, September 1943," Folder 101: "Interracial Study: Virginia, 1940–1946," Box 9. In Los Angeles, conflicts arose between Japanese and African American residents. One observer wrote about Pilgrim House that "we have a new and potentially dangerous situation; there is need of acquaintance and common purpose; the many agencies in this field now have a sharp challenge and a golden opportunity to work out something constructive." Kingsley to Kennedy, October 8, 1945, and unidentified clipping called "Small Talk," by Yamamoto, *Los Angeles Tribune*, in Kennedy Papers, SWHA.

28. Trolander, *Professionalism and Social Change*, pp. 67, 139–57.

29. Berry, quoted in ibid., p. 67; ibid., p. 225.

30. Drake foresaw this damaging effect of separatism in the 1960s: *Race Relations*, pp. 75–108, 126–34, 145–51.

31. Ibid., pp. 129–35, 146–51, 159–60.

32. Ibid.; King, *Where Do We Go from Here*, p. 50.

Bibliography

Manuscript Collections

Amherst, Massachusetts
Tower Library, University of Massachusetts
  Claude Barnett/Associated Negro Press Papers (microfilm)
  W. E. B. Du Bois Papers (microfilm)
  John and Lugenia Hope Papers (microfilm)
  National Association for the Advancement of Colored People Papers (microfilm)

Atlanta, Georgia
Robert W. Woodruff Library, Atlanta University Center
  Neighborhood Union Papers, Special Collections/Archives

Cambridge, Massachusetts
Arthur and Elizabeth Schlesinger Library, Radcliffe College
  Black Women Oral History Project

Chapel Hill, North Carolina
Southern Historical Collection, University of North Carolina
  Penn School Papers
  Southern Oral History Program Collection

Chicago, Illinois
University Library, University of Illinois at Chicago
  Jane Addams Memorial Collection

Cleveland, Ohio
Case Western Reserve Historical Society
  Jelliffe/Karamu Collection

Detroit, Michigan
Walter P. Reuther Library, Wayne State University
  Detroit Federation of Settlements Papers, United Community Services Collection
  Carrie Burton Overton Papers
  Mary White Ovington Papers

Hampton, Virginia
Hollis Burke Frissell Library, Hampton University
  Calhoun Colored School and Social Settlement Papers

Janie Porter Barrett Papers
Penn School Papers
People's Village School Papers

Minneapolis, Minnesota
Social Welfare History Archives, University of Minnesota
    Albert J. Kennedy Papers
    National Federation of Settlements Papers

Montgomery, Alabama
Alabama Department of Archives and History
    Calhoun Clipping File

Northampton, Massachusetts
Sophia Smith Collection, Smith College
    College Settlements Collection
    Young Women's Christian Associations Papers

Philadelphia, Pennsylvania
Urban Archives Center, Temple University
    Southwest Belmont Branch YWCA Papers
    Wharton Centre Papers

Pittsburgh, Pennsylvania
Archives of Industrial Society, University of Pittsburgh
    Soho Community House, Annual Reports

Talladega, Alabama
Savery Library, Talladega College
    Calhoun Colored School Records

Washington, D.C.
Bethune Museum and Archives
    National Council of Negro Women Records
Library of Congress, Manuscript Division
    National Urban League Records
    Booker T. Washington Papers
Moorland-Spingarn Research Center, Howard University
    Civil Rights Documentation Project

Primary Sources

Addams, Jane. *The Second Twenty Years at Hull-House*. New York: Macmillan, 1930.
———. "Social Control." *The Crisis*, 1, 3 (January 1911): 22–23.
———. *Twenty Years at Hull-House*. 1910. Reprint. New York: New American Library,
    1981.
Addams, Jane, and Ida B. Wells. "Lynching and Rape: An Exchange of Views," edited
    by Bettina Aptheker. Reprinted in *Occasional Paper* 25. New York: American Institute
    for Marxist Studies, 1977.

Adler, Felix. "The Persistence of Race Prejudice." *The Standard* 9, 6 (February 1923): 205–8.

——— . "The Question of an Ethical Creed." *The Standard*, 32, 6 (March 1946): 161–64.

——— . "What Should Be the Attitude of a Religious Society Toward the Great Issues of the Day." *The Standard* 4, 3 (December 1917): 87–92.

Ames, Jessie Daniel, and Bertha Payne Newell. *"Repairers of the Breach": A Story of Interracial Cooperation Between Southern Women, 1935–1940.* Atlanta: Women's Department of the Commission on Interracial Cooperation, 1940.

Annals of the American Academy of Political and Social Science 140 (November 1928): entire issue, on "The American Negro."

Annual Reports of the Principal of the Calhoun Colored School. Boston: George H. Ellis, 1901–1933.

"Appreciation of Colored Women: Resolution Agreed to by the House and Senate February 6, 1918." *Southern Workman* 47, 6 (June 1918): 315.

Aptheker, Herbert, ed. *The Education of Black People: Ten Critiques by W. E. B. Du Bois.* Amherst: University of Massachusetts Press, 1973.

Armstrong, Samuel Chapman. *Education for Life.* Hampton, Va.: Press of the Hampton Normal and Agricultural Institute, 1914.

Baker, Ray Stannard. *Following the Color Line: American Negro Citizenship in the Progressive Era.* 1908. Reprint. New York: Harper and Row, 1964.

Baldwin, William H. "Negroes in the Cities." *The Standard* 13, 6 (February 1927): 174–81.

Barnett, Samuel, and Mrs. S. A. Barnett. *Towards Social Reform.* New York: Macmillan, 1909.

Barrett, Janie Porter (Mrs. Harris). "Negro Women's Clubs and the Community." *Southern Workman* 39, 1 (January 1910): 33–34.

——— . "Social Settlement for Colored People." *Southern Workman* 41, 9 (September 1912): 511–18.

Bartholomew, Frances R. "A Northern Social Settlement for Negroes." *Southern Workman* 35, 2 (February 1906): 99–102.

Bell, Juliet O., and Helen J. Wilkins. *Interracial Practices in Community YWCAs.* New York: The Woman's Press, 1944.

Bell, W. A. *Missions and Cooperation of the Methodist Episcopal Church, South.* N.p.: 1933.

Bennett, Belle H., John W. Gilbert, and Ellen Young. "Paine College and Its Annex." *Our Homes* 19, 3 (March 1910): 6–9.

Berry, Margaret. "Civil Rights and Social Welfare." *The Social Welfare Forum, 1963: Official Proceedings, 90th Annual Forum, National Conference on Social Welfare, Cleveland, Ohio, May 19–24, 1963*, pp. 84–96. New York: Columbia University Press, 1963.

"Blacklisting the YWCA." *The Survey* 45, 19 (February 5, 1921): 668.

Blascoer, Frances. *Colored School Children in New York.* 1915. Reprint. New York: Negro Universities Press, 1970.

Boas, Franz. "The Negro and the Demands of Modern Life." *Charities* 15, 1 (October 7, 1905): 85–88.

Bowen, Louise de Koven. "The Colored People of Chicago." *The Survey* 31, 5 (November 1, 1913): 117–20.

Bowles, Eva. "Negro Women and the War." *Southern Workman* 47, 9 (September 1918): 425–26.

Brawley, Benjamin. "Atlanta Striving." *The Crisis* 8, 1 (May 1914): 28–30.

Brown, Esther F. "The Southern Educational Conference." *Southern Workman* 35, 6 (June 1906): 331–34.

Bruno, Frank J. "Using a Case Technique." In *Christianity and Social Adventuring*, edited by Jerome Davis, pp. 179–90. New York: Century, 1927.

Carroll, Charles. *The Negro a Beast.* 1900. Reprint. Miami: Mnemosyne, 1969.

Center for Racial Justice and Services to Student Associations Unit, National Board, YWCA. *Some Highlights of Steps along the Way to the One Imperative.* Boston: Boston Young Women's Christian Associations, n.d.

Chapin, Caroline. "Settlement Work among Colored People." *Annals of the American Academy of Political and Social Science* 21, 2 (March 1903): 184–85.

Charities, 15, 1 (October 7, 1905). Entire issue on "The Negro."

Chicago Commission on Race Relations. *The Negro in Chicago: A Study of Race Relations and a Race Riot.* 1922. Reprint. New York: Arno and the New York Times, 1968.

Circular of Information for Students and Applicants, Calhoun Colored School. Boston: George H. Ellis Co., 1919.

Clark, William E. "The Katy Ferguson Home." *Southern Workman* 52, 5 (May 1923): 221–27.

Clarke, John Henrik, ed. *Marcus Garvey and the Vision of Africa.* New York: Vintage–Random House, 1974.

Coit, Stanton. "Character and Conduct." Reprinted in *The Standard* 32, 8 (May 1946): 230.

"Colored Girls in Cleveland." *The Crisis* 36, 12 (December 1929): 411–12.

"Colored Social Workers." *Southern Workman* 49, 8 (August 1920): 348.

"Colored Women's Federation Meeting." *Southern Workman* 41, 7 (July 1912): 398–99.

"Community House for Colored People." *Southern Workman* 48, 10 (October 1919): 473–76.

Cooley, Rossa B. "The Farm Demonstrator." *The Survey* 44, 18 (August 16, 1920): 40.

———. *School Acres: An Adventure in Rural Education.* 1930. Reprint. Westport, Conn.: Negro Universities Press, 1970.

Crossland, William. *Industrial Conditions among Negroes in St. Louis.* St. Louis: Mendle Printing, 1914.

Curtis, Julia Childs. "A Girls' Clubhouse." *The Crisis* 6, 6 (October 1913): 294–96.

Daniels, John. *In Freedom's Birthplace: A Study of the Boston Negroes.* 1914. Reprint. New York: Negro Universities Press, 1968.

Davis, Elizabeth Lindsay. *Lifting as They Climb: The National Association of Colored Women.* Washington, D.C.: National Association of Colored Women, 1933.

De Bardeleben, Mary. "Training for Christian Negro Workers." *Our Homes* 19, 3 (March 1910): 10–12.

Dewey, John. "The School as a Social Settlement." In *Schools of Tomorrow*, by John Dewey and Evelyn Dewey, pp. 150–66. 1915. Reprint. New York: E. P. Dutton, 1962.

Dillingham, Pitt. "The Settlement Idea in the Cotton Belt." *Outlook* 70, 15 (April 12, 1902): 920–22.

"Distinctive Ideals in Settlement Work: Addresses by Headworkers." *The Standard* 3, 1 (October 1916): 17–19.

Drake, St. Clair. *Race Relations in a Time of Rapid Social Change.* New York: National Federation of Settlements and Neighborhood Centers, 1966.

Du Bois, W. E. B. "Back to Africa." *Century* (February 1923). Reprinted in *Marcus Garvey and the Vision of Africa*, edited by John Henrik Clarke, pp. 105–19. New York: Vintage, 1974.

————. *The Philadelphia Negro: A Social Study.* 1899. Reprint. Millwood, N.Y.: Kraus-Thompson, 1973.

————. *The Souls of Black Folk: Essays and Sketches.* 1903. Reprint. Greenwich, Conn.: Fawcett, 1961.

————. "Thomas Jesse Jones." *The Crisis* 22, 6 (October 1921): 252–56.

————, ed. *Atlanta University Publications.* 2 vols. 1896–1906. Reprint. New York: Octagon, 1968.

Dunbar, Paul Lawrence. *The Sport of the Gods.* New York: Dodd, Mead, 1902.

Dunn, Mary Noreen. *Women and Home Missions.* Nashville, Tenn.: Cokesbury Press, 1936.

Duster, Alfreda M., ed. *Crusade for Justice: The Autobiography of Ida B. Wells.* Chicago: University of Chicago Press, 1970.

Elliot, Charles William. "The Churches and the Prevailing Social Sentiment." *Harvard Theological Review.* 6: 397–406. 1913. Reprint. New York: Kraus Reprint, 1968.

Elliott, John Lovejoy. "After Twenty Years in the Tenement Houses of New York." *The Standard* 1, 9 (May 1915): 250–54.

————. "The Supreme Problem of Ethical Education: The Combination of the Theoretical and the Practical." *The Standard* 9, 2 (October 1922): 57–60.

Fauset, Jessie. "The 'Y' Conference at Talladega." *The Crisis* 26, 5 (September 1923): 213–15.

"Federation of Colored Women." *Southern Workman* 40, 8 (August 1911): 453–55.

Fernandis, Sarah C. "Hampton's Relation to the Constructive Needs of the Negro." *Southern Workman* 39, 4 (April 1910): 202.

————. "Inter-racial Activities of Baltimore Women." *Southern Workman* 51, 10 (October 1922): 482–84.

"For Community Betterment." *Southern Workman* 49, 7 (July 1920): 296–98.

Frank, Glenn. "An American Looks at His World: Unsettling the Social Settlement." *The Century Magazine* 84 (May–October 1923): 317–20.

Frazier, E. Franklin. "The Pathology of Race Prejudice." *The Forum* 77, 6 (June 1927): 856–62.

————. "Psychological Factors in Negro Health." *Journal of Social Forces* 3, 3 (March 1925): 488–90.

Gladden, Washington. *Social Salvation.* 1902. Reprint. New York: Regina, 1975.

[Goerner], Mrs. Paul. "A Window and an Open Door: Bethlehem Community Center, Augusta, Georgia, 1912–1952." Photocopy at the Bethlehem Community Center.

"The Good Neighbor Committee." *The Standard* 26, 1 (October 1939): 3.

Hall, Helen. "Creativeness in Settlement Work." *The Standard* 23, 4 (January 1937): 85–86.

————. *Unfinished Business: In Neighborhood and Nation.* New York: Macmillan, 1971.

Hammond, L. H. *In Black and White: An Interpretation of Southern Life.* New York: Fleming H. Revell, 1914.

————. *In the Vanguard of a Race.* New York: Council of Women for Home Missions and Missionary Education Movement of United States and Canada, 1922.

————. *Southern Women and Race Adjustment.* Lynchburg, Va.: J. P. Bell, 1917.

Hansen, Edna. "The Child Guidance Clinic of Abraham Lincoln Centre." *Individual Psychology Bulletin* 4 (1944–1945): 49–58.

Harlan, Louis R., Stuart B. Kaufman, and Raymond W. Smock, eds. *The Booker T. Washington Papers*. Vol. 3. Urbana: University of Illinois Press, 1974.

Harper, Elsie D. *The Past Is Prelude: Fifty Years of Social Action in the Young Women's Christian Associations*. New York: National Board of the Young Women's Christian Associations of the United States of America, 1963.

Hartshorn, W. N., ed. *An Era of Progress and Promise: The Religious, Moral and Educational Development of the American Negro since His Emancipation*. Boston: Priscilla, 1910.

Haskin, Sarah Estelle. *The Upward Climb: A Course in Negro Achievement*. New York: Council of Women for Home Missions, 1927.

Hawkins, Gaynell. *Educational Experiments in Social Settlements*. New York: American Association for Adult Education, 1937.

Hawkins, Hugh, ed. *Booker T. Washington and His Critics: Black Leadership in Crisis*. 2d ed. Lexington, Mass.: D. C. Heath, 1974.

Haynes, Birdye H. "Lincoln House: Its Work for Colored Americans." *The Standard* 6, 4 (December 1919): 122–24.

Haynes, George Edmund. "The Church and Negro Progress." *Annals of the Academy of Political and Social Science* 140 (November 1928): 264–71.

———. *The Negro at Work in New York City: A Study in Economic Progress*. 1912. Reprint. New York: Arno, 1968.

Height, Dorothy I. *Step by Step with Interracial Groups*. 2d ed. New York: The Woman's Press, 1948.

Herskovits, Melville J. "Christianity and the Race Problem." *Journal of Social Forces* 3, 3 (March 1925): 490–92.

Hill, Ruth Edmonds, ed. *The Black Women Oral History Project*. 10 vols. Westport, Conn.: Meckler, 1991.

Holmes, John Haynes. "The Community Church: A Reply." *The Standard* 9, 6 (February 1923): 190–94.

Holmes, Josephine Pinyon. "Youth Cannot Wait." *The Crisis* 28, 3 (July 1924): 128–31.

"The Homemakers' Community Fair." *Southern Workman* 41, 12 (December 1912): 663–64.

Hope, John. "The Colored YMCA." *The Crisis* 31, 1 (November 1925): 14–17.

Hunton, Mrs. W. A. "Women's Clubs: Caring for Young Women." *The Crisis* 2, 3 (July 1911): 121–22.

"Industrial Home School." *Southern Workman* 48, 10 (October 1919): 473–76.

Ingram, Frances. "The Settlement Movement in the South." *World Outlook* 37 (May 1937): 12–14, 38.

"Interesting and Significant Gains in Program and Community Relations Noted in Annual Report to Membership." *The YWCA News* 12, 2 (February 1936): 5–8.

Johnson, F. Ernest, ed. *The Social Work of the Churches: A Handbook of Information*. New York: Federal Council of Churches, 1930.

"Keeping the New Blood Pure." *Outlook* 79 (1905): 219–21.

Kellogg, Paul. Introduction to *School Acres: An Adventure in Rural Education*, by Rossa B. Cooley, ix–xx. 1930. Reprint. Westport, Conn.: Negro Universities Press, 1970.

Kellor, Frances. "Assisted Emigration From the South: The Women." *Charities* 15, 1 (October 1905): 11–14.

———. "The Criminal Negro: A Sociological Study." *Arena* 25, 1–5 (January–May 1901): 59–68, 190–97, 308–16, 419–28, 510–20.

———. *Neighborhood Americanization: A Discussion of the Alien in a New Country and of the Native American in His Home Country*. New York: National Americanization Committee, 1918.

———. *Out of Work: A Study of Employment Agencies*. New York: Putnam, 1904.

King, Martin Luther, Jr. *Where Do We Go from Here: Chaos or Community?* New York: Harper and Row, 1967.

Krehbiel, Edward. "The Attack on the Los Angeles YWCA." *The Survey* 44, 18 (August 16, 1920): 611–13.

Lasker, Bruno. *Race Attitudes in Children*. 1929. Reprint. New York: Greenwood, 1968.

Lattimore, Florence. *A Palace of Delight*. Hampton, Va.: Hampton Institute Press, 1915.

Lerner, Gerda, ed. *Black Women in White America: A Documentary History*. New York: Vintage–Random House, 1973.

Letzig, Betty J. *Expressions of Faith: A Background Paper on the Origins of Social Welfare Institutions Related to the National Program Division of the General Board of Global Ministries of the United Methodist Church*. New York: General Board of Global Ministries, the United Methodist Church, n.d.

Lewis, Sinclair. *Babbitt*. 1922. Reprint. New York: New American Library, 1961.

Lindenberg, Sidney J., and Ruth Ellen Zittel. "The Settlement Scene Changes." *Social Forces* 14, 4 (May 1936): 559–66.

"A Lost Friend." *The Crisis* 9, 4 (February 1915): 183–84.

Lumpkin, Katharine Du Pre. *The Making of a Southerner*. 1946. Reprint. Athens: University of Georgia Press, 1981.

McCulloch, James, ed. *Battling for Social Betterment: The Southern Sociological Congress, Memphis, Tennessee, May 6–10, 1914*. Nashville, Tenn.: Southern Sociological Congress, 1914.

MacDonell, Mrs. R. W. "Wesley Houses and the Social Work of the Woman's Home Mission Society." *Missionary Voice* 1, 3 (March 1911): 46–49.

McGinley, A. A. "A New Field for the Convent Graduate In the Social Settlement." *Catholic World* 71, 423 (June 1900): 396–401.

———. "The Scope of the Catholic Social Settlement." *Catholic World* 71, 422 (May 1900): 145–60.

Mann, Albert R. "Co-operative Community Building." *Southern Workman* 49, 8 (August 1920): 374–77.

Marshall, Troward H. "From Provincialism to Catholicity." *The Standard* 4, 6 (March 1918): 159–62.

Martin, Alfred W. "The Community Church and the Ethical Movement." *The Standard* 7, 8 (April 1921): 225–34.

Meeker, Ruth Esther. *Six Decades of Service, 1880–1940: A History of the Woman's Home Missionary Society of the Methodist Episcopal Church*. 1927. Reprint. Cincinnati: Steinhauser, 1969.

Moore, Rosa Hunter. "A Pioneer Settlement Worker." *Southern Workman* 52, 7 (July 1923): 320–31.

Moss, R. Maurice. "The Frederick Douglass Community Center." *Southern Workman* 52, 5 (May 1923): 221–27.

Moynihan, Daniel P. *The Negro Family in America: The Case for National Action*. Washington, D.C.: U.S. Government Printing Office, 1965.

Muzzey, David Saville. "Spiritual Provincialism." *The Standard* 29, 6 (March 1943): 152–56.

"My Neighbor." *Our Homes* 17, 7 (August 1908): 6–7.

"National Association of Colored Women." *Southern Workman* 49, 9 (September 1920): 391–92.

"National Division Institutional Ministries Historical Perspective." Photocopy at National Program Division, General Board of Global Ministries, the United Methodist Church, New York City.

National Program Division Handbook: A Handbook of Programs, Projects and Relationships. New York: General Board of Global Ministries, the United Methodist Church, n.d.

" 'Neighbors'—a Visitation." *The Standard* 16, 1 (July 1929): 20–23.

Nutt, Martha. "Bethlehem Center, Nashville, Tennessee." *Southern Workman* 53 (September 1924): 401–4.

Olcott, Jane, comp. *The Work of Colored Women.* New York: National Board of the Young Women's Christian Associations, 1919.

Our Homes 19, 3 (March 1910): entire issue, on "Our Duty to the Negro."

"Our Negro Schools." *Our Homes* 17, 7 (August 1908): 7–11.

Ovington, Mary White. *Half a Man: The Status of the Negro in New York.* 1911. Reprint. New York: Negro Universities Press, 1969.

———. "The Negro Home in New York." *Charities* 15, 1 (October 7, 1905): 25–30.

———. "The Negro in America: Today and Tomorrow." *Survey* 28, 6 (May 18, 1912): 318–20.

———. *Portraits in Color.* 1927. Reprint. Freeport, N.Y.: Books for Libraries Press, 1971.

———. *The Walls Came Tumbling Down.* 1947. Reprint. New York: Schocken, 1970.

Pemberton, Caroline. "The Barbarization of Civilization." *Arena* 23, 1 (January 1900): 5–15.

Pierce, John B. "Hamptonians in Extension Service." *Southern Workman* 52, 8 (August 1923): 387–409.

Quillin, Frank U. *The Color Line in Ohio: A History of Race Prejudice in a Typical Northern State.* 1913. Reprint. New York: Negro Universities Press, 1969.

"Race Suicide and Common Sense." *North American Review* 176, 559 (June 1903): 892–900.

Rauschenbusch, Walter. *Christianizing the Social Order.* New York: Macmillan, 1914.

Riis, Jacob. "The Black Half." *The Crisis* 5, 6 (April 1913): 298–99.

Ross, Edward A. "Causes of Race Superiority." *Annals of the American Academy of Political and Social Science* 18 (1901): 85–86.

Settlement Goals for the Next Third of a Century: A Symposium. Boston: National Federation of Settlements, 1926.

Simkhovitch, Mary Melinda (Kingsbury). *The Settlement Primer.* Boston: National Federation of Settlements, 1926.

Sims, Mary S. "The YWCA at Detroit." *The Crisis* 37, 10 (October 1930): 335, 356.

"Social Settlements and the Church." *Nashville Christian Advocate,* June 18, 1903: 1.

Spencer, Anna Garlin. "The Social Challenge." Reprinted in *The Standard* 32, 8 (May 1946): 231.

"State Federation of Colored Women's Clubs." *Southern Workman* 37, 12 (December 1908): 647–48.

Stillman, Bessie W. " 'Life, Liberty and the Pursuit of Happiness': An Appeal for Justice to the Negro." *The Standard* 6, 2 (October 1919): 47–51.

Strong, Josiah. *The New Era, or the Coming Kingdom.* 1893. Reprint. New York: Regina, 1975.

Taylor, Graham. *Chicago Commons through Forty Years.* Chicago: Chicago Commons Association, 1936.

———. *Pioneering on Social Frontiers.* Chicago: University of Chicago Press, 1930.

———. "The Social Settlement Religion and the Church." *Christianity and Social Adventuring,* edited by Jerome Davis, pp. 165–75. New York: Century, 1927.

———. "The Southern Social Awakening." *Survey* 28, 22 (September 14, 1912): 744–45.

Tobias, C. H. "The Colored YMCA." *The Crisis* 9, 1 (November 1914): 33–36.

———. "A Decade of Student YMCA Work." *The Crisis* 24, 6 (October 1922): 265–67.

Tyler, Ralph W. "The Phyllis Wheatley Association: A Negro Woman's Achievement." *Southern Workman* 49, 3 (March 1920): 121–26.

Vance, Catherine S. *The Girl Reserve Movement of the Young Women's Christian Association: An Analysis of the Educational Principles and Procedures Used throughout Its History.* New York: Bureau of Publications, Teachers College, Columbia University, 1937.

"Virginia Federation of Colored Women." *Southern Workman* 44, 9 (September 1915): 467–68.

" 'Voice of the Churches.' " *The Survey* 45, 26 (March 26, 1921): 912–13.

"W. E. B. Du Bois' Confrontation with White Liberalism during the Progressive Era: A Phylon Document." *Phylon* 35, 3 (September 1974): 241–58.

Wald, Lillian D. *The House on Henry Street.* 1915. Reprint. New York: Henry Holt, 1938.

Walling, William English. "The Founding of the NAACP." *The Crisis* 36, 1 (July 1929): 226.

———. "The Race War in the North." *Independent* 65 (September 3, 1908): 529–34.

Washington, Booker T. "The Fruits of Industrial Training." *Atlantic Monthly* 92, 552 (October 1903): 453–62.

———. "Why Should Negro Business Men Go South." *Charities* 15, 1 (October 7, 1905): 17–19.

———. *Working with the Hands.* 1904. Reprint. New York: Arno and the New York Times, 1969.

Washington, James Melvin, ed. *A Testament of Hope: The Essential Writings of Martin Luther King, Jr.* San Francisco: Harper and Row, 1986.

Washington, Margaret Murray (Mrs. Booker T.). "The Tuskegee Woman's Club." *Southern Workman* 49, 8 (August 1920): 365–69.

What Hampton Graduates Are Doing: 1868–1904. Hampton, Va.: Hampton Institute Press, 1904.

White, Gaylord. "The Social Settlement after Twenty-Five Years." *Harvard Theological Review* 5: 47–70. 1911. Reprint. New York: Kraus Reprint, 1968.

"Why the Women Ask the Rights of the Laity." *Our Homes* 18, 12 (December 1909): 23–24.

Williams, Emily. "The National Association of Colored Women." *Southern Workman* 43, 9 (September 1914): 481–83.

Williams, Fannie Barrier. "Club Movement among Negro Women." In *The Colored American from Slavery to Honorable Citizenship,* edited by J. W. Gibson and W. H. Crogman, pp. 197–231. Atlanta: J. L. Nichols, 1903.

———. "Colored Women of Chicago." *Southern Workman* 43, 10 (October 1914): 564–66.

———. "The Frederick Douglass Center." *Southern Workman* 35, 6 (June 1906): 334–36.

———. "The Social Bonds in the 'Black Belt' of Chicago." *Charities* 15, 1 (October 7, 1905): 40–44.

Williams, W. T. B. "Hampton Graduates as Teachers." *Southern Workman* 48, 10 (October 1919): 503–7.

———. Review of *In Black and White: An Interpretation of Southern Life*, by L. H. Hammond. *Southern Workman* 43, 8 (August 1914): 460–62.

Wilson, Elizabeth. *Fifty Years of Association Work among Young Women: A History of Young Women's Christian Associations in the United States of America*. New York: National Board of the Young Women's Christian Associations of the United States of America, 1916.

Wittenberg, Rudolph. "Therapeutic Values of Groupwork." *The Standard* 26, 3 (December 1939): 64–66.

"Women of All Nations." *The Survey* 45, 10 (December 4, 1920): 351.

Woods, Robert. Introduction to *In Freedom's Birthplace: A Study of the Boston Negroes*, by John Daniels, ix–xiii. 1914. Reprint. New York: Negro Universities Press, 1968.

———. *The Neighborhood in Nation-Building: The Running Comment of Thirty Years at the South End House*. Boston: Houghton-Mifflin, 1923.

———, ed. *The City Wilderness: A Settlement Study by Residents and Associates of the South End House*. 1898. Reprint. New York: Garrett, 1970.

Woods, Robert, and Albert J. Kennedy, eds. *Handbook of Settlements*. New York: Charities Publication Committee, 1911.

Wright, Arthur D., ed. *The Negro Rural School Fund, Inc., Anna T. Jeanes Foundation, 1907–1933*. Washington, D.C.: Negro Rural School Fund, 1933.

Wright, R. R., Jr. *The Negro in Pennsylvania: A Study in Economic History*. 1912. Reprint. New York: Arno, 1969.

"YMCA." *The Crisis* 9, 2 (December 1914): 77–80.

"YWCA." *Survey Graphic* 52, 5 (June 1, 1924): 311–12.

"The YWCA under Fire." *The Survey* 44, 18 (August 16, 1920): 603.

Secondary Sources

Abell, Aaron I. *American Catholicism and Social Action: A Search for Social Justice, 1865–1950*. Notre Dame, Ind.: University of Notre Dame Press, 1960.

———. *The Urban Impact on American Protestantism, 1865–1900*. Hamden, Conn.: Archon, 1962.

Anderson, James D. *The Education of Blacks in the South, 1860–1935*. Chapel Hill: University of North Carolina Press, 1988.

———. "The Hampton Model of Normal School Industrial Education, 1868–1900." In *New Perspectives on Black Educational History*, edited by Vincent P. Franklin and James D. Anderson, pp. 61–96. Boston: G. K. Hall, 1978.

———. "Northern Foundations and the Shaping of Southern Black Rural Education, 1902–1935." In *The Social History of American Education*, edited by B. Edward

McClellan and William J. Reese, pp. 287–312. Urbana: University of Illinois Press, 1988.

Anderson, M. Christine. "Home and Community for a Generation of Women: A Case Study of the Cincinnati Y.W.C.A. Residence, 1920–1940." *Queen City Heritage* 43, 4 (Winter 1985): 34–41.

Aptheker, Bettina. *Woman's Legacy: Essays on Race, Sex and Class in American History.* Amherst: University of Massachusetts Press, 1982.

Baker, Paula. "The Domestication of Politics: Women and American Political Society, 1780–1920." *American Historical Review* 89 (June 1984): 620–47.

Banner, Lois W. "Religious Benevolence as Social Control: A Critique of an Interpretation." *Journal of American History* 60, 1 (June 1973): 23–41.

Berry, Benjamin D., Jr. "Plymouth Settlement House and the Development of Black Louisville, 1900–1930." Ph.D. dissertation, Case Western Reserve University, 1977.

Blassingame, John. *The Slave Community: Plantation Life in the Antebellum South.* New York: Oxford University Press, 1979.

Blauch, Lloyd E. *Federal Cooperation in Agricultural Extension Work, Vocational Education, and Vocational Rehabilitation.* New York: Arno, 1969.

Bliss, R. K., et al., comps. *The Spirit and Philosophy of Extension Work.* Washington, D.C.: United States Department of Agriculture and Epsilon Sigma Phi, 1952.

Bodnar, John E., Roger D. Simon, and Michael P. Weber. *Lives of Their Own: Blacks, Italians, and Poles in Pittsburgh, 1900–1960.* Urbana: University of Illinois Press, 1982.

Bogin, Ruth. "Elizabeth Ross Haynes." In *Notable American Women: The Modern Period,* edited by Barbara Sicherman et al., pp. 324–25. Cambridge, Mass.: Harvard University Press, Belknap Press, 1980.

Bond, Horace Mann. *The Education of the Negro in the American Social Order.* 1934. Reprint. New York: Octagon, 1970.

Boyd, Nancy. *Emissaries: The Overseas Work of the American YWCA, 1895–1970.* New York: Woman's Press, 1986.

Boyer, Paul. *Urban Masses and Moral Order in America, 1820–1920.* Cambridge, Mass.: Harvard University Press, 1978.

Brady, Marilyn Dell. "Organizing Afro-American Girls' Clubs in Kansas in the 1920s." *Frontiers* 9, 2 (1987): 69–73.

Bremner, Robert H. *From the Depths: The Discovery of Poverty in the United States.* New York: New York University Press, 1956.

Brooks, Evelyn. "Religion, Politics, and Gender: The Leadership of Nannie Helen Burroughs." *Journal of Religious Thought* 44, 2 (Winter-Spring 1988): 7–22.

Brown, Elsa Barkley. "African-American Quilting: A Framework for Conceptualizing and Teaching African-American Women's History." *Signs* 14, 4 (Summer 1989): 921–38.

———. "Womanist Consciousness: Maggie Lena Walker and the Independent Order of Saint Luke." In *Unequal Sisters: A Multicultural Reader in U.S. Women's History,* edited by Ellen DuBois and Vicki Ruiz, pp. 208–23. New York: Routledge, 1990.

Brown, Hallie Q. *Homespun Heroines and Other Women of Distinction.* 1926. Reprint. New York: Oxford University Press, 1988.

Brunner, Edmund deS., and E. Hsin Pao Yang. *Rural America and the Extension Service: A History and Critique of the Cooperative Agricultural and Home Economics Extension Service.* New York: Columbia University Bureau of Publications, 1949.

Bullock, Henry Allen. *A History of Negro Education in the South, From 1619 to the Present.* Cambridge, Mass.: Harvard University Press, 1967.

Byrd, Alicia D. "Adult Educational Efforts of the American Black Church, 1600–1900." *Journal of Religious Thought* 44, 2 (Winter-Spring 1988): 83–93.

Carby, Hazel V. "It Jus Be's Dat Way Sometime: The Sexual Politics of Women's Blues." *Radical America* 20, 4 (1986): 9–22.

Carson, Mina. *Settlement Folk: Social Thought and the American Settlement Movement, 1885–1930.* Chicago: University of Chicago Press, 1990.

Carter, Paul A. *The Decline and Revival of the Social Gospel: Social and Political Liberalism in American Protestant Churches, 1920–1940.* Ithaca, N.Y.: Cornell University Press, 1956.

Cash, W. J. *The Mind of the South.* New York: Vintage–Random House, 1941.

Chambers, Clarke. "The 'New' Social History, Local History and Community Empowerment." *Minnesota History* 49, 1 (Spring 1984): 14–18.

――――. *Seedtime of Reform: American Social Service and Social Action, 1918–1933.* Minneapolis: University of Minnesota Press, 1963.

――――. "Social Service and Social Reform: A Historical Essay." *Social Service Review* 37, 1 (March 1963): 76–90.

――――. "Toward a Redefinition of Welfare History." *Journal of American History* 73, 2 (September 1986): 407–33.

Clark, Kenneth. *Dark Ghetto: Dilemmas of Social Power.* New York: Harper and Row, 1965.

Cohen, Lizabeth. *Making a New Deal: Industrial Workers in Chicago, 1919–1939.* Cambridge: Cambridge University Press, 1990.

Collins, Patricia Hill. *Black Feminist Thought: Knowledge, Consciousness, and the Politics of Empowerment.* 1990. Reprint. New York: Routledge, 1991.

Conway, Jill. "Women Reformers and American Culture, 1870–1930." *Journal of Social History* 5 (Winter 1971–1972): 164–77.

Cott, Nancy F. *The Bonds of Womanhood: "Woman's Sphere" in New England, 1780–1835.* New Haven, Conn.: Yale University Press, 1977.

――――. *The Grounding of Modern Feminism.* New Haven, Conn.: Yale University Press, 1987.

――――. "What's in a Name? The Limits of 'Social Feminism'; or, Expanding the Vocabulary of Women's History." *Journal of American History* 76 (1989): 809–29.

Cremin, Lawrence A. *The Transformation of the School: Progressivism in American Education, 1876–1957.* New York: Vintage–Random House, 1961.

Crocker, Ruth Hutchinson. *Social Work and Social Order: The Settlement Movement in Two Industrial Cities, 1889–1930.* Urbana: University of Illinois Press, 1992.

――――. "Sympathy and Science: The Settlement Movement in Gary and Indianapolis to 1930." Ph.D. dissertation, Purdue University, 1982.

Cruse, Harold. *The Crisis of the Negro Intellectual: A Historical Analysis of the Failure of Black Leadership.* New York: Quill, 1984.

Cryer, Daniel. "Mary White Ovington." In *Notable American Women: The Modern Period,* edited by Barbara Sicherman et al., pp. 517–19. Cambridge, Mass.: Harvard University Press, Belknap Press, 1980.

――――. "Mary White Ovington and the Rise of the NAACP." Ph.D. dissertation, University of Minnesota, 1977.

Curti, Merle. *The Social Ideas of American Educators*. 1935. Reprint. Paterson, N.J.: Pageant, 1959.

Dabney, Charles William. *Universal Education in the South*. 2 vols. 1936. Reprint. New York: Arno and the New York Times, 1969.

Daise, Ronald. *Reminiscences of Sea Island Heritage*. Orangeburg, S.C.: Sandlapper, 1986.

Davis, Allen. *The American Heroine: The Life and Legend of Jane Addams*. New York: Oxford University Press, 1973.

————. "Social Welfare History." *Reviews in American History* 12, 3 (September 1984): 343–47.

————. *Spearheads for Reform: The Social Settlements and the Progressive Movement, 1890–1914*. New York: Oxford University Press, 1967.

Davis, Allen, and Mary Lynn McCree, eds. *Eighty Years at Hull House*. Chicago: Quadrangle, 1969.

Davis, Angela Y. *Women, Race and Class*. New York: Vintage–Random House, 1983.

Deegan, Mary Jo. *Jane Addams and the Men of the Chicago School, 1892–1918*. New Brunswick, N.J.: Transaction Books, 1988.

Degler, Carl. *At Odds: Women and the Family in America from the Revolution to the Present*. New York: Oxford University Press, 1980.

Dickson, Lynda F. "Toward a Broader Angle of Vision in Uncovering Women's History: Black Women's Clubs Revisited." *Frontiers* 9, 2 (1987): 62–68.

Dill, Bonnie Thornton. "The Dialectics of Black Womanhood." *Signs* 4, 3 (Spring 1979): 543–55.

Diner, Hasia R. *In the Almost Promised Land: American Jews and Blacks, 1915–1935*. Westport, Conn.: Greenwood, 1977.

Diner, Stephen. "Chicago Social Workers and Blacks in the Progressive Era." *Social Service Review* 44, 4 (December 1970): 393–410.

————. "Scholarship in the Quest for Social Welfare: A Fifty-Year History of the *Social Service Review*." *Social Service Review* 51, 1 (March 1977): 1–66.

Douglas, Ann. *The Feminization of American Culture*. New York: Knopf, 1977.

Drake, St. Clair, and Horace Cayton. *Black Metropolis: A Study of Negro Life in a Northern City*. New York: Harcourt, Brace, 1945.

DuBois, Ellen, et al. "In Women's History: A Symposium." *Feminist Studies* 6, 1 (Spring 1980): 26–64.

DuBois, Ellen, and Vicki Ruiz, eds. *Unequal Sisters: A Multicultural Reader in U.S. Women's History*. New York: Routledge, 1990.

Dykeman, Wilma, and James Stokely. *Seeds of Southern Change: The Life of Will Alexander*. New York: Norton, 1976.

Ehrenreich, John H. *The Altruistic Imagination: A History of Social Work and Social Policy in the United States*. Ithaca, N.Y.: Cornell University Press, 1985.

Eighmy, John Lee. *Churches in Cultural Captivity: A History of the Social Attitudes of Southern Baptists*. Knoxville: University of Tennessee Press, 1972.

————. "Religious Liberalism in the South during the Progressive Era." *Church History* 38, 3 (September 1969): 359–72.

Ellis, Rose Herlong. "The Calhoun School: Miss Charlotte Thorn's 'Lighthouse on the Hill' in Lowndes County, Alabama." *Alabama Review* (July 1984): 183–201.

Ellison, Ralph. *Going to the Territory*. New York: Vintage–Random House, 1987.

Elshtain, Jean Bethke. *Public Man, Private Woman: Women in Social and Political Thought*. Princeton, N.J.: Princeton University Press, 1981.

Enck, Henry S. "Black Self-Help in the Progressive Era: The 'Northern Campaigns' of Smaller Southern Black Industrial Schools, 1900–1915." *Journal of Negro History* 61, 1 (January 1976): 73–87.

Epstein, Barbara Leslie. *The Politics of Domesticity: Women, Evangelism, and Temperance in Nineteenth-Century America*. Middletown, Conn.: Wesleyan University Press, 1981.

Eugene, Toinette. "Moral Values and Black Womanists." *Journal of Religious Thought* 44, 2 (Winter-Spring 1988): 23–34.

Findlay, James F. "Religion and Politics in the Sixties: The Churches and the Civil Rights Act of 1964." *Journal of American History* 77, 1 (June 1990): 66–92.

Fisher, Jacob. *The Response of Social Work to the Depression*. Boston: G. K. Hall, 1980.

Flynt, Wayne. "Dissent in Zion: Alabama Baptists and Social Issues, 1900–1914." *Journal of Southern History* 35, 4 (November 1969): 523–42.

Foner, Eric. *Nothing But Freedom: Emancipation and Its Legacy*. Baton Rouge: Louisiana State University Press, 1983.

Foner, Philip S. *Organized Labor and the Black Worker, 1619–1981*. 2d ed. New York: International Publishers, 1982.

Ford, James, Katherine Morrow, and George Thompson. *Slums and Housing: With Special Reference to New York City*. Cambridge, Mass.: Harvard University Press, 1936.

Foucault, Michel. *Power/Knowledge: Selected Interviews and Other Writings, 1972–1977*. Edited and translated by Colin Gordon. New York: Pantheon, 1980.

Franklin, John Hope, and Alfred A. Moss, Jr. *From Slavery to Freedom: A History of Negro Americans*. 6th ed. New York: Knopf, 1988.

Franklin, Vincent P., and James D. Anderson, eds. *New Perspectives on Black Educational History*. Boston: G. K. Hall, 1978.

Frazier, E. Franklin. *The Negro Church in America*. 1964. Reprint. New York: Schocken, 1974.

Frederickson, George. *The Black Image in the White Mind: The Debate on Afro-American Character and Destiny, 1817–1914*. New York: Harper and Row, 1972.

Frederickson, Mary E. " 'Each One Is Dependent on the Other': Southern Church-women and the Process of Transformation, 1880–1940." In *Visible Women: New Essays on American Activism*, edited by Nancy Hewitt and Suzanne Lebsock. Urbana: University of Illinois Press, forthcoming.

Gaston, Paul M. *The New South Creed: A Study in Southern Mythmaking*. New York: Knopf, 1970.

Genovese, Eugene. *Roll, Jordan, Roll: The World the Slaves Made*. New York: Pantheon, 1974.

Giddings, Paula. *When and Where I Enter: The Impact of Black Women on Race and Sex in America*. Toronto: Bantam–William Morrow, 1985.

Goldman, Eric F. *Rendezvous with Destiny: A History of Modern American Reform*. New York: Vintage–Random House, 1956.

Gordon, Linda. "Black and White Visions of Welfare: Women's Welfare Activism, 1890–1945." *Journal of American History* 78, 2 (September 1991): 559–90.

———. *Heroes of Their Own Lives: The Politics and History of Family Violence, Boston 1880–1960*. New York: Viking, 1988.

Gossett, Thomas F. *Race: The History of an Idea in America*. New York: Schocken, 1965.

Grabowski, John J. "From Progressive to Patrician: George Bellamy and Hiram House Social Settlement, 1896–1914." *Ohio History* 87 (Winter 1978): 37–52.

Grantham, Dewey W., Jr., ed. *The South and the Sectional Image: The Sectional Theme since Reconstruction*. New York: Harper and Row, 1967.

Griffin, Farah Jasmine. "'A Layin' on of Hands': Organizational Efforts among Black Women, 1790–1930." *Sage: A Scholarly Journal on Black Women*, Student Supplement (1988): 23–39.

Grob, Gerald N. "Reflections on the History of Social Policy in America." *Reviews in American History* 7, 3 (September 1979): 293–306.

Gutman, Herbert. *The Black Family in Slavery and Freedom, 1750–1925*. New York: Pantheon, 1976.

Haley, Alex, narrator. *The Autobiography of Malcolm X*. New York: Ballantine, 1973.

Hall, Jacquelyn Dowd. *Revolt against Chivalry: Jessie Daniel Ames and the Women's Campaign against Lynching*. New York: Columbia University Press, 1979.

Harlan, Louis R. *Booker T. Washington, The Wizard of Tuskegee, 1901–1915*. New York: Oxford University Press, 1983.

———. *Separate and Unequal: Public School Campaigns and Racism in the Southern Seaboard States, 1901–1915*. New York: Atheneum, 1968.

Harley, Sharon. "Beyond the Classroom: Organizational Lives of Black Women Educators." *Journal of Negro Education* 51 (Summer 1983): 254–65.

———. "For the Good of Family and Race: Gender, Work, and Domestic Roles in the Black Community, 1880–1930." *Signs* 15, 2 (Winter 1990): 336–49.

Harrington, Michael. *The Other America: Poverty in the United States*. New York: Macmillan, 1962.

Harris, William H. *The Harder We Run: Black Workers since the Civil War*. New York: Oxford University Press, 1982.

Hartmann, Edward George. *The Movement to Americanize the Immigrant*. New York: Columbia University Press, 1948.

Hawks, Joanne, and Sheila Skemp, eds. *Sex, Race, and the Role of Women in the South*. Jackson: University Press of Mississippi, 1983.

Henri, Florette. *Black Migration: Movement North, 1900–1920*. Garden City, N.Y.: Anchor Press, 1975.

Hess, Jeffrey. "Black Settlement House, East Greenwich, 1902–1914." *Rhode Island History* 29, 3–4 (August/November 1970): 113–27.

Hewitt, Nancy A. "Beyond the Search for Sisterhood: American Women's History in the 1980s." *Social History* 10, 3 (October 1985): 299–321.

Higham, John. *Strangers in the Land: Patterns of American Nativism, 1860–1925*. New York: Atheneum, 1963.

Hill, Howard C. "The Americanization Movement." *American Journal of Sociology* 24, 6 (May 1919): 609–42.

Hill, Samuel S., Jr., et al. *Religion and the Solid South*. Nashville, Tenn.: Abingdon Press, 1972.

Hine, Darlene Clark. "Protest: The Savannah Men's Sunday Club." *Phylon* 35, 2 (Summer 1974): 193–202.

———. "Rape and the Inner Lives of Black Women in the Middle West: Preliminary Thoughts on the Culture of Dissemblance." *Signs* 14, 4 (Summer 1989): 912–20.

———, ed. *Black Women in American History*. 16 vols. Brooklyn: Carlson, 1990.

Hofstadter, Richard. *The Age of Reform: From Bryan to F.D.R.* New York: Vintage–Random House, 1955.

Holley, Donald. "The Negro in the New Deal Resettlement Program." *Agricultural History* 45, 3 (July 1971): 179–93.

Hopkins, Charles Howard. *The Rise of the Social Gospel in American Protestantism, 1865–1915.* 1940. Reprint. New Haven, Conn.: Yale University Press, 1967.

Husock, Howard. "America's First War on Poverty." *Wilson Quarterly* 14, 2 (Spring 1990): 78–91.

Hutchinson, William R. "Cultural Strain and Protestant Liberalism." *American Historical Review* 76, 2 (April 1971): 386–411.

Jackson, Philip. "Black Charity in Progressive Era Chicago." *Social Service Review* 52, 3 (September 1978): 400–417.

Jacobs, Claude F. "Benevolent Societies of New Orleans Blacks during the Late Nineteenth and Early Twentieth Centuries." *Louisiana History* 29, 1 (Winter 1988): 21–33.

Jacoway, Elizabeth. *Yankee Missionaries in the South: The Penn School Experiment.* Baton Rouge: Louisiana State University Press, 1980.

James, Edward T., Janet Wilson James, and Paul S. Boyer. *Notable American Women, 1607–1950.* 3 vols. Cambridge, Mass.: Harvard University Press, Belknap Press, 1971.

Jones, Adrienne Lash. *Jane Edna Hunter: A Case Study of Black Leadership, 1910–1950.* Brooklyn: Carlson, 1990.

Jones, Jacqueline. *Labor of Love, Labor of Sorrow: Black Women, Work, and the Family, From Slavery to the Present.* 1985. Reprint. New York: Vintage–Random House, 1986.

Jones-Jackson, Patricia. *When Roots Die: Endangered Traditions on the Sea Islands.* Athens: University of Georgia Press, 1987.

Kaplan, Temma. "Female Consciousness and Collective Action: The Case of Barcelona, 1910–1918." *Signs* 7, 3 (Spring 1982): 545–66.

Karger, Howard Jacob. "Phyllis Wheatley House: A History of the Minneapolis Black Settlement House, 1924–1940." *Phylon* 47, 1 (March 1986): 79–90.

———. *The Sentinels of Order: A Study of Social Control and the Minneapolis Settlement House Movement, 1915–1950.* Lanham, Md.: University Press of America, 1987.

Kelley, Robin D. *Hammer and Hoe: Alabama Communists during the Great Depression.* Chapel Hill: University of North Carolina Press, 1990.

Klein, Philip. *From Philanthropy to Social Welfare: An American Cultural Perspective.* San Francisco: Jossey-Bass, 1971.

———. "Services to Neighborhoods: The Settlement Movement." In *From Philanthropy to Social Welfare: An American Cultural Perspective,* pp. 114–24. San Francisco: Jossey-Bass, 1971.

Kogut, Alvin B. "The Negro and the Charity Organization Society in the Progressive Era." *Social Service Review* 44, 1 (March 1970): 11–21.

Korman, Gerd. *Industrialization, Immigrants, and Americanizers: The View from Milwaukee, 1866–1921.* Madison: State Historical Society of Wisconsin, 1967.

Kornbluh, Andrea Tuttle. "Woman's City Club: A Pioneer in Race Relations." *Queen City Heritage* 44, 2 (Summer 1986): 21–38.

Koven, Seth, and Sonya Michel. "Gender and the Origins of the Welfare State." *Radical History Review* 43 (Winter 1989): 112–19.

Kusmer, Kenneth. *A Ghetto Takes Shape: Black Cleveland, 1870–1930.* Urbana: University of Illinois Press, 1976.

LaCapra, Dominick. *History and Criticism.* Ithaca, N.Y.: Cornell University Press, 1985.

Lasch, Christopher. "Jane Addams: The College Woman and the Family Claim." In *The New Radicalism in America, 1889–1963: The Intellectual as a Social Type*, pp. 3–37. New York: Chatto and Windus, 1966.

Layng, Anthony. "Voluntary Associations and Black Ethnic Identity." *Phylon* 39, 2 (Summer 1978): 171–79.

Lears, T. J. Jackson. "The Concept of Cultural Hegemony: Problems and Possibilities." *American Historical Review* 90, 3 (June 1985): 567–93.

Lerner, Gerda. "Black and White Women in Interaction and Confrontation." In *The Majority Finds Its Past: Placing Women in History*, pp. 94–111. New York: Oxford University Press, 1979.

———. "Community Work of Black Club Women." In *The Majority Finds Its Past: Placing Women in History*, pp. 83–93. Oxford: Oxford University Press, 1979.

———. *The Majority Finds Its Past: Placing Women in History*. Oxford: Oxford University Press, 1979.

Levine, Lawrence. *Black Culture and Black Consciousness: Afro-American Folk Thought from Slavery to Freedom*. New York: Oxford University Press, 1977.

Lewis, David Levering. "Parallels and Divergences: Assimilationist Strategies of Afro-American and Jewish Elites from 1910 to the Early 1930s." *Journal of American History* 71, 3 (December 1984): 543–64.

Lincoln, C. Eric. "The Black Church in the Context of American Religion." In *Varieties of Southern Religious Experience*, edited by Samuel Hill, pp. 52–75. Baton Rouge: Louisiana State University Press, 1988.

Lindsay, Inabel B. "Adult Education Programs for Negroes in Settlement Houses." *Journal of Negro Education* 14 (1945): 347–52.

Lissak, Rivka Shpak. *Pluralism and Progressives: Hull House and the New Immigrants, 1890–1919*. Chicago: University of Chicago Press, 1989.

Lubove, Roy. *The Professional Altruist: The Emergence of Social Work as a Career, 1880–1930*. 1965. Reprint. New York: Atheneum, 1980.

———. *The Progressives and the Slums: Tenement House Reform in New York City, 1890–1917*. 1962. Reprint. Westport, Conn.: Greenwood, 1974.

Luker, Ralph E. "The Social Gospel and the Failure of Racial Reform, 1877–1898." *Church History* 46, 1 (March 1977): 80–99.

———. *The Social Gospel in Black and White: American Racial Reform, 1885–1912*. Chapel Hill: University of North Carolina Press, 1991.

McCree, Mary Lynn. "Louise de Koven Bowen." In *Notable American Women: The Modern Period*, edited by Barbara Sicherman et al., pp. 99–101. Cambridge, Mass.: Harvard University Press, Belknap Press, 1980.

McDowell, John Patrick. *The Social Gospel in the South: The Woman's Home Mission Movement in the Methodist Episcopal Church, South, 1886–1939*. Baton Rouge: Louisiana State University Press, 1982.

McPherson, James. *The Abolitionist Legacy: From Reconstruction to the NAACP*. Princeton, N.J.: Princeton University Press, 1975.

———. "White Liberals and Black Power in Negro Education, 1865–1915." *American Historical Review* 75, 5 (June 1970): 1357–86.

Mandle, Jay R. *The Roots of Black Poverty: The Southern Plantation Economy after the Civil War*. Durham, N.C.: Duke University Press, 1978.

Matthews, Fred. " 'Hobbesian Populism': Interpretive Paradigms and Moral Vision in

American Historiography." *Journal of American History* 72, 1 (June 1985): 92–115.

May, Henry F. *Protestant Churches and Industrial America*. 1949. Reprint. New York: Octagon, 1963.

Meacham, Standish. *Toynbee Hall and Social Reform, 1880–1914: The Search for Community*. New Haven, Conn.: Yale University Press, 1987.

Meier, August. *Negro Thought in America, 1880–1915: Racial Ideologies in the Age of Booker T. Washington*. Ann Arbor: University of Michigan Press, 1966.

Melvin, Patricia Mooney, ed. *American Community Organizations: A Historical Dictionary*. Westport, Conn.: Greenwood, 1986.

Mohl, Raymond A. "Mainstream Social Welfare History and Its Problems." *Reviews in American History* 7, 4 (December 1979): 469–76.

Montalto, Nicholas V., comp. *The International Institute Movement: A Guide to Records of Immigrant Service Agencies in the United States*. St. Paul: Immigration History Research Center, University of Minnesota, 1978.

Mumford, Lewis. "Love and Integration." In *The Human Prospect*. 1955. Reprint. Carbondale: Southern Illinois University Press, 1965.

Muraskin, William. "The Social-Control Theory in American History: A Critique." *Journal of Social History* 9 (1976): 559–69.

Naipaul, V. S. "How the Land Lay." *The New Yorker*, June 6, 1988, pp. 94–105.

Nasstrom, Kathryn L. *Women's Voices in the Southern Oral History Program Collection*. Chapel Hill: University of North Carolina Southern Oral History Program and Manuscripts Department, 1992.

Neverdon-Morton, Cynthia. *Afro-American Women of the South and the Advancement of the Race, 1895–1925*. Knoxville: University of Tennessee Press, 1989.

Newby, I. A. *Jim Crow's Defense: Anti-Negro Thought in America, 1900–1930*. Baton Rouge: Louisiana State University Press, 1965.

Norrell, Robert. *Reaping the Whirlwind: The Civil Rights Movement in Tuskegee*. New York: Vintage, 1986.

O'Connell, Lucille. "Frances Kellor." In *Notable American Women: The Modern Period*, edited by Barbara Sicherman et al., pp. 393–95. Cambridge, Mass.: Harvard University Press, Belknap Press, 1980.

Odum, Howard W. *American Social Problems: An Introduction to the Study of the People and Their Dilemmas*. 1945. Reprint. Freeport, N.Y.: Books for Libraries Press, 1970.

O'Neill, William L. *Everyone Was Brave: The Rise and Fall of Feminism in America*. New York: Quadrangle, 1969.

Osofsky, Gilbert. *Harlem, the Making of a Ghetto: Negro New York, 1890–1930*. New York: Harper and Row, 1968.

Pacey, Lorene, ed. *Readings in the Development of Settlement Work*. New York: Association, 1950.

Palmer, Phyllis Marynick. "White Women/Black Women: The Dualism of Female Identity and Experience in the United States." *Feminist Studies* 9, 1 (Spring 1983): 151–70.

Parsons, Talcott. "Racial and Religious Differences as Factors in Group Tensions." In *Approaches to National Unity: Fifth Symposium*, edited by Lyman Bryson, Louis Finkelstein, and Robert M. Maciver, pp. 182–99. 1945. Reprint. New York: Kraus Reprint, 1971.

Peterson, Jon A. "From Social Settlement to Social Agency: Settlement Work in

Columbus, Ohio, 1898–1958." *Social Service Review* 39, 2 (June 1965): 191–208.

Philpott, Thomas. *The Slum and the Ghetto: Neighborhood Deterioration and Middle-Class Reform, Chicago, 1880–1930.* New York: Oxford University Press, 1978.

Platt, Tony, and Susan Chandler. "Constant Struggle: E. Franklin Frazier and Black Social Work in the 1920s." *Social Work* 33, 4 (July–August 1988): 293–97.

Quarles, Benjamin. *The Negro in the Making of America.* Rev. ed. New York: Collier-Macmillan, 1969.

Rabinowitz, Howard N. *Race Relations in the Urban South, 1865–1890.* New York: Oxford University Press, 1978.

Ransom, Roger L., and Richard Sutch. *One Kind of Freedom: The Economic Consequences of Emancipation.* New York: Cambridge University Press, 1977.

Reid, Ira De A. "The Development of Adult Education for Negroes in the United States." *Journal of Negro Education* 14 (1945): 299–311.

Richardson, Joe M. "The Failure of the American Missionary Association to Expand Congregationalism among Southern Blacks." *Southern Studies* 18, 1 (Spring 1979): 51–73.

Robbins, Gerald. "Rossa B. Cooley and Penn School: Social Dynamo in a Negro Rural Subculture, 1901–1930." *Journal of Negro Education* 33, 1 (Winter 1964): 43–51.

Robinson, William H. "The Relevancy of Church Social Work to the Black Revolution." *Lutheran Social Welfare Quarterly* 9 (Spring 1969): 11–20.

Rose, Willie Lee. *Rehearsal for Reconstruction: The Port Royal Experiment.* Indianapolis: Bobbs-Merrill, 1964.

Rosenberg, Rosalind. *Beyond Separate Spheres: Intellectual Roots of Modern Feminism.* New Haven, Conn.: Yale University Press, 1982.

Ross, B. Joyce. *J. E. Spingarn and the Rise of the NAACP.* New York: Atheneum, 1972.

Ross, Edyth L. "Black Heritage in Social Welfare: A Case Study of Atlanta." *Phylon* 37, 4 (Winter 1976): 297–307.

Rouse, Jacqueline Anne. *Lugenia Burns Hope: Black Southern Reformer.* Athens: University of Georgia Press, 1989.

Rousmaniere, John P. "Cultural Hybrid in the Slums: The College Woman and the Settlement House, 1889–1894." *American Quarterly* 22 (Spring 1970): 45–66.

Rudwick, Elliott. *Race Riot at East St. Louis, July 2, 1917.* Carbondale: Southern Illinois University Press, 1964.

Salem, Dorothy. *To Better Our World: Black Women in Organized Reform, 1890–1920.* Brooklyn: Carlson, 1990.

Sandburg, Carl. *The Chicago Race Riots, July 1919.* New York: Harcourt, Brace, 1919.

Scott, Anne Firor. "Most Invisible of All: Black Women's Voluntary Associations." *Journal of Southern History* 56, 1 (February 1990): 3–22.

———. *Natural Allies: Women's Associations in American History.* Urbana: University of Illinois Press, 1991.

———. *The Southern Lady: From Pedestal to Politics, 1830–1930.* Chicago: University of Chicago Press, 1970.

Selby, John. *Beyond Civil Rights.* Cleveland: World Publishing, 1966.

Sherer, Robert G. *Subordination or Liberation?: The Development and Conflicting Theories of Black Education in Nineteenth Century Alabama.* University, Alabama: University of Alabama Press, 1977.

Shivery, Louie Davis. "The Neighborhood Union: A Survey of the Beginnings of

Social Welfare Movements among Negroes in Atlanta." *Phylon* 3, 1 (Spring 1942): 149–62.

Shlomowitz, Ralph. "The Origins of Southern Sharecropping." *Agricultural History* 53 (July 1979): 557–75.

Sicherman, Barbara, et al., eds. *Notable American Women: The Modern Period*. Cambridge, Mass.: Harvard University Press, Belknap Press, 1980.

Sklar, Kathryn Kish. *Catharine Beecher: A Study in American Domesticity*. New York: Norton, 1976.

———. "Hull House in the 1890s: A Community of Women Reformers." *Signs* 10, 4 (Summer 1985): 658–77.

Smith-Rosenberg, Carroll. *Disorderly Conduct: Visions of Gender in Victorian America*. New York: Knopf, 1985.

Sorin, Gerald. *The Nurturing Neighborhood: The Brownsville Boys Club and Jewish Community in Urban America, 1940–1990*. New York: New York University Press, 1990.

Spear, Allan. *Black Chicago: The Making of a Negro Ghetto, 1890–1920*. Chicago: University of Chicago Press, 1967.

Speizman, Milton D. "The Movement of the Settlement Idea into the South." *Southwestern Social Science Quarterly* 44, 3 (December 1963): 237–46.

Spivey, Donald. *Schooling for the New Slavery: Black Industrial Education, 1868–1915*. Westport, Conn.: Greenwood, 1978.

Stanfield, John H. *Philanthropy and Jim Crow in American Social Science*. Westport, Conn.: Greenwood, 1985.

Stehno, Sandra M. "Public Responsibility for Dependent Black Children: The Advocacy of Edith Abbott and Sophonisba Breckinridge." *Social Service Review* 62, 3 (September 1988): 485–503.

Sternsher, Bernard, ed. *The Negro in Depression and War: Prelude to Revolution, 1930–1945*. Chicago: Quadrangle, 1969.

Stewart, Ruth Ann. "Charlotte Hawkins Brown." In *Notable American Women: The Modern Period*, edited by Barbara Sicherman et al., pp. 111–13. Cambridge, Mass.: Harvard University Press, Belknap Press, 1980.

Strickland, Arvarh E. *History of the Chicago Urban League*. Urbana: University of Illinois Press, 1966.

Stueck, William. "Progressivism and the Negro: White Liberals and the Early NAACP." *The Historian* 38, 1 (November 1975): 58–78.

Taylor, Frances Sanders. "'On the Edge of Tomorrow': Southern Women, the Student YWCA, and Race, 1920–1944." Ph.D. dissertation, Stanford University, 1984.

Terborg-Penn, Rosalyn, and Sharon Harley, eds. *The Afro-American Woman: Struggles and Images*. Port Washington, N.Y.: Kennikat, 1978.

Tillman, James A., and Mary Norman Tillman. "Black Intellectuals, White Liberals and Race Relations: An Analytic Overview." *Phylon* 33, 1 (September 1972): 54–66.

Tindall, George Brown. *The Ethnic Southerners*. Baton Rouge: Louisiana State University Press, 1976.

Trattner, Walter. *From Poor Law to Welfare State, A History of Social Welfare in America*. 2d ed. New York: Free Press, 1979.

———. "The Settlement House Movement." In *From Poor Law to Welfare State: A History of Social Welfare in America*, pp. 147–72. 3d ed. New York: Free Press, 1984.

Trolander, Judith. *Professionalism and Social Change: From the Settlement House Move-

ment to Neighborhood Centers, 1886 to the Present. New York: Columbia University Press, 1987.

——— . *Settlement Houses and the Great Depression.* Detroit: Wayne State University Press, 1975.

Turner, Richard B. "The Ahmadiyya Mission to Blacks in the United States in the 1920s." *Journal of Religious Thought* 44, 2 (Winter/Spring 1988): 50–66.

Vicinus, Martha. "Settlement Houses: A Community Ideal for the Poor." In *Independent Women: Work and Community for Single Women, 1850–1920*, pp. 211–46. Chicago: University of Chicago Press, 1985.

Walker, Alice. *In Search of Our Mothers' Gardens: Womanist Prose.* New York: Harcourt Brace Jovanovich, 1983.

Weatherford, Willis D., and Charles S. Johnson. *Race Relations: Adjustment of Whites and Negroes in the United States.* 1934. Reprint. New York: Negro Universities Press, 1969.

Weiss, Nancy J. *The National Urban League, 1910–1940.* New York: Oxford University Press, 1974.

Welter, Barbara. "The Cult of True Womanhood: 1820–1860." In *The American Family in Social-Historical Perspective*, edited by Michael Gordon, pp. 313–33. New York: St. Martin's, 1978.

White, Deborah Gray. "The Cost of Club Work, The Price of Black Feminism." In *Visible Women: New Essays on American Activism*, edited by Nancy Hewitt and Suzanne Lebsock. Urbana: University of Illinois Press, forthcoming.

White, George Carey. "Social Settlements and Immigrant Neighbors, 1886–1914." *Social Service Review* 33 (March 1959): 55–66.

Wiener, Jonathan M. *Social Origins of the New South: Alabama, 1860–1885.* Baton Rouge: Louisiana State University Press, 1978.

Wilkerson, Doxey A. "The Participation of Negroes in the Federally-Aided Program of Agricultural and Home Economics Extension." *Journal of Negro Education* 7, 3 (July 1938): 331–44.

Williams, Lillian S. "And I Still Rise: Black Women and Reform, Buffalo, New York, 1900–1940." *Afro-Americans in New York Life and History* 14, 2 (July 1990): 7–33.

——— . "To Elevate the Race: The Michigan Avenue YMCA and the Advancement of Blacks in Buffalo, New York, 1922–1940." In *New Perspectives on Black Educational History*, edited by Vincent P. Franklin and James D. Anderson, pp. 129–48. Boston: G. K. Hall, 1978.

Williams, Raymond. *Marxism and Literature.* Oxford: Oxford University Press, 1977.

Williamson, Joel. *The Crucible of Race: Black-White Relations in the American South since Emancipation.* New York: Oxford University Press, 1984.

Wisner, Elizabeth. "The Howard Association of New Orleans." *Social Service Review* 41, 4 (1967): 411–18.

Wolters, Raymond. *Negroes and the Great Depression: The Problem of Economic Recovery.* Westport, Conn.: Greenwood, 1970.

Woofter, T. J., Jr. *Black Yeomanry: Life on St. Helena Island.* 1930. Reprint. New York: Octagon, 1978.

Yancey, William L., Eugene P. Ericksen, and Richard N. Juliani. "Emergent Ethnicity: A Review and a Reformulation." *American Sociological Review* 41, 3 (June 1976): 391–403.

Yarros, Victor S. "Hull House." *Jewish Social Service Quarterly* 2, 4 (June 1926): 245–50.

Index

Clifton, Mass.: conference in (1908), 27, 55
Club movement. *See* Women
Club work. *See* Group work
Colored Protective Association (Philadelphia, Pa.), 68
Commission on Interracial Cooperation (Atlanta, Ga.), 97, 114; women's committee of, 115
Committee for Improving the Industrial Conditions of Negroes in New York, 39
Committee on Urban Conditions, 39
Commons, John R., 20
Community: building and transformation of, 5, 7, 11, 46, 73, 76, 77, 78, 80, 81, 84, 88, 89, 100, 104–5, 109, 162; self-sufficiency of, 88, 96, 99, 106, 107–8, 109; power of, 108; competition of black men and women in sphere of, 117; fragmentation of, 143–44; spiritual dimension of, 145; meaning of, 156
Community Chest, 59, 61, 62–63, 69, 173 (n. 40)
Community churches, 59
Conference for Education in the South (Lexington, Ky.), 115
"Conference on the Status of the Negro in the United States" (1909), 42
Congregationalists, 58, 69
Conservatism, 4, 11, 39, 61, 173 (n. 40); of teachers trained at Hampton Institute, 78; of benefactors of industrial schools, 80
Conspiracy thesis, 80
Cooley, Rossa B., 106, 107–9
Cooper, Charles: on blacks' denominationalism, 57; on direction of settlement movement, 63
Cooperatives, 89, 103, 108
Corbin, Sam, 158–59, 160
Corporate welfarism, 13, 59
Cosmopolitan Club (New York, N.Y.) dinner, 46
Cosmopolitanism, 7, 9, 58, 66, 67, 74, 112, 115
Cotton farming, 87, 89, 99; and schooling, 102, 180 (n. 99)
Council House (New York, N.Y.), 72

Council of Jewish Women, 67
Counseling, 72
Crime, 12, 17, 44, 122
Criminology: environmental school of, 16
Crisis, The, 13, 133
Crocker, Ruth, 3
Crop-lien system, 79, 90, 91. *See also* Sharecropping
Crozer Theological Seminary, 72
"Cult of true womanhood." *See* Domesticity

Daniels, John, 10, 12, 13, 168 (n. 27); *In Freedom's Birthplace*, 13, 20–21; on "social intermixture," 20; on slavery, 21; on blacks, 22; on "racial advancement," 22, 23
Davis, Allen, 3, 4; on founding of NAACP, 42; on southern settlements, 48; on decline of settlement movement, 154
Davis, Jackson, 96
De Bardeleben, Mary, 127
Democracy, 143, 146, 155, 160, 161, 162; Christian, 112–13, 135, 145–46; and integration, 163
Denominationalism, 55, 56, 58, 64, 73
Dewey, John, 85
Dickinson, Thorn, 87, 98
Dillingham, John, 72
Dillingham, Mabel Wilhelmina, 82, 83–84, 100, 101
Dillingham, Pitt, 84
Discrimination: and settlement house policy, 10; job, 12, 41; in education, 12, 74; racial, 17, 41, 112, 117, 126, 129, 133, 146, 149; by the courts, 75; economic, 76, 79; "privatization" of, 177, 183 (n. 19)
Disfranchisement. *See* Voting
Dodge, Grace, 133
Doggett, John N., Jr.: memories of Wharton Centre, 35
Domesticity, 111, 113, 114, 116, 139, 181 (n. 5). *See also* Separate spheres
Domestic science, 87, 124, 133
Douglass Community Center (Springfield, Ill.), 41; vocational opportunity campaign of, 41

Lee Plantation Church (Lowndes County, Ala.), 82
Lewis, Sinclair: *Babbitt*, 60
Liberalism, 4, 7, 27, 47, 48, 59, 96, 100, 101, 172 (n. 22)
Lincoln, C. Eric: on black churches, 47
Lincoln House (New York, N.Y.), 29
Lincoln University, 80
Lindenberg, Sidney, 23
Locust Street Settlement (Hampton, Va.), 27
Loud, Joseph, 96
Lowndes County, Ala., 82, 83, 88, 97, 99. *See also* Agricultural demonstration work; Calhoun Colored School and Social Settlement
Lowndes County Board of Education, 99
Lowndes County Teachers' Institute, 88
Luker, Ralph, 4
Lutherans, 72
Lynching, 78, 117, 118, 149. *See also* Anti-lynching

McCall, James Edward, 145
McDowell, John, 158–60
McLennan, William, 54
McMain, Eleanor, 48
McPherson, James, 80
Manual training, 11, 79–81, 85, 87. *See also* Industrial education
Maternalism, 125, 161. *See also* Motherhood
Memphis, Tenn.: interracial women's conference (1920), 114–15
Men's sphere, 117. *See also* Separate spheres
Methodist Episcopal Church, South: women's home missions, 5, 7, 54, 64, 67, 72–73, 111, 112–13, 115, 118,128–31, 150, 184 (nn. 45, 46); on spiritual dimension of settlement work, 53–54; and equal rights, 58; and Women's Missionary Council convention (1920), 114; attempts to integrate settlements, 156. *See also* Bethlehem Houses; Settlement house activities

Methodists, 130, 185 (n. 63). *See also* Methodist Episcopal Church, South
Migrant workers, 67. *See also* Black migration
Miscegenation, 14
Missions, 172 (n. 22); contrasted with settlements, 7, 48, 50–52, 58–59, 61–62; and admission to NFS, 62; as models for settlement work, 154. *See also* Methodist Episcopal Church, South: women's home missions
Model tenement, 44–45
Modernism, 58
Montgomery Industrial School, 92
Morality: of blacks, 10, 16, 17, 18, 19, 21, 22, 23, 28, 29, 47, 56; education in, 11, 17, 18, 27, 39–40; social, 14, 37, 58, 67, 69, 74, 76, 78, 119; of dominant group, 31; and women, 111, 116–18, 125
Morehouse College, 80, 114, 120, 122, 124
Moskowitz, Henry, 42
Motherhood: as imperative for reform, 111–13, 115–16, 120, 122, 125–26, 131, 134, 139, 150, 160. *See also* Domesticity; Separate spheres; Womanhood
Mothers' Clubs. *See* Settlement house activities: Mothers' Clubs
Mothers' Conference (People's Village School), 103
Moynihan, Daniel Patrick: *The Negro Family in America*, 167 (n. 8)
Murray, Ellen, 106

Nashville, Tenn.: interracial women's conference (1920), 120
Nashville Christian Advocate, 53
National Association for the Advancement of Colored People (NAACP), 11, 13, 14, 25, 29, 39, 40, 42, 46, 75, 133, 155, 170 (n. 86)
National Association of Colored Women, 118, 119; biennial conference, 114
National Conference of Colored Women, 119
National Conference of Social Work (1934), 151
National Council of Negro Women, 146